OECD Public Governance Reviews

Effective Delivery of Large Infrastructure Projects

THE CASE OF THE NEW INTERNATIONAL AIRPORT OF MEXICO CITY

OECD
BETTER POLICIES FOR BETTER LIVES

Please cite this publication as:
OECD (2015), *Effective Delivery of Large Infrastructure Projects: The Case of the New International Airport of Mexico City*, OECD Public Governance Reviews, OECD Publishing, Paris.
http://dx.doi.org/10.1787/9789264248335-en

ISBN 978-92-64-24832-8 (print)
ISBN 978-92-64-24833-5 (PDF)

Series: OECD Public Governance Reviews
ISSN 2219-0406 (print)
ISSN 2219-0414 (online)

Photo credits: Cover © FP-FREE, S. DE R.L. DE C.V.

Corrigenda to OECD publications may be found on line at: *www.oecd.org/about/publishing/corrigenda.htm*.

Foreword

Infrastructure projects are central to government mandates. Their benefits and risks can be seen as two sides of the same coin. One side holds a vision and a promise: increased national competitiveness, better public service delivery and inclusive growth. On the other side there are risks of mismanagement, waste of public money and corruption. Because major infrastructure projects can represent the legacy of governments for generations to come, governments must be particularly attentive to ensure their social value.

Much of the success of such projects depends on transparency, efficiency and skills. International experience shows that implementing these principles often remains a challenge.

The Government of Mexico has called on the OECD to assist the state-owned entity Airport Group of Mexico City (*Grupo Aeroportuario de la Ciudad de México, GACM)* to deliver on its mandate to manage the construction of the New International Airport of Mexico City. In responding to this request, the OECD brought together practices and expertise from Member countries on the governance of infrastructure projects, public procurement, integrity frameworks and the related communication strategies.

This report is part of OECD's mandate to help governments at all levels design and implement strategic, evidence-based and innovative policies to strengthen public governance, respond effectively to diverse and disruptive economic, social and environmental challenges and deliver on government's commitments to citizens.

While the GACM is committed to applying international best practices of integrity, transparency and open government, additional efforts are necessary. The report identifies several areas for improvement based on international experience.

The report demonstrates the imperative of co-ordinated action from different institutions and levels of government, as well as systematic stakeholder engagement. A corporate governance structure replacing GACM's current organisation would better address this complex environment. In addition, procurement processes should be tailored to the magnitude and specificities of the project to ensure effective delivery. Also, a comprehensive integrity strategy including public and private stakeholders would reduce the risk of corruption. Finally, strategic and frequent communications are needed to secure vital social and political support.

Infrastructure projects are multidimensional by nature. Progress made in one area not only represents an improvement in itself, but also contributes to strengthening other dimensions that together pave the way for effective delivery of large infrastructure projects. By providing assistance to the Mexican authorities in this unique project, the OECD aims to support the government in reaping the direct benefits of better policies for better lives without taking unnecessary risks and ensuring that the outcomes of the project reflect the right side of the coin.

Rolf Alter
OECD Director for Public Governance and Territorial Development

Acknowledgements

Under the direction of Rolf Alter, OECD Director for Public Governance and Territorial Development, and János Bertók, Head of the Public Sector Integrity Division, this review was led by Paulo Magina, Head of the Procurement Unit; Jacobo Pastor García Villarreal, Senior Specialist on Integrity and Procurement Policies (Chapter 2); Matthieu Cahen, Policy Analyst (Chapter 3); and Emma Cantera, Policy Analyst (Chapter 4). Chapter 5 was written by Luis Carlos Ugalde and Luis Antonio Espino.

Valuable comments were received from Julio Bacio Terracino, Hans Christiansen, and various staff members from Mexico's Ministry of Public Administration. Editorial assistance was provided by Julie Harris. Anaisa Goncalves provided administrative assistance.

Special thanks are attributed to Mexico's Ministry of Communications and Transport, in particular, Gerardo Ruiz Esparza, Minister; and Yuriria Mascott, Deputy Minister, who took the initiative to establish the project with the OECD.

The OECD expresses its gratitude to the Airport Group of Mexico City for the constructive leadership and open dialogue held with the OECD and with procurement leaders, in particular to Federico Patiño, Director General; Jose Luis Romo, Corporate Director for Planning, Evaluation, and Outreach; Sandra Gonzalez, Deputy Director for Planning; and all of the Corporate Directors and their staff.

The OECD also thanks Manuel Ángel Núñez Soto, former Director General of the Airport Group of Mexico City; Ambassador Dionisio Pérez-Jácome Friscione and Maya Camacho, from the Permanent Delegation of Mexico to the OECD, who were instrumental in facilitating the co-ordination of the review.

This review is part of a series of governance reviews in OECD and G20 countries. It benefited from input provided by senior public procurement officials who participated in discussions in Mexico City.

Particular thanks are given to the reviewers Alan Couzens, Head of Infrastructure Tracking and Performance, Infrastructure UK, Airports Commission; Chris Howe, Buildings Procurement Director, Heathrow; Neill Stansbury, Co-founder and Director, Global Infrastructure Anti-corruption Centre (GIACC); and Denise Bower, Executive Director, Major Projects Association, who also participated in a series of OECD workshops to build capacities in the Airport Group of Mexico City.

The OECD Mexico Centre for Latin America, under the leadership of Roberto Martínez and the staff in charge of publications, notably Alejandro Camacho, were instrumental in co-ordinating the editorial process for the Spanish publication.

Table of contents

Tables

Figures

Boxes

Acronyms and abbreviations

AICM	International Airport of Mexico City *Aeropuerto Internacional de la Ciudad de México*
APF	Federal Public Administration *Administración Pública Federal*
ASA	Airports and Auxiliary Services *Aeropuertos y Servicios Auxiliares*
ASF	Supreme audit institution of Mexico *Auditoría Superior de la Federación*
ASPA	Pilot and Flight Attendant Union *Asociación Sindical de Pilotos Aviadores de México*
BBI	Berlin-Brandenburg International Airport
CANAERO	Air Transport National Chamber *Cámara Nacional de Aerotransportes*
CEMDA	Environmental Law Mexican Centre *Centro Mexicano de Derecho Ambiental*
CINAM	Environmental Engineers Board *Colegio de Ingenieros Ambientales de México*
CMIC	Mexican Chamber of the Construction Industry *Cámara Mexicana de la Industria de la Construcción*
COFECE	National Economic Competition Commission *Comisión Federal de Competencia Económica*
COMPRANET	Mexico's electronic procurement system
CONAGUA	National Water Commission *Comisión Nacional del Agua*
CONASMI	National Commission on Minimum Salary *Comisión Nacional de los Salarios Mínimos*
CPEUM	Mexico's Constitution *Constitución Política de los Estados Unidos Mexicanos*
DCA (GACM)	Corporate Directorate for Administration and Real Estate Management (GACM) *Dirección Corporativa de Administración y Gestión Inmobiliaria (GACM)*
DCF (GACM)	Corporate Directorate for Finance (GACM) *Dirección Corporativa de Finanzas (GACM)*

DCI (GACM)	Corporate Directorate for Infrastructure (GACM) *Dirección Corporativa de Infraestructura (GACM)*
DCP (GACM)	Corporate Directorate for Planning, Evaluation, and Outreach (GACM) *Dirección Corporativa de Planeación, Evaluación y Vinculación (GACM)*
DGAC	Civil Aeronautics General Directorate *Dirección General de Aeronaútica Civil*
FPDT	Front of Towns to Defend their Lands *Frente de Pueblos en Defensa de la Tierra*
GACM	Airport Group of Mexico City *Grupo Aeroportuario de la Ciudad de México, S.A. de C.V.*
IATA	International Airport Transport Association
II - UNAM	Engineering Institute of the National Autonomous University *Instituto de Ingeniería de la UNAM*
IMCO	Mexico's Competitiveness Institute *Instituto Mexicano para la Competitividad*
INAI	National Institute for Freedom of Information *Instituto Nacional de Transparencia, Acceso a la Información y Protección de Datos Personales*
INM	National Immigration Institute *Instituto Nacional de Migración*
ISSSTE	State's Employees' Social Security and Social Services Institute *Instituto de Seguridad y Servicios Sociales de los Trabajadores del Estado*
KPIs	Key Performance Indicators
LAASSP	Law on Acquisitions, Leasing and Services of the Public Sector *Ley de Adquisiciones, Arrendamientos y Servicios del Sector Público*
LFACP	Federal Anti-Corruption Law on Public Procurement *Ley Federal Anticorrupción en Contrataciones Públicas*
LFEP	Federal Law for Quasi-state Entities *Ley Federal de las Entidades Paraestatales*
LFEP Bylaws	Bylaws of the Federal Law for Quasi-state Entities *Reglamento de la Ley Federal de las Entidades Paraestatales*
LFPRH	Federal Law of Budget and Fiscal Responsibility *Ley Federal de Presupuesto y Responsabilidad Hacendaria*
LFRASP	Federal Law on Administrative Responsibilities of Public Servants *Ley Federal de Responsabilidades Administrativas de los Servidores Públicos*

LOPSRM	Law on Public Works and Associated Services *Ley de Obras Públicas y Servicios Relacionados con las Mismas*
MAAGMAASSP	Administrative Manual for General Application concerning Acquisitions, Leasing and Services of the Public Sector *Manual Administrativo de Aplicación General en Materia de Adquisiciones, Arrendamientos y Servicios del Sector Público*
MAAGMOPSRM	Administrative Manual for General Application concerning Public Works and Associated Services *Manual Administrativo de Aplicación General en Materia de Obra Públicas y Servicios Relacionados con las Mismas*
NAICM	New International Airport of Mexico City *Nuevo Aeropuerto Internacional de la Ciudad de México*
OIC	Internal Control Unit *Órgano Interno de Control*
ONC	National Citizen Observatory *Observatorio Nacional Ciudadano*
PEMEX	Mexican Petroleum *Petróleos Mexicanos*
PGR	General Attorney's Office *Procuraduría General de la República*
POBALINES Acquisitions (GACM)	Policies and guidelines on acquisitions, leasing and services (GACM) *Políticas, bases y lineamientos en materia de adquisiciones, arrendamientos y servicios (GACM)*
POBALINES Public Works (GACM)	Policies and guidelines regarding public works and related services (GACM) *Políticas, bases y lineamientos en materia de Obras Públicas y Servicios Relacionados con las Mismas (GACM)*
PM	Project Manager
PPPs	Public-Private Partnerships
RAN	National Agrarian Registry *Registro Agrario Nacional*
ROPSRM	Regulation on Public Works and Associated Services *Reglamento de la Ley de Obras Públicas y Servicios Relacionados con las Mismas*
RTA	Network for Transparency and Freedom of Information of Latin America *Red de Transparencia y Acceso a la Información Pública*
SAGARPA	Ministry of Agriculture, Livestock, Rural Development, Fishing, and Food *Secretaría de Agricultura, Ganadería, Desarrollo Rural, Pesca y Alimentación*

SAT	Revenue Service *Servicio de Administración Tributaria*
SCT	Ministry for Communication and Transport *Secretaría de Comunicaciones y Transportes*
SEDATU	Ministry of Rural, Territorial, and Urban Development *Secretaría de Desarrollo Agrario, Territorial y Urbano*
SEDENA	Ministry of National Defence *Secretaría de la Defensa Nacional*
SEGOB	Ministry of the Interior *Secretaría de Gobernación*
SEMARNAT	Ministry of the Environment and Natural Resources *Secretaría de Medio Ambiente y Recursos Naturales*
SENASICA	National Service for Vegetal and Animal Health *Servicio Nacional de Sanidad, Inocuidad y Calidad Agroalimentaria*
SENEAM	Navigational Services in Mexico's Aerial Space *Servicios a la Navegación en el Espacio Aéreo Mexicano*
SFP	Ministry of Public Administration *Secretaría de la Función Pública*
SHCP	Ministry of Finance and Public Credit *Secretaría de Hacienda y Crédito Público*
SST	Deputy Ministry of Transport *Subsecretaría de Transporte*
TUA	Airport Departure Tax *Tarifa de Uso de Aeropuerto*
UNAM	National Autonomous University of Mexico *Universidad Nacional Autónoma de México*
UNAOPSPF	Regulatory Unit on Goods, Public Works, Services and Federal Assets *Unidad de Normatividad de Adquisiciones, Obras Públicas, Servicios y Patrimonio Federal*

Executive summary

The New International Airport of Mexico City (*Nuevo Aeropuerto Internacional de la Ciudad de México,* NAICM) project responds to a 20 year-old need to expand the capacity of Mexico City's International Airport (AICM). Currently the largest infrastructure project in the country, it aims to position Mexico as a regional hub and improve its competitiveness.

The Airport Group of Mexico City (*Grupo Aeroportuario de la Ciudad de México S.A. de C.V.*, GACM) received a mandate from the Government of Mexico to design, build, and open the NAICM by 2020. GACM is an enterprise with majority state participation, part of the quasi-state public administration.

This report provides the GACM with a comprehensive assessment and analysis of the project and offers recommendations in four critical dimensions: governance, procurement, integrity and communication. It also provides an action plan for addressing the recommendations designed in collaboration with GACM and including the corresponding managing unit in charge of its implementation.

Governance is of vital importance in such megaprojects, not only to keep them on time and on budget, but also to avoid corruption and mismanagement. GACM's governance model is that of a public institution; a more corporatised structure would allow GACM to make efficiency and operational gains. GACM's organisational structure was designed in line with principles of austerity and public spending discipline. However, it faces serious capacity and human resources constraints, which become evident when benchmarking against other airport projects. A project of this magnitude requires co-ordinated action among different public institutions and several levels of government. In addition, good governance of NAICM calls for systematic stakeholder engagement. Risk assessment and management, for example, should include civil society and benefit from its expertise.

Procurement in infrastructure projects, although offering advantages, is a very sensitive activity due to the amount of resources involved and the close interaction between the public and private spheres. To make the most of its potential, the GACM should seize existing opportunities to adapt standard processes to the magnitude and complexity of the project.

The choice of procurement as the delivery mode for NAICM, as opposed to public-private partnership or concession, was a strategic one shaping the distribution of risks. Public procurement in infrastructure limits the risk of unsustainable long-term relationships with economic operators based on over-optimistic assumptions. Yet, it reduces the suppliers' ownership in the project, which could be mitigated by effective contract management. In a second strategic decision, GACM decided to phase the main construction activities into a series of 21 procurement packages, in order to meet an extremely ambitious timeline. The aim is to encourage the participation of Mexican companies, establish clear rules from the start, identify the largest number of qualified participants, and ensure transparency. This model also offers the possibility to tailor each procurement strategy to meet market capabilities and appetites, and deliver the best value for money, not only to GACM and the Mexican Government, but to society as a whole. Defining tender specifications commensurate with the complexity of the works and appropriate award criteria, and ensuring a transparent, thorough analysis of submissions is also crucial to both achieving efficient results and reinforcing citizen trust.

Worldwide experience suggests that infrastructure projects are particularly prone to corruption. The construction of the Mexico's new airport is not exempt from this risk. A comprehensive strategy should be put in place to prevent corruption and mismanagement during the different phases of the project. Despite measures by the Mexican Government in early 2015 to promote integrity in the public sector and reinforce the fight against corruption, more needs to be done within GACM. Not doing so puts the credibility and effectiveness of the project at risk. For example, GACM could better promote openness and enhance its culture of integrity by setting common standards and norms of conduct, investing in training and guidance. In addition, GACM could establish tailored conflict-of-interest policies for public officials, bidders, and suppliers; create conditions for internal reporting of wrongdoing; and develop tools and mechanisms such as standard bidding documents, integrity monitors, and "red flags". Furthermore, establishing and empowering the Internal Control Office will help clarify the risk environment in which the project operates and provide the necessary tools to protect the project from those risks through, for example, an accurate risk map. Finally, GACM could improve the transparency of all its procurement activities by proactively publishing on its webpage all the relevant information such as annual procurement programmes, tender procedures (solicitation documents, minutes of the clarification meetings, and of the opening of tenders), contract awards history, modification to contracts, and formal complaints.

Given the potential long-term benefits of this project, building broad social and political support should be a priority, and can only be achieved through an effective communications strategy. Developing sound communication strengthens the foundations for good governance by promoting open government, increased accountability and the active engagement of civil society. A common weakness in many projects is the lack of a coherent and effective communications strategy linking the needs, expectations, and concerns of the project's different stakeholder interests. Besides controversy, symptoms of underfunded communication functions include ad hoc approaches and a lack of upfront communication and strategic planning. Unlike most government agencies, GACM's organisational structure does not include a dedicated communication role and a comprehensive strategy is still needed to change negative perceptions among several stakeholders.

NAICM is at the core of the current administration's (2012-18) infrastructure plan and public opinion is vastly in favour of the project. An adequate governance model, effective and efficient management of procurement, integrity safeguards to reduce opportunities for corruption, and a comprehensive communications strategy are all critical elements of successful megaprojects. Not honouring the project's time and budget commitments would imply huge costs for the country. Conversely, successful development would greatly improve the competitiveness of the country and the well-being of its citizens. Major infrastructure projects such as the NAICM are highly visible and provide a unique opportunity for governments to implement an infrastructure governance framework promoting an innovative, completely accountable and "clean" approach that optimises the spending of public resources and benefits the public interest.

Chapter 1

The NAICM project in perspective

*On 3 September 2014, Mexico's President announced the construction of the New International Airport of Mexico City (*Nuevo Aeropuerto Internacional de la Ciudad de México, *NAICM). This project is one of the three largest airport infrastructure projects worldwide. It responds to a constant need of over 20 years to expand the capacity of Mexico City's current airport, which is reaching its operational capacity limit. The construction of the NAICM will be funded with a mix of public and private funds, with around 60% coming from the federal budget. This chapter will introduce the nature and main features of the project, setting the stage for a deep analysis of its governance, procurement structure, integrity approach, and communications strategy.*

The New International Airport of Mexico City (*Nuevo Aeropuerto Internacional de la Ciudad de México*, NAICM) is currently one of the three largest airport infrastructure projects worldwide (see Table 1.1). Its construction costs are estimated at USD 13 billion and should be built within a four-year timeframe, followed by a series of tests and certifications. The Government anticipates this infrastructure being operational in 2020.

Table 1.1. **The NAICM in perspective**

Airport	Passengers per year (million)	Type of project
Istanbul New Airport (Turkey)	150	New construction
NAICM (Mexico)	120	New construction
New International Airport of Beijing (China)	75	New construction
Hamid International Airport (Qatar)	50	New construction
Berlin Brandenburg International Airport (Germany)	45	New construction
Dubai International Airport	28	Expansion
Heathrow-Terminal 5 (United Kingdom)	27	Expansion

Source: Presentation "*Visión Integral*", www.aeropuerto.gob.mx/documentos/05092014-sct-visionintegral.pdf, consulted on 18 September 2015.

The decision to launch the NAICM project was announced on 3 September 2014 by President Enrique Peña Nieto. The first stage is to be operational in 2020 and the project is estimated to be self-financed, with revenues coming from Mexico City's International Airport (AICM) plus NAICM when it starts operation through the resources obtained by the payment of the Fee Use of the Airport (TUA).

The NAICM will be built in the Texcoco Valley, located on the eastern border of Mexico City. The location decision was reached after assessing several alternatives. The first alternative was to expand the capacity of nearby airports to create a metropolitan system. This choice would have required a new runway at the Toluca Airport (to reach two runways); works in other airports surrounding Mexico City to be able to use three runways; and two runways currently in use at the AICM. This choice implied several setbacks, such as long distances between the different airports to Mexico City and complicated simultaneous operations. A second choice was the construction of a new airport in Tizayuca, Hidalgo with two runways and the potential of expansion for two more, plus the two currently operating at AICM. However, the new airport would have been located approximately 80 kilometres from Mexico City and also implied complications with regard to simultaneous operations. The third choice, the one preferred in the end, implies access to an area six times the size of AICM, allowing for six runways and the closure of AICM. NAICM will be located approximately 25 kilometres from the city centre, which compares favourably with the location of other airports in the world (see Figure 1.1 as well as Box 1.1 for more information about the characteristics of the area where NAICM will be located).

Figure 1.1. **Distance from the airport to the city centre (km)**

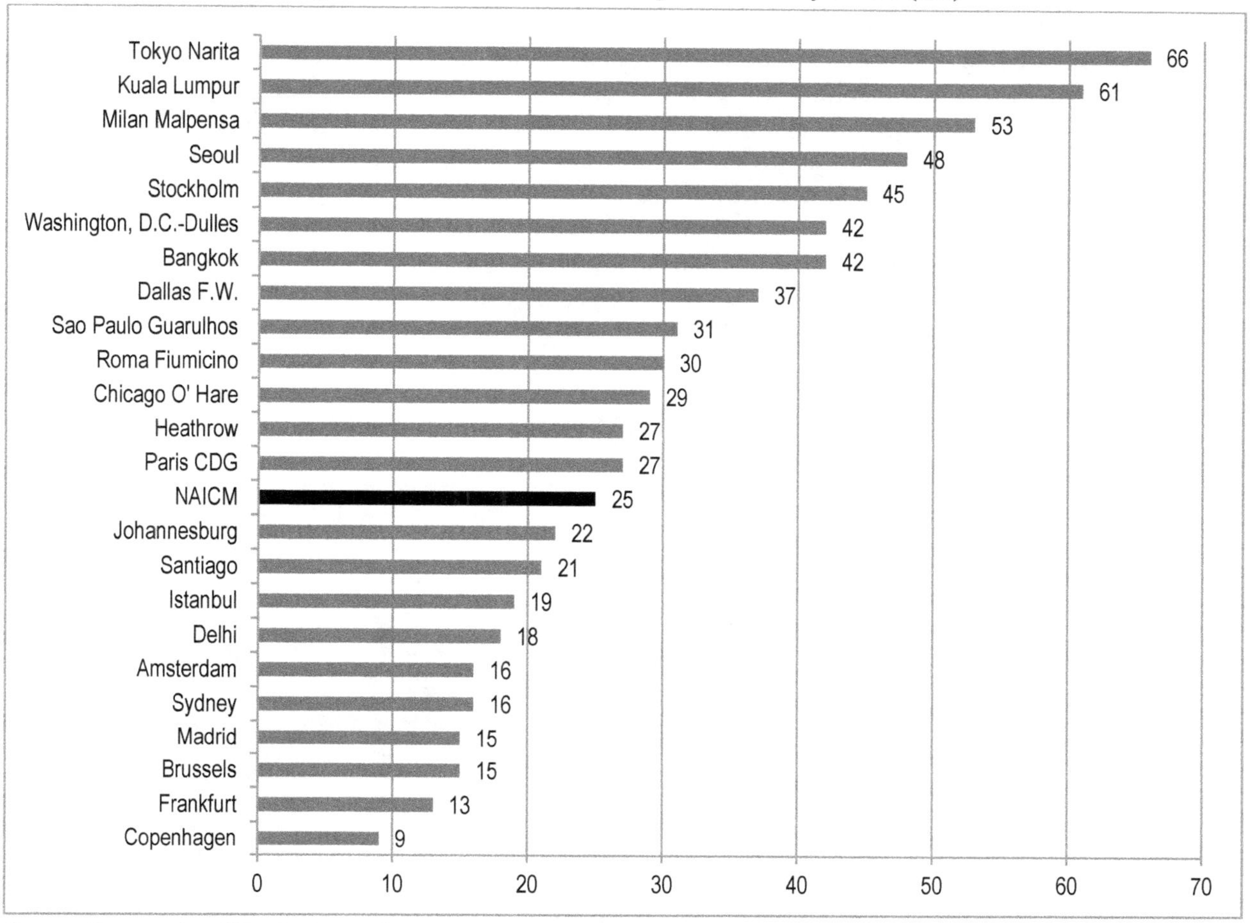

Source: Presentation "*Visión Integral*", www.aeropuerto.gob.mx/documentos/05092014-sct-visionintegral.pdf, consulted on 18 September 2015.

Box 1.1. **Characteristics of the area where NAICM will be located**

The area where NAICM will be located belongs to the municipalities of Texcoco and Atenco, in the State of Mexico. It limits with the solar evaporation deposit "*El Caracol*" to the north, the *Peñon-Texcoco* highway to the south, rural land for agriculture to the east, and urban areas of the municipality of Ecatepec to the west. The soil is lacustrine, alluvial, and sedimentary, and so is used for agriculture and pasture. More than 75% of the area is partially or totally covered by salty pasture.

The flora of the area consists of 24 species, with five dominant ones. Their preservation and relocation is envisioned in the "Programme for flora preservation of the NAICM". The fauna consists of five species of mammals, four species of reptiles, and five species of amphibious animals, which are covered by a "Programme for fauna preservation and relocation of the NAICM". Likewise, the area hosts 14 species of birds, which will be considered in the "Action and follow up plan for the preservation of birds".

The area of the Lake of Texcoco is considered a stressed ecosystem, as it has gone through alterations during long periods, impacting the physical and biological characteristics, which have not allowed it to recover its original structure. Such alterations impeded the passive or natural regeneration of the ecosystem, leaving behind a highly salty soil. The project anticipates improving the conditions of the soil, which should lead to the assisted restoration of the ecosystem in the long run.

Source: GACM (2015), "*Plan de Restauración Ecológica*", www.aeropuerto.gob.mx/documentos/plan-de-restauracion-ecologica-naicm1.pdf.

The NAICM responds to a constant need of over 20 years to expand the AICM's capacity according to the country's rate of growth. In fact, recent works at AICM include the remodelling and opening of a new international terminal building (1994), the construction and remodelling to expand capacity for check-in, passenger services, migration, and baggage, among others (2001-04), and the opening of Terminal 2 (2007). Indeed, AICM operations are reaching the technical limit, which is set at 394 000 operations per year (see Figure 1.2).[1] This is because airport activity has grown faster than the economy. While the annual growth in real gross domestic product (GDP) was 3.5% between 2009 and 2013, the annual growth in passengers in Mexico was 5.4% during the same period. Likewise, while the annual growth of the industrial activity indicator was 2.5% between 2009 and 2013, the annual growth of cargo was 5.2% during the same period.[2]

Figure 1.2. **Number of AICM operations (thousands)**

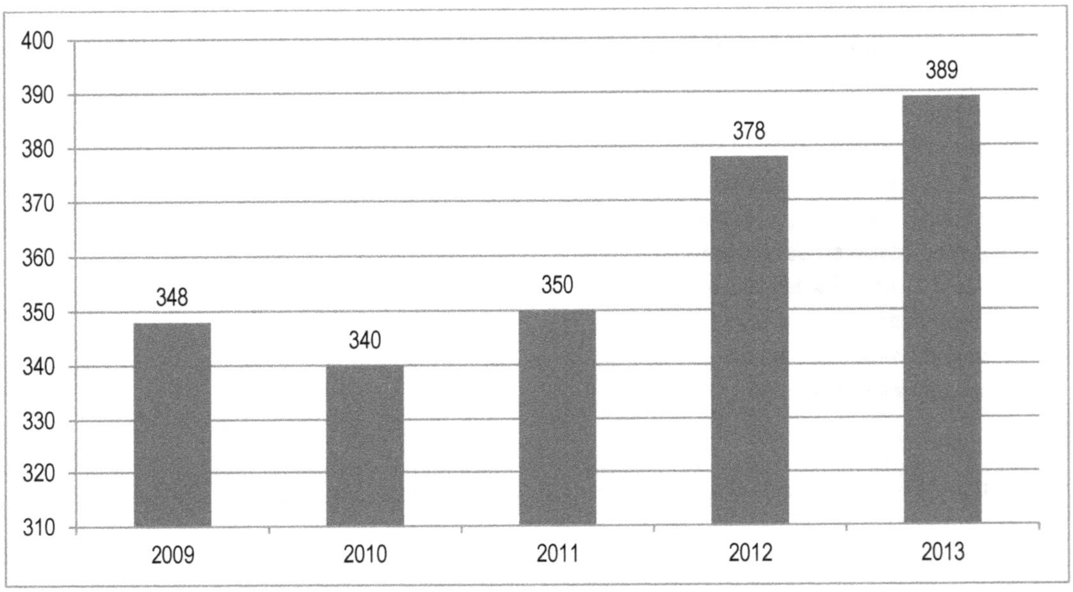

Source: Presentation "*Visión Integral*", www.aeropuerto.gob.mx/documentos/05092014-sct-visionintegral.pdf, consulted on 18 September 2015.

The fact that AICM is reaching its operational capacity causes trade and passengers to connect via alternative airports, losing the potential of Mexico City to become a regional hub. Panama, for example, handles more than double the transit passengers Mexico does (see Figure 1.3).

Figure 1.3. **Percentage of total transit passengers**

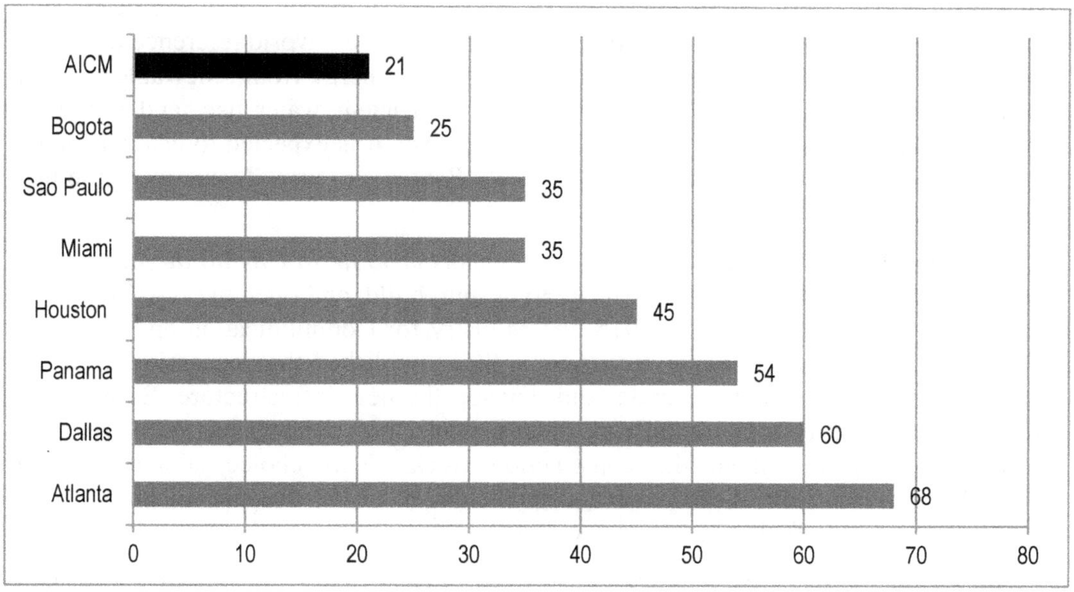

Source: Presentation "*Visión Integral*", www.aeropuerto.gob.mx/documentos/05092014-sct-visionintegral.pdf, consulted on 18 September 2015.

AICM is the number one means of air transportation in Mexico. It is the strategic point that connects the country internally and with the rest of the world. Not only does it serve 34% of the passengers in Mexico, but it is also the main port of entry for tourists and business travellers. In addition, it concentrates 56% of the merchandise that is air-transported abroad. The NAICM will have in its maximum development phase six runways and will transport around 120 million passengers annually, which is four times the current capacity of AICM (Table 1.2).

Table 1.2. **NAICM capacity**

First phase	Maximum development
50 million passengers per year	120 million passengers per year
550 000 operations per year	1 000 000 operations per year
3 parallel runways operating simultaneously	6 runways with triple simultaneous operation
94 contact and 42 remote stands[1]	
4 430 ha of land	

1. Estimated to be sufficient for the next ten years.

Source: Presentation "*Visión Integral*", www.aeropuerto.gob.mx/documentos/05092014-sct-visionintegral.pdf, consulted on 18 September 2015.

The five-year National Development Plan 2013-18 published in the Official Journal on 20 May 2013 indicates that Mexico shall be equipped with modern airport infrastructure to augment connectivity between regions and increase the competitiveness of the country. Infrastructure is found to be one important factor that enhances the overall competitiveness of countries.

Mexico is currently ranked 61 out of 144 countries in terms of global competitiveness and 65 in terms of infrastructure (WEF, 2014).

The new airport is designed to be one of the world's most sustainable airports and a showcase for Mexican innovation built by national contractors and engineers. The Federal Government has set the objective for the airport to be a world reference in design, construction, and sustainable operation. It will use clean energy from renewable sources; it will operate with green technologies promoting efficient water use; and will have ventilation and air conditioning that optimise energy use. It is expected to take advantage of the biogas generated in the dump of the *Bordo Poniente* to provide energy to the new airport.

A previously existing entity, the *Grupo Aeroportuario de la Ciudad de México S.A. de C.V.* (GACM) has received the mandate to design, build, and open the NAICM by the Mexican Government. In January 2015, the Ministry for Communication and Transport (*Secretaria de Comunicaciones y Transportes*, SCT) published the concession in favour of GACM, to build, manage, operate, and develop the new infrastructure. Between the different types of infrastructure delivery modes, public procurement has been identified as the means to implement the construction works. This choice, along with the surrounding environment of the project, entails choices on the structure of procurement operations and trade-offs between various objectives.

The vision for the project is that it will not only be a state-of-the-art emblematic infrastructure in terms of design, construction, and operation, but that it will also define how major infrastructure projects are carried out in Mexico. In this sense, NAICM is seen as much more than just infrastructure, but as a lever to improve the quality of life of the inhabitants of central Mexico, in particular, and of Mexicans in general. Consequently, the development of the airport is accompanied by a set of measures dealing with the environment, mobility, water management and urban development, among others.

The construction of the NAICM will be funded with a mix of public and private funds, with around 60% coming from the federal budget. The cost of the project is estimated to amount to USD 13 billion for the first phase of construction (2014-18), with about 50% concentrated in 2015 and 2016 (Figure 1.4).

In order to guarantee the long-term financial sustainability of the project, GACM, together with the Ministry of Finance, designed a comprehensive financial strategy taking into account the situation in international financial markets and the recent evolution of the commodities market. In 2015, MXN 5.4 billion were allocated by the Federal Government to initiate preliminary work. At the same time, a credit line of USD 1 billion (MXN 16.7 billion) has been negotiated with private banks (HSBC, BBVA, Citibank and Inbursa).

Government revenues in Mexico are significantly exposed to fluctuations of oil prices since almost 30% of public resources are drawn from oil revenues. Although stabilisation mechanisms (i.e. exchange rate depreciation when oil prices fall, oil stabilisation fund, financial hedge on prices) in place prevent public resources from dramatically fluctuating with the oil market, this factor could however induce a greater recourse to private financing if public funds are scarcer than anticipated.

Due to the recent downtrend in oil prices and to accommodate possible changes in the funding from public resources, GACM upgraded the initial financial strategy to resist similar circumstances. The revised strategy includes a revolving credit facility of USD 3 billion, which was closed on 7 October 2015 and the forthcoming bond issuance of long-term bonds with international investment grade up to the amount of USD 6 billion.

Figure 1.4. **Total NAICM investment and planned funding sources**

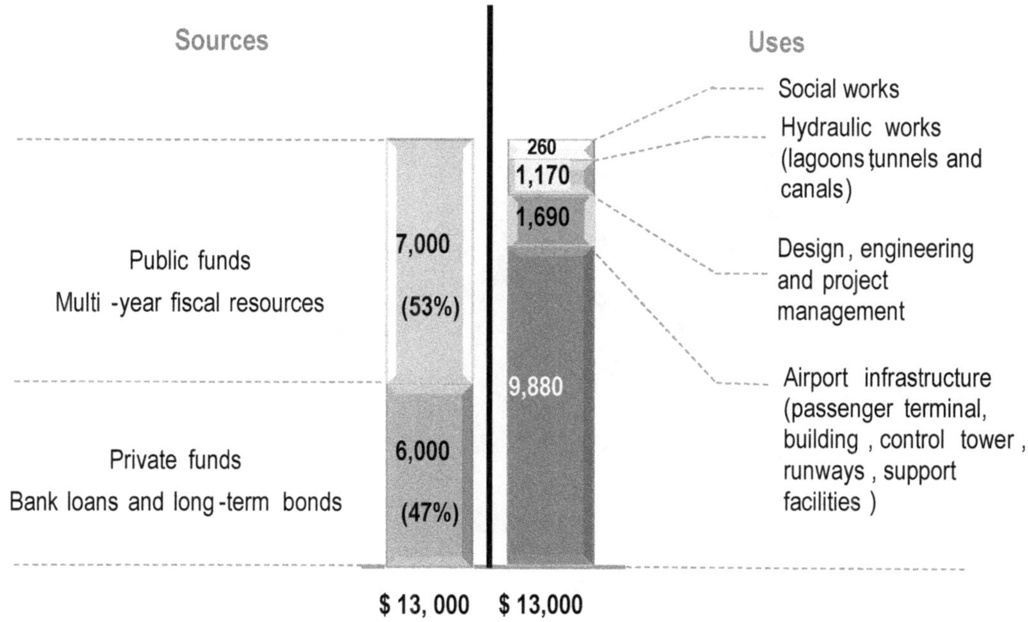

Source: Adapted from www.aeropuerto.gob.mx/financing-scheme-for-the-new-mexico-city-international-airport.php (accessed on 26 August 2015).

Both public and private investments should be reimbursed through cash flow generated by the current and future airport. Returns on investment will therefore largely depend on the completion date of the construction of the airport. Although GACM is not experiencing any difficulties in attracting private funding for the project, as evidenced by the interim results of a checklist sent to members of the G20/OECD Task Force on Institutional Investors and Long-Term Financing, the expected return and risk of investment projects is a core consideration in attracting private financing (OECD, 2015).

When investment decisions relate to infrastructure projects, securing private financing can be seriously affected by the absence, perceived or real, of two main components. The first is a lack of planning in infrastructure projects. In efforts to create a framework conducive to private sector investment in infrastructure projects, the Mexican Government designed a national infrastructure investment plan for the period 2014-18. The second component is the absence of demonstration of the capacity to prepare and execute projects successfully. While this element will be assessed in the light of past successes or failures in infrastructure projects, it could also be influenced, according to the phasing of construction activities (see Chapter 4), by the success or failure of previous construction phases.

International experience illustrates that governance is a key issue for the success of this type of megaproject, not only to keep them on time and on budget, but also to avoid corruption. Chapter 2 deals with the governance structure of GACM and the different entities and stakeholders involved in the project. Chapter 3 addresses procurement practices and strategies. Procurement is, without a doubt, a very sensitive activity due to the amount of resources involved and the close interactions between the public and private sectors. By way of example, the OECD analysed a set of 427 foreign bribery cases concluded between February 1999 and June 2014 and found that 57% are related to public procurement (Figure 1.5).

Figure 1.5. **Purpose of foreign bribery cases between 1999 and 2014**

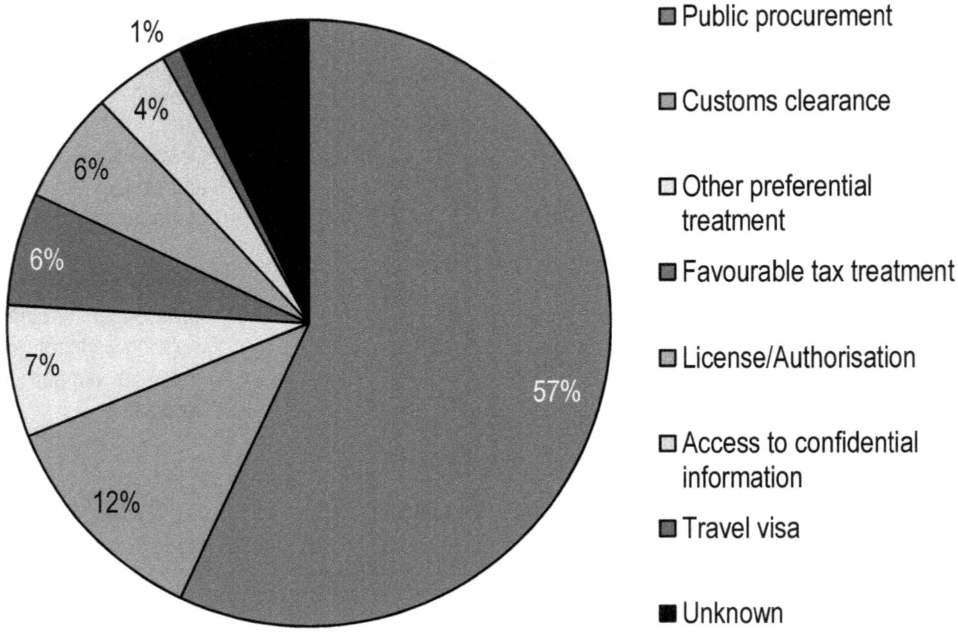

Source: Based on OECD (2014), *OECD Foreign Bribery Report: An Analysis of the Crime of Bribery of Foreign Public Officials*, OECD Publishing, Paris, http://dx.doi.org/10.1787/9789264226616-en.

The dimension of these risks calls for the implementation of preventive measures to safeguard integrity. Corruption not only implies economic costs, but also hinders trust in government and may result in risks for citizens (i.e. due to poor quality infrastructure). Chapter 4 proposes tools and measures to mitigate the risks of corruption and waste.

Successful megaprojects are accompanied by a robust communications strategy, which serves not only to inform, but also to engage citizens and business. Chapter 5 will describe to what extent the NAICM communications strategy abides by good OECD practices. Finally, Chapter 6 represents a route map for the implementation of the recommendations contained throughout this report.

Notes

1. The operational limit translates into about 32 million passengers per year.
2. Information provided by GACM.

References

GACM (*Grupo Aeroportuario de la Ciudad de México*) (2015), "*Plan de Restauración Ecológica*", www.aeropuerto.gob.mx/documentos/plan-de-restauracion-ecologica-naicm1.pdf.

OECD (2015), "Updated report on G20/OECD checklist on long-term investment financing strategies and institutional investors", https://g20.org/wp-content/uploads/2015/05/G20-OECD-Report-on-Checklist-on-Long-Term-Investment-Financing-Strategies-and-Institutional-Investors-April-2015.pdf.

OECD (2014), *OECD Foreign Bribery Report: An Analysis of the Crime of Bribery of Foreign Public Officials*, OECD Publishing, Paris, http://dx.doi.org/10.1787/9789264226616-en.

WEF (World Economic Forum) (2014), *The Global Competitiveness Report 2014-2015*, www.weforum.org/reports/global-competitiveness-report-2014-2015.

Chapter 2

The governance of the NAICM project

*As a result of austerity policies, the Government of Mexico, via the Ministry of Finance and Public Credit (*Secretaría de Hacienda y Crédito Público, *SHCP) decided to leverage on an existing body, specifically a quasi-state entity (*entidad paraestatal*), to lead the development of the New International Airport of Mexico City* (Nuevo Aeropuerto Internacional de la Ciudad de México, *NAICM), avoiding the need to create new public institutions. The Government decided to activate the enterprise with majority state participation, Airport Group of Mexico City (*Grupo Aeroportuario de la Ciudad de México, S.A. de C.V., *GACM), to be in charge of the design, construction, and launching of operations of NAICM. This chapter will analyse the governance of the project in two dimensions: the internal dimension (GACM's corporate governance) and the external one (the relationships and interactions with stakeholders).*

Background of the *Grupo Aeroportuario de la Ciudad de México* (GACM)

In 1998, different concessions of air terminals to the private sector were carried out in Mexico, as part of the restructuring and disincorporation of the national airports network, which until then had been managed by Airports and Auxiliary Services (*Aeropuertos y Servicios Auxiliares*, ASA).[1] As a result, four airport groups emerged: Southeast Airport Group, Airport Group of the Pacific, Airport Group Center-North, and GACM. The GACM was formally established as an enterprise with state participation on 28 May 1998, being the unique shareholder the Federal Government, via the Ministry for Communication and Transport (*Secretaria de Comunicaciones y Transportes*, SCT) and ASA. GACM was, in fact, created as an enterprise to hold shares, but until its appointment as the leader of the NAICM project it had not completed any operation and did not have an organisational structure.

GACM has two subsidiary entities in charge of the management, operations, maintenance, and organisation of airport services, provided in the Benito Juárez International Airport of Mexico City. These entities are International Airport of Mexico City (*Aeropuerto Internacional de la Ciudad de México*, S.A. de C.V., AICM) and Airport Services of Mexico City (*Servicios Aeroportuarios de la Ciudad de México*, S.A. de C.V.).

GACM's vision is to be the entity in charge of co-ordinating and successfully carrying out the integral development of the airport infrastructure of the Mexico Valley, following good international practices in a framework of social and environmental responsibility in order to contribute to Mexico's sustainable development. Its mission is to undertake the necessary actions to provide the required modern and efficient infrastructure to launch operations of the airport infrastructure of the Mexico Valley, following the principles of legality, transparency, and opportunity, to address the current and future needs of national and international air transport, supporting the economy, the environment, tourism and safety.[2]

GACM corporate governance

The GACM Board is GACM's governing body. It is responsible for establishing general policies and defining priorities regarding production, productivity, marketing, finance, research, technology development, and management, in line with the Government's programmes for the transport sector. Likewise, it reviews and approves GACM programmes and budgets, financial statements and its organisational structure.

The GACM Board is led by the Minister of Communications and Transport and is composed of the following officials:

- the Head of the Legal Affairs Unit of SCT, who serves as the Secretariat
- the Head of the Legal Co-ordination for Transport of SCT, who serves as Deputy Secretariat
- the Deputy Minister for Transport (SCT)
- the Deputy Minister for Population, Migration, and Religious Affairs of the Ministry of the Interior (*Secretaría de Gobernación*, SEGOB)
- the Deputy Minister for Trade and Industry of the Ministry of Economy

- the Deputy Minister for Tourism Policy and Planning of the Ministry of Tourism
- ASA's Director General
- the Head of the National Agrarian Registry (*Registro Agrario Nacional*, RAN)
- the Director General for Legal Affairs of the RAN
- the Director General for Environmental Impacts and Risks of the Ministry of the Environment and Natural Resources (*Secretaría de Medio Ambiente y Recursos Naturales*, SEMARNAT)
- the Director General "B" for Programming and Budgeting of the Ministry of Finance and Public Credit (*Secretaría de Hacienda y Crédito Público*, SHCP)
- the Deputy Director General for Programming and Budgeting for Social Development, Labour, Economy, and Communications of SHCP
- the Director General for Planning of the Ministry of Tourism
- GACM's Director General.

GACM's corporate governance responds to the logic of the governance of public institutions, which prevents it from benefiting from the efficiency gains and operational benefits associated with a more corporatised structure. Indeed, GACM's corporate governance is not aligned with key issues outlined in the OECD Guidelines on Corporate Governance of State-Owned Enterprises (Box 2.1).[3] Even though GACM is not considered as an enterprise, it issues shares, which are fully owned by Mexico's Federal Government.[4] The general principle is that when governments conduct financially important projects, they should allocate these undertakings to a state-owned enterprise (SOE) if and only if they seek to benefit from the corporate form. Otherwise it is better left to a public institution.

Box 2.1. **The OECD Guidelines on Corporate Governance of State-Owned Enterprises**

The OECD Guidelines on Corporate Governance of State-Owned Enterprises are recommendations to governments on how to ensure that SOEs operate efficiently, transparently, and in an accountable manner. They are the internally agreed standard for how governments should exercise the state ownership function to avoid the pitfalls of both passive ownership and excessive state intervention. The guidelines were first developed in 2005 as a complement to the OECD Principles on Corporate Governance. They are being updated to reflect the decade of experience with their implementation and address new issues that have arisen concerning SOEs in the domestic and international context.

The document is divided into two main parts. The guidelines presented in the first part of the document cover the following themes: *i)* rationales for state ownership; *ii)* the state's role as an owner; *iii)* SOEs in the marketplace; *iv)* equitable treatment of shareholders and other investors; *v)* stakeholder relations and responsible business; *vi)* disclosure and transparency; and *vii)* the responsibilities of the boards of SOEs. In the second part of the document, the guidelines are supplemented by annotations that are intended to help readers understand their rationale. The annotations also contain descriptions of dominant trends and offer a range of implementation methods and examples that may be useful in making the guidelines operational.

See www.oecd.org/daf/ca/2014-review-oecd-corporate-governance-principles.htm for more information.

First, there is a possibility to increase the degree for vertical separation of powers in GACM's relationship with SCT (within GACM and between GACM and the government ownership). It is critical that which type of decision is made at which level is made clear (see Figure 2.1). Policy disagreements should be discussed at a whole-of-government level and, under no circumstances, carried into the boardroom of GACM. If the Government cannot, or will not, grant this degree of autonomy to the board, then the corporate form is not suitable and the Government may opt to establish a more traditional public agency. In other words, an unclear vertical separation of powers increases the risk of bringing inherently political disagreements to be settled in the boardroom, rather than decided at a whole-of-government level and communicated to GACM.

Figure 2.1. **Vertical separation of powers**

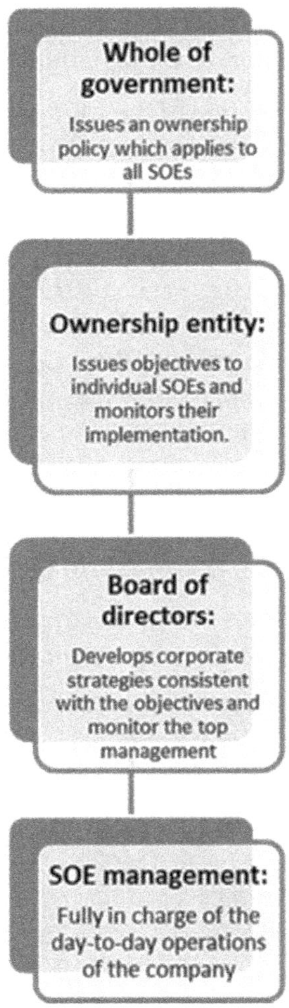

Source: OECD (2013c), *Boards of Directors of State-Owned Enterprises: An Overview of National Practices*, OECD Publishing, Paris.

SCT involvement in day-to-day operations of GACM would illustrate the lack of vertical separation. In such a case, the ownership entity validates, for example, communications to be issued by the SOE. *De facto*, the ownership entity makes the important decisions concerning, for example, the procurement and financial strategies of the SOE. Hence, the SOE does not have the flexibility to make decisions as they do in many OECD countries (see Box 2.2).

Box 2.2. **The evolution of PEMEX's Board**

The Law of PEMEX (*Petróleos Mexicanos*, Mexico's state-owned oil enterprise), published in the Official Gazette on 11 August 2014, establishes in Article 15 that its board will be composed by the following:

- the Minister of Energy, who presides over the Board, and the Minister of Finance
- three members representing the Federal Government, appointed by the Federal Executive
- five independent members, appointed by the Federal Executive and ratified by the Senate, who will exercise the position on a part-time basis and are not public officials.

Overall, the reform is an improvement in relation to the OECD Guidelines on Corporate Governance of State-Owned Enterprises. The diversification of the board to include independent members is in accordance with internationally recommended good practices. Care must however be taken to ensure the actual independence of the individuals appointed. Previous to this reform, the board was composed of the following:

- six representatives of the state, appointed by the Federal Executive
- five representatives from the Petroleum Workers' Union, who had to be active members and permanent employees of PEMEX
- four members appointed by the Federal Executive and ratified by the Senate, who represented the State and, in this capacity, were considered as public officials.

Source: OECD (2013a), *Corporate Governance and Board Arrangements at* Petroleos Mexicanos, *Evaluation and recommendations*, OECD Publishing, Paris; and Law of Pemex, available at www.diputados.gob.mx/LeyesBiblio/pdf/LPM_110814.pdf, consulted on 29 September 2015.

A management that lacks clear direction and powers to act, subject to reasonable checks and balances, might lead to a dysfunctional organisation. Good practice would suggest a corporate governance arrangement that is similar to the following:

- Business strategy, operational issues, investment decisions, and procurement would be the responsibility of GACM's management and its Board.
- Airport policy is managed by SCT as part of an integrated transport policy.
- Sectoral or specific regulatory concerns would be the responsibility of the relevant ministries and government agencies.

Another issue of concern is that the GACM Board does not have the adequate support in terms of internal audit. This could foster distrust between the Board and GACM's management and invite the Board to micromanage. OECD good practices suggest that SOEs should develop efficient internal audit procedures and establish an internal audit function that is monitored by, and responds directly to, the Board. Currently, there are two main entities involved in the auditing and oversight of GACM, namely the Ministry of Public Administration (*Secretaría de la Función Pública*, SFP) through the Internal

Control Body (*Órgano Interno de Control*, OIC) of SCT and the Superior Audit Office (*Auditoría Superior de la Federación*, ASF), which is the auditing body that oversees all parts of the general government sector, reports to Congress, and is completely independent of GACM and the Executive Branch of Government. These two oversight bodies complement, but should not replace, the internal audit function suggested above and, in fact, neither of the two report to GACM's board.

Board composition and nomination is also problematic when benchmarked against the OECD Guidelines. As established in the Federal Law for Quasi-state Entities (*Ley Federal de las Entidades Paraestatales,* LFEP*)* members of the board of enterprises with majority state participation representing the Federal Public Administration (*Administración Pública Federal*, APF) are appointed and can be replaced by the President, through the sector leader. LFEP states that these members should always represent more than 50% of the board and they should be public servants or recognised individuals with experience in the corresponding field. In other words, the law does not require that all members representing the APF are public servants, however, in GACM's case, all board members are indeed public officials.[5] LFEP or its Bylaws do not elaborate on alternative procedures for the President to appoint board members (i.e., nomination committees, pools of qualified candidates, headhunting firms), while OECD good practice suggests that such appointments should be based on competitive and merit-based procedures. This is clearly not the case for GACM and hence there is a risk of politicising the nominations. Furthermore, contrary to good practices in OECD countries, no compulsory or voluntary board training programmes are in place in GACM.

The LFEP Bylaws (*Reglamento de la Ley Federal de las Entidades Paraestatales*) establish that members of the board should register alternate members in case they cannot participate in board meetings. This is a common practice in Latin America that should be managed with care and restricted to really extreme circumstances since it might prevent the Board from acting as a truly collegial and professional body.

Finally, in another departure from good corporate practices, no evaluation or self-evaluation mechanism exists for the GACM Board.

GACM organisational structure

The GACM's organisational structure was designed with the knowledge that as many functions as possible would be outsourced and in line with principles of austerity and public spending discipline. As it will be mentioned in the assessment section, outsourcing without proper controls can imply serious risks. The organisational structure was revised and approved, as legally required, by both SHCP and SFP.

As illustrated in Figure 2.2, GACM's organisational structure is led by its Director General and four corporate directors: *i)* planning, evaluation, and outreach; *ii)* infrastructure; *iii)* finance; and *iv)* administration and real estate management. The structure also includes the establishment of an Internal Control Office (OIC), subordinated to the SFP.[6]

Figure 2.2. **Organisational structure of the GACM**

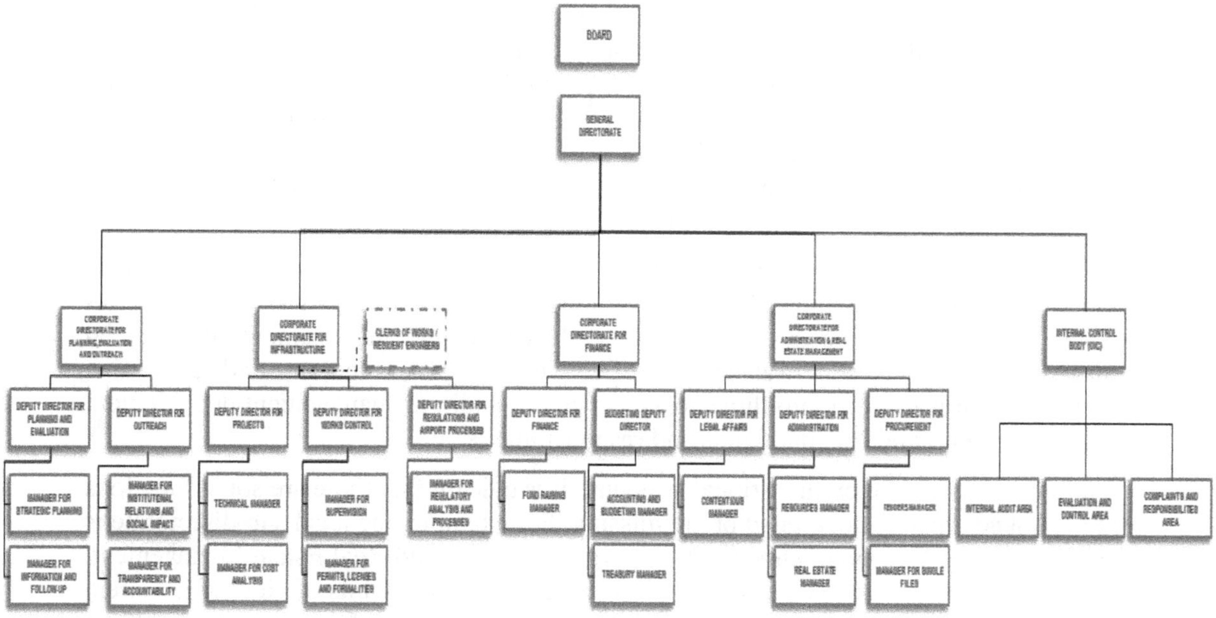

Source: GACM website, www.aeropuerto.gob.mx/gacm/estructura-organizacional.php (accessed on 18 September 2015).

The Director General co-ordinates and executes the necessary measures so that every stage in the development of the airport infrastructure of the Mexico Valley is completed on time and in compliance with the applicable regulatory frameworks, in co-ordination with other entities of the APF and the state and municipal governments concerned.

The Corporate Directorate for Planning, Evaluation, and Outreach is responsible for strategic planning in the development of the airport infrastructure of the Mexico Valley, its evaluation, and following up the actions to be undertaken in every stage of the project to facilitate institutional development, as well as easing co-ordination and engagement between the different GACM areas and with external stakeholders. Likewise, it is responsible for compliance with transparency and freedom of information regulations. It is divided into two sub-directorates: *i)* planning and evaluation; and *ii)* outreach.

The Corporate Directorate for Infrastructure is responsible for organising and managing the studies, projects, works, and related services, by preparing terms of reference, managing investment contracts, supervising works, and ensuring an adequate infrastructure for the operation of the airport infrastructure of the Mexico Valley, while ensuring compliance with national and international aeronautic and safety regulations and the approved budgets. It is divided into three sub-directorates: *i)* projects; *ii)* control of works; and *iii)* airport regulations and processes.

The Corporate Directorate for Finance is responsible for planning, defining, and co-ordinating strategies and guidelines for the adequate programming, budgeting, and financial strategy by controlling the budget exercise and accounting of the assigned and spent resources, as well as for identifying, analysing, and proposing mechanisms to obtain the necessary resources and funding for the development of the airport infrastructure of the Mexico Valley. It is divided into two sub-directorates: *i)* finance; and *ii)* budget.

The Corporate Directorate for Administration and Real Estate Management is responsible for GACM's legal representation and undertaking the necessary measures to ensure compliance with the applicable regulatory frameworks; leading the planning, integration, direction, and control of human resources, real estate, buildings, and general services; carrying out procurement of public works, acquisitions, and related services; as well as the real estate management strategy. It is divided into three sub-directorates: *i)* legal; *ii)* management; and *iii)* procurement.

Finally, the OIC is responsible for the monitoring and surveillance of the authorised programmes and budgets through prevention measures and verification of operations, as well as for reviewing the systems for internal control and management of financial information to advance a transparent, effective, efficient, modern, and simplified organisation.[7] It is divided into three areas: *i)* internal audit; *ii)* management development and improvement; and *iii)* complaints and responsibilities.

After reviewing the organisational structure, it is evident that there are some functions that are not adequately positioned or are missing. For example, the legal sub-directorate is placed within the Corporate Directorate for Administration and Real Estate Management. This might not only lead to conflicts of interest (i.e. sustaining points of view of its parent directorate *vis-à-vis* those of the other), but also misrepresents a function that should be transversal and serve the whole organisation. Likewise, there is nothing resembling a Chief Information Officer (CIO) in charge of the information systems and platforms of GACM. Again, this is a transversal function that could very well report directly to the Director General.

Since GACM staff are hired on temporary contracts that have to be renewed every three months, it is advisable to take a close look at the profiles of each professional and assess whether skills, rank, and compensations are coherent with the tasks to be undertaken. For example, for NAICM to be a world-class project, it requires its senior staff to have the skills to understand the implications of such a megaproject (i.e. technical and management skills dealing with finance, project administration, negotiation, leadership) and to communicate the attractiveness and virtues of the project to an international audience (i.e. speaking English and other languages).

The organisational structure also depends on the work of three other actors, working hand-in-hand with GACM: the project manager (PM, a company called Parsons International Limited), the master design architect (a company called Romero-Foster & Partners), and the master civil design engineer (a group of companies integrated by Netherlands Airports Consultants-TADCO and SACMAG). GACM is, *vis-à-vis* these actors, the owner of the NAICM project and integrates all aspects of it, with the support of the PM. The PM is tasked with developing the programme implementation plan, which is used as the guiding document for execution. It oversees, guides, and manages the master design architect, the master civil design engineer, and other key consultants to make sure objectives and milestones are met. The PM is also responsible for the programme budget, schedule, and overall controls. In fact, it has developed a plan to track all achievements and provide early warnings that pose risks to the project. The project leverages on a Dashboard Control System, which allows for the follow up of progress at any stage, measuring the work done, and identifying critical elements and work to be done, providing warning flags when there are elements that may impact progress. However, as the PM is not part of the Government, it has limited decision-making powers. The master design architect provides design and architectural services for executive projects that lead to the construction of NAICM, as well as follow up. This includes the architectural projects for the terminal, the control tower, and the parking lots. The master civil design engineer provides the executive projects of design and conceptual engineering for runways, platforms, and navigational support.

Regulatory framework governing GACM

The operations of GACM are governed by a series of regulatory instruments, ranging from the Political Constitution of the United Mexican States (*Constitución Política de los Estados Unidos Mexicanos*, hereinafter the Constitution) to guidelines and manuals issued by GACM itself.

The Constitution, in its Article 90, establishes that the APF is divided into central and quasi-state (*paraestatal*), according to the Organic Law of the APF, which elaborates on how the administrative functions are allocated in the different ministries and defines the criteria to establish quasi-state entities and determine the intervention of the Executive in their operations. The Organic Law of the APF, in its Article 46, defines as enterprises with majority state participation those in which the Federal Government or one or more quasi-state entities, jointly or separately, hold more than 50% of the social capital and/or those for which the Federal Government has the power to appoint most of the members of the board and/or its President or General Director. Both conditions are met in the case of the GACM, since the Federal Government, via SCT, holds 99.999% of the shares and ASA holds 0.001%.[8]

Likewise, according to the Organic Law of the APF, the President will group the quasi-state public administration by sector, bearing in mind the objectives of each entity. Consequently, the GACM is grouped in the transport sector, which is led by SCT. Sector leaders co-ordinate the programming and budgeting of the entities under their umbrellas, have the duty to know their operations, evaluate their results, and participate in their boards.

The LFEP also elaborates on the mandates of Article 90 of the Constitution. Its objective is to regulate the organisation, functioning, and control of quasi-state entities. Chapter III refers specifically to the governance of enterprises with majority state participation. For example, it dictates how the members of the board are appointed (i.e. by the President through the sector leader, in the GACM case, SCT), how frequently the board should meet (at least four times per year) and the powers granted to general directors.

In addition to these primary regulations,[9] GACM has issued the main secondary rules and guidelines that govern its organisation and functions, including the following:

- *Organisation Manual:* It establishes the functions and attributions of the different administrative units of GACM.
- *Salary scales:* This document defines the salaries and compensations of GACM personnel.
- Policies and guidelines regarding public works and related services ([*Políticas, bases y lineamientos en materia de Obras Públicas y Servicios Relacionados con las Mismas*, POBALINES] public works): This piece regulates the acts and procedures for planning, budgeting, hiring, executing, following up, and

controlling public works and related services, as well as the units and officials responsible for undertaking these activities.

- *Procedures manual for planning, contracting, and executing public works and related services:* It regulates specific details concerning the public works annual plan and procedures for open tendering, invitation to at least three suppliers by exception, direct adjudications by exception, invitation to at least three suppliers by amount, direct adjudication by amount, and contract management.
- *Manual for the integration and functioning of the Committee on Public Works and Related Services:* This manual provides the normative framework for the composition, operations, and functions of the Committee on Public Works and Related Services of GACM, as well as the responsibilities of its members, in line with Article 25 of the Law on Public Works and Related Services.
- *Policies and guidelines regarding acquisitions, leasing, and services (POBALINES acquisitions):* This piece regulates the acts and procedures for acquisitions, leasing, and other services, as well as the units and officials responsible for undertaking these activities.
- *Procedures manual for planning, contracting, and managing acquisitions, leasing, and services:* It regulates specific details concerning the acquisitions, leasing, and services annual plan, the preparation of calls for tender, and procedures for open tendering, invitation to at least three suppliers by exception, direct adjudications by exception, invitation to at least three suppliers by amount, direct adjudication by amount, and contract management.
- *Manual for the integration and functioning of the Committee on Acquisitions, Leasing, and Services of the Public Sector:* This manual provides the normative framework for the composition, operations, and functions of the Committee on Acquisitions, Leasing, and Services of GACM, as well as the responsibilities of its members, in line with Article 22 of the Law on Acquisitions, Leasing, and Services of the Public Sector.
- *Budgeting administrative procedures manual:* It regulates the procedures for programming and budgeting, spending and control, and accountability mechanisms.
- *Budgeting administrative procedures policies:* It establishes policies for the management of the revolving fund, obtaining and justifying travel expenses, remunerations corresponding to Chapter 1000 of the national budget, procedures to request payments for the acquisition of goods and services and the contracting of public works and related services, and contributions to funds, mandates, and similar contracts.
- *Procedures manual* to elaborate, evaluate, and update the strategic plan.
- *Operational guidelines for the revolving fund:* This regulation establishes criteria and measures for the management of the revolving fund, aiming at providing certainty to the public officials in charge of it.
- *Guidelines for obtaining and using services cards for expenses incurred in national and international travel.*

Table 2.1 sets out the regulatory framework applicable to the governing of GACM.

Table 2.1. **Regulatory framework applicable to the governing of GACM**

Government-wide regulations	GACM-specific regulations
On general governance: • Constitution (Article 90) • Organic Law of the AP. • Federal Law for Quasi-State Entities.	On general governance: • Organisation Manual • Salary scales • Budgeting administrative procedures manual • Budgeting administrative procedures policies • Procedures manual to elaborate, evaluate, and update the strategic plan • Operational guidelines for the revolving fund • Guidelines for obtaining and using services cards for expenses incurred in national and international travel.
On procurement: • Law on acquisitions, leasing, and services of the public sector • Bylaws (*Reglamento*) of the Law on acquisitions, leasing and services of the public sector • Law on public works and related services • Bylaws (*Reglamento*) of the Law on public works and related services.	On procurement: • POBALINES Public works • Procedures manual for planning, contracting, and executing public works and related services • Manual for the integration and functioning of the Committee on public works and related services • POBALINES Acquisitions • Procedures manual for planning, contracting, and managing acquisitions, leasing, and services • Manual for the integration and functioning of the committee on acquisitions, leasing, and services of the public sector.

Source: Author's own work with information provided by GACM.

The regulatory framework governing GACM resembles that of other quasi-state entities and therefore includes rules that are common to find in Mexico's APF. Hence, one important challenge is to adapt the framework to the needs of a megaproject. This is particularly relevant for the regulations dealing with procurement. But it is also true for others to allow the incorporation of good international practices concerning, for example, corporate governance.

Another challenging dilemma is preventing wrongdoing and guaranteeing integrity while keeping structures flexible and simple. This is not an easy balance to strike. The issuance of GACM specific rules could provide certainty but it is important to communicate about such regulations among staff and provide support and training for their interpretation and implementation, particularly for those rules recently approved, such as POBALINES. Indeed, other entities in Mexico's government (i.e. the State's Employees' Social Security and Social Services Institute, ISSSTE) have reported benefits from the issuance of detailed and consolidated regulations. It will be important in the future that the issuance of GACM specific regulations or their reforms be accompanied by consultation to GACM officials in order to address common situations faced by them. Consultation would provide information to determine practicability and to design compliance strategies. This is a widely applied practice in OECD countries.[10]

Governance and co-ordination with other government entities

The stakeholders of NAICM, influencing the external dimension of the governance of the project, can be classified into three groups: *i)* government institutions directly linked to NAICM; *ii)* airport users; and *iii)* the wider public.

A project the magnitude of NAICM has multiple implications and impacts requiring the co-ordinated action of different public institutions and several levels of government (see Figure 2.3 for a mapping of the government institutions involved).

Figure 2.3. **Mapping of the government institutions involved in the development of NAICM**

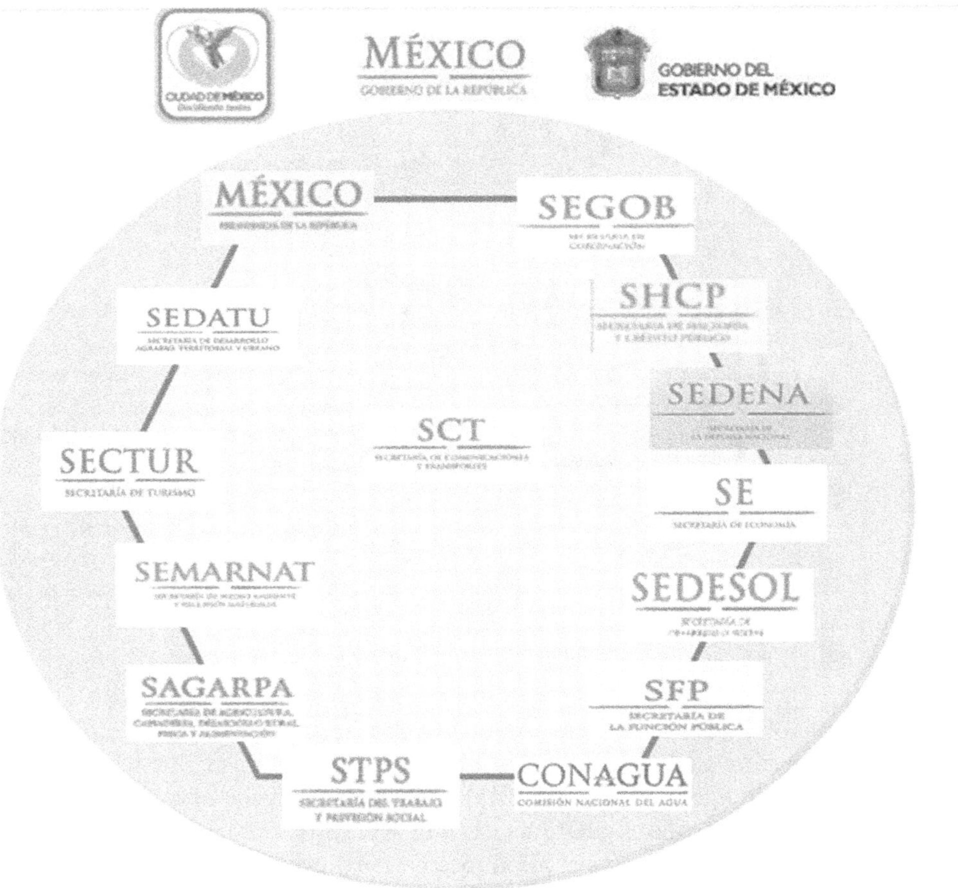

Source: Presentation "*Visión Integral*", www.aeropuerto.gob.mx/documentos/05092014-sct-visionintegral.pdf, consulted on 18 September 2015.

The following five impacts require the co-ordinated action of the different public institutions and several levels of the Mexican Government:

1. *Environmental:* Pollution and noise will be generated not only during the construction phase, but also once NAICM is operational. As recommended in the resolution to the Environmental Impact Statement, issued by SEMARNAT,[11] mitigation measures have been anticipated in order to address potential impacts to fauna and flora that have their habitats in the airport site and its surroundings. Furthermore, the airport and the businesses and neighbourhoods that will follow its construction and operation will require water, which calls for investments that are being co-ordinated by the National Water Commission (CONAGUA).

   The NAICM project is addressing these concerns with plans to rescue an ecologically degraded zone by developing green areas, particularly the Metropolitan Forest, which will comprise 670 hectares and become the region's main lung. In addition, 5 000 hectares will be reforested within the Valley of

Mexico. The Environmental Master Plan (co-ordinated by SEMARNAT) set ambitious goals for NAICM, such as obtaining the LEED certification,[12] being the first non-European airport to operate with a neutral carbon fingerprint, and using 100% of its energy from clean local sources. In this regard, the plans include the construction of a plant of biogas and taking advantage of solar intake conditions, which are much better than those of other airports (5.1 KWh/m^2 per day for NAICM versus 3.8 for Chicago O'Hare, 3.7 for Indianapolis, and 3.5 for Kasai-Osaka). Likewise, the Hydraulic Master Plan (co-ordinated by CONAGUA) anticipates the development of the biggest water body of the Metropolitan Area with more than 2 700 hectares and 300 hectares devoted for aquatic birds.[13] In summary, GACM will launch a series of more than 20 measures and programmes to address the issues raised in the resolution to the Environmental Impact Assessment and put forward a deposit for MXN 770 million as a guarantee to comply with such measures.

2. *Social:* During the 2000-06 administration, social unrest was strong enough to question the need for a new airport and block its construction. The movement was led by inhabitants of the municipality of Atenco, State of Mexico, who did not agree to the terms proposed to sell their lands for the project. The situation is different now as NAICM will be constructed on land that is property of the Federal Government and that public opinion is vastly in favour of it, despite the fact that there are still minority political and social movements in disagreement with its construction. On the side of social benefits, for example, the project will trigger works for hydraulic solutions, by increasing three times, up to 38 million cubic meters, water regulation capacity, which should help reduce risks of flooding. In 2010, 585 schools in the State of Mexico and 120 in the Federal District were temporarily closed as a result of flooding.

   NAICM will mainly impact the eastern side of Mexico City, including three of its delegations and 11 municipalities of the State of Mexico. The East Zone has significantly lower standards of living relative to the metropolitan area of Mexico City (see Table 2.2). The NAICM is seen as an opportunity to raise the standards of living in the East Zone.

Table 2.2. **Standard of living in the East Zone vs. the metropolitan area of Mexico City (2010)**

Indicator	East Zone	Metropolitan area of Mexico City
Economically active population with income below two times the minimum salary	33%	22%
Unemployment rate	5.1%	4.9%
Informality rate	45%	41%
Population below the poverty line	39%	34%
Average school years	9.6	10

Source: Presentation "*Visión Integral*", www.aeropuerto.gob.mx/documentos/05092014-sct-visionintegral.pdf, consulted on 18 September 2015.

Indeed, this might be one of the main reasons why public opinion polls show strong and steady support for the project. In a poll commissioned by GACM carried out in the Federal District, 57% of respondents were in favour of the NAICM project in late August 2014 and 60% in early September 2015. Those claiming to be against were 18% at both periods. Likewise, a poll carried out in the central region of the country, and particularly the State of Mexico, reported 56% and 62% in favour and 14% against, respectively.[14] The conclusion of strong support towards the project is consistent with another poll carried out by *El Universal* newspaper, in which 65% of those surveyed approved the construction of NAICM and 18% disapproved.[15]

3. *Economic:* Competitiveness, investment, and jobs are some of the main benefits justifying the construction of NAICM. During the construction phase, for example, the NAICM will create 160 000 jobs. Currently, for example, the ministries of Labour and Social Development are implementing a Plan of Action with Direct Impact, which includes a temporary work programme and a data collection programme, benefiting 800 inhabitants of Atenco and Texcoco. In its ultimate development phase, the NAICM will have six runways and will transport 120 million passengers annually, four times the current capacity of the Benito Juárez International Airport of Mexico City.

4. *Mobility:* The NAICM will require transport means to make it accessible, not only for the air travellers themselves, but also for the people working on site and the businesses operating in the vicinity to the airport. Roads connecting to the airport, metro, bus lines, and some other transport options are being considered to facilitate mobility to and from the airport. Access is also necessary for the construction phase in order to allow the materials and equipment to get to the construction site. Such challenges will require co-ordination, for example, with the authorities of the State of Mexico and the Federal District, as well as those of their municipalities and delegations.

5. *Urban development:* The NAICM project will give birth to a new centre of economic and social activity. However, this does not come without risks and challenges. The three levels of government need to be co-ordinated to ensure an adequate supply of services, such as schools, hospitals, cultural and recreation centres, and public spaces. State and local governments will have to incorporate new dynamics into their urban development plans or, for those municipalities that do not even have one or when it is clearly outdated, new plans will have to be conceived.

The government institutions directly linked to NAICM participate in the project in order to support the construction and/or anticipate the necessary needs to carry out their duties. This is the case, for example, of control and surveillance institutions, such as the Customs Office, which reports to the Revenue Service (*Servicio de Administración Tributaria*, SAT); the National Immigration Institute (*Instituto Nacional de Migración*, INM), which reports to the Ministry of the Interior (SEGOB); the National Service for Vegetal and Animal Health (*Servicio Nacional de Sanidad, Inocuidad y Calidad Agroalimentaria*, SENASICA), which reports to the Ministry of Agriculture, Livestock, Rural Development, Fishing, and Food (*Secretaría de Agricultura, Ganadería, Desarrollo Rural, Pesca y Alimentación*, SAGARPA); and police bodies such as the General Attorney's Office (*Procuraduría General de la República*, PGR) and the Federal Police. Likewise, the military, via the Ministry of National Defence (*Secretaría de la Defensa Nacional,* SEDENA) is working on the project as it will use one of the runways for military purposes. Budget and fiscal control institutions, such as the Ministry of Public Administration (*Secretaría de la Función Pública*, SFP) and the Superior Audit of the Federation (*Auditoría Superior de la Federación*, ASF) are also engaged to exercise their surveillance and audit powers.

Co-ordination seems to be working well, at least concerning the federal institutions. There is a high-level group that gathers the heads of the main federal ministries taking part in NAICM. This group incorporates the participation of the governments of the State of Mexico and the Federal District. This has been a good mechanism to co-ordinate high-level decisions. However, the OECD team has heard about cases of information asymmetries, which should be addressed to avoid duplication, overlaps, or even contradictory measures. For example, the Ministry of Rural, Territorial, and Urban Development (*Secretaría de Desarrollo Agrario, Territorial y Urbano*, SEDATU) has developed several studies on the urban impact of the NAICM. These studies could be shared with GACM to benefit from its input.[16] It might be the case that while the high-level group ensures strategic co-ordination, there might still remain gaps at the technical level.

Within the group of public institutions, state and municipal governments also play an important role. In meetings with government entities of Mexico City and its delegations (April, July, and August 2015), they expressed having limited information on the plans to advance mobility and implications for urban planning. This might be particularly important for municipalities, as their capacities to collect and analyse information are limited and may have to rely on data provided by the Federal Government. While sensitive issues discussions (i.e. land use and commercial plans) might be kept to a small group of officials to avoid speculation, it is also true that good international practices suggest that urban and mobility planning, for example, are anticipated before the actual approval of megaprojects, such as an airport.

Mention should also be made of co-ordination with autonomous entities, particularly the National Institute for Freedom of Information (*Instituto Nacional de Transparencia, Acceso a la Información y Protección de Datos*, INAI) and the National Economic Competition Commission (*Comisión Federal de Competencia Económica*, COFECE). Late in 2014, GACM expressed its intention to sign agreements with these two institutions. The objective of the agreement with INAI was to advance a pro-active strategy for transparency and access to information, as well as have INAI advise GACM on building a web portal to maximise transparency. Likewise, the agreement with COFECE would aim to provide advice to GACM concerning market studies and prevention of bid rigging, in line with the mandate of the Federal Law on Economic Competition. As of April 2015, very little had been done to establish an agreement with COFECE. On the contrary, INAI and SCT agreed upon a programme to guarantee the transparency and informative disclosure of the infrastructure project known as New International Airport of Mexico City (*Programa para garantizar la transparencia y apertura informativa del proyecto de infraestructura conocido como "Nuevo Aeropuerto Internacional de la Ciudad de México*) (Box 2.3).

Decisions are typically made at multiple levels, however, there are strategic and operational decisions that will be vetted and discussed as part of the programme objectives. In terms of the approval process, the programme will implement technical committees to approve challenging proposals/recommendations concerning the technical aspects of design. In addition, GACM will form a review committee that will analyse all contract documents for compliance with the normative framework and due diligence. A number of authorities of the Federal Government participate in the typical approval process of the design and construction phases, such as SCT, the Civil Aeronautics General Directorate (*Dirección General de Aeronaútica Civil*, DGAC), and the bureau of Navigational Services in Mexico's Aerial Space (*Servicios a la Navegación en el Espacio Aéreo Mexicano*, SENEAM).

Box 2.3. The programme to guarantee the transparency and informative disclosure of the NAICM infrastructure project

The objective of the programme is to create the conditions for transparency and accountability to be a transversal policy that contributes to informed citizens, who participate in the initiatives carried out by the authorities in the development of NAICM in order for the project to have credibility among Mexico's society and the international community.

Among others, the specific actions to be undertaken to fulfil the objective of the programme are the following:

- complying with all the resolutions of INAI's Board related to challenges regarding the negative to disclose NAICM information
- training public officials and citizens
- developing the one-stop portal to access information concerning NAICM
- implementing a control board of requests for information
- organising academic events on transparency, freedom of information, and accountability
- implementing the model for archives management developed by the Network for Transparency and Freedom of Information of Latin America (*Red de Transparencia y Acceso a la Información Pública*, RTA).

Source: Information provided by GACM.

Financial strategy decisions are formally taken at the GACM Board of Directors and executed by GACM's General Director or the person specifically appointed by him. The General Director shall inform the Board of Directors of all actions executed by such authorisation. As a practical example, as part of the process of executing the first stage of the financing plan for NAICM, consisting on a loan for up to USD 1 billion granted to the development bank *Nacional Financiera* (NAFIN) Trust, AICM and GACM had to obtain the following authorisations and confirmations:

- authorisation from SCT, DGAC, and COFECE, with respect to granting the concession to GACM for the construction and operation of NAICM
- authorisation from the Deputy Ministry of Transport (*Subsecretaría de Transporte*, SST), with respect to the absolute assignment by AICM and GACM of the Airport Departure Tax (*Tarifa de Uso de Aeropuerto*, TUA) collection rights to the NAFIN Trust
- confirmation by the SAT, with respect to the tax regime applicable to AICM and GACM
- authorisation from AICM and GACM shareholders and Board of Directors to assign TUA collection rights to the NAFIN Trust.

Stakeholder engagement

In addition to the co-ordination with multiple public entities and the different levels of government, the governance of NAICM calls for systematic stakeholder engagement. Risk assessment and management, for example, should involve civil society and take advantage of its expertise (OECD, 2014). This is a key element in facilitating the sustainability of the project and mega-infrastructure projects generally speaking. New airports in particular are often accompanied by controversy and opposition (Alberts, Bowen, Jr. and Cidell, 2009) (Box 2.4). In other words, "megaprojects often come draped in a politics of mistrust" (OECD, 2014).

Box 2.4. **Challenges in the development of the Berlin-Brandenburg International Airport (BBI)**

After German reunification the two most affected federal states–the city of Berlin and Brandenburg–and the Federal Government created the Berlin-Brandenburg Airport Holding. This placed Berlin's three airports under a joint administration for the first time. Even more importantly, the holding was created to co-ordinate and facilitate the planning of BBI.

The year 1996 promised to be a breakthrough as politicians finally agreed on a location for BBI. Federal Minister of Transportation, Berlin's Mayor, and Brandenburg's Premier reached a consensus decision to build the new international airport in Schönefeld with private investments. Tempelhof would be closed as soon as possible, and Tegel would cease operating as soon as BBI opened. After these plans were made public, the airlines serving Tempelhof immediately stated that they would not move from Tempelhof to Schönefeld. A move to Tegel, however, was impossible because the airport could not handle any more passengers due to the terminal's circular outline.

Once there was consensus that BBI would be built in Schönefeld, the draft plan was presented to the public for comment. In total, citizens filed more than 132 000 complaints against the expansion of Schönefeld, focusing on noise pollution, the expected decline in property values, and the impact on the ground transportation infrastructure. According to German planning law, hearings have to be organised to listen and respond to all the complaints brought forward by citizens. The sheer volume (approximately 4 000 separate arguments) meant that the beginning of construction of the airport (scheduled for 2003) was delayed. At the same time as the hearings were taking place, a new Federal Government initiative reduced permissible noise levels around airports. These stricter regulations meant that BBI could not be operated late at night and that a significant amount of money had to be budgeted to provide citizens with mandatory noise insulation. Since the noise evaluation had been done based on the previous regulations, it was questionable whether it was still valid.

The debate concerning the financing of BBI also went on. According to the consensus decision, private investors should pay for the airport. After several potential investors dropped out early in the process, two serious contenders remained–*Hochtief* (an international construction services provider with experience in numerous large infrastructure projects) and IVG (one of the largest real estate companies in Europe). In 2000, *Hochtief* was excluded from consideration because of charges that it had obtained an unfair advantage in the competitive bid. However, just months later the regional court in Brandenburg overruled the decision and said that *Hochtief* should be allowed to bid. Rather than restarting the entire privatisation procedure again with IVG and *Hochtief* as competitors, a consensus was reached that the two companies should co-operate on the airport project. It appeared as if the privatisation issue was solved. However, in 2001, the consortium of the two companies made its offer, which was significantly lower than expected: DM 50 million, rather than the DM 650 million first offered by *Hochtief* and the DM 350 million originally promised by the IVG. After additional negotiations and extended deadlines this amount was increased to DM 70 million. This unacceptably low offer ended all hopes for privatisation.

Box 2.4. **Challenges in the development of the Berlin-Brandenburg International Airport (BBI)** ***(continued)***

Assuming that the investors were hesitant because of the large risk involved in building BBI–after all there was a possibility that lawsuits would stop the entire project– the Airport Holding now considered building the airport with government loans and privatising it once it was fully operational. By 2003, the estimated cost for the airport alone was EUR 1.7 billion. Additional funds would be needed to connect it to the highway and rail system and pay for noise protection measures and environmental clean-up at the site. Berlin and Brandenburg were heavily indebted, so they needed the help of the Federal Government to build BBI.

While these controversies were based on the assumption that BBI would be built in Schönefeld, a variety of different parties continued to argue in favour of other locations including Sperenberg, other Brandenburg sites, and even a military airfield in Poland. The lack of consensus was hardly resolved when, in 2004, the results of the hearings were made public. The 1 200-page document imposed strict limitations on night flights in Schönefeld and mandated that 42 000 people were entitled to receive noise-proof windows. Immediately, citizens started to compile a list of points against BBI for a lawsuit at the upper court in Leipzig. The lawyers representing the citizens were positive that the ten-point list addressing issues such as noise, pollution and other environmental hazards, and safety concerns would stop the project–in their opinion every single point would be enough to convince the judge. However, the supporters of BBI were equally convinced that they would receive permission to build the airport. In April 2005, the Federal Administrative Court (*Bundesverwaltungsgericht*) stopped the construction until a final decision could be reached, a step never before taken in Germany in the planning phase of a large infrastructure project. However, the airport opponents celebrated their victory prematurely: in March 2006, the court announced its final decision that the airport could be built in Schönefeld.

Source: ITF (2013), "The development of Berlin Brandenburg and the expansion of the Beijing Capital International Airport", working paper.

The second group of stakeholders to consider is airport users. Although their interests comprise a diverse set of elements, the common denominator is that they benefit from an efficient and effective operation of NAICM. Some of the main actors in this group include the following:

- *Passengers:* 34.2 million in 2014, who struggle with saturation problems in the current Benito Juárez International Airport of Mexico City. Estimates indicate that passengers in NAICM will reach 125 million, with an average of 342 465 per day, at its maximum development.[17]
- *Airlines:* Currently, 6 national airlines and 14 foreign ones serve passengers, while 34 are in the freight business.
- *Service providers:* Air side (baggage handling, catering, plane loading and unloading, cleaning, fuelling, airplane maintenance, etc.) and land side (taxis, buses, rent-a-car companies, etc.).
- *Freight area services:* Customs brokers, freight transport, fiscal warehouses, etc. About 14 000 workers are included in this group.
- *Employees:* Currently at 25 000. Unions and professional associations, such as the Pilots Association (*Colegio de Pilotos*), are also part of this group.

- *Businesses to be hosted in the airport terminals and their surroundings:* These include hotels, restaurants, duty-free shops, business parks, and various types of stores and businesses.
- *Investors:* Mainly banking institutions providing financing for the project.

This group of airport users, with the exceptions of businesses and employees, has been consulted extensively and continuously in order to align the design of the airport to the operative criteria of future users and make NAICM more attractive as a regional hub for airlines and passengers. The consultation process collected the technical, functional, and operative requirements of the 60 main users of NAICM (see Table 2.3 for examples), which are being considered in the design of the terminal, runways, and other facilities. CANAERO and IATA, for example, were consulted specifically on customs and migration issues.

Table 2.3. **Consulted airport users and government institutions**

20 airlines	15 government institutions	Service providers	Others
Aeromexico	Customs	Mexico's Postal Service	CANAERO (Air transport National Chamber)
Interjet	National Migration Institute	Aerocharter	IATA (International Air Transport Association)
Volaris	SENASICA	AGN	Pilots Association
Vivaaerobus	CISEN (Intelligence and National Security Centre)	Menzies	Aeronautics Engineers Association
United	Federal Police	Globalia	Air Traffic Controllers Association
American	PGR	AMACARGA (Mexico's Association of Freight Agents)	
Delta	PROFEPA (Federal Attorney for Environmental Protection)	ANAFAC (Fiscal Warehouses National Association)	
Magnicharter	SEDENA / Air Force	AAADAM (Association of Customs Brokers of Mexico City Airport)	
Aeromar	SEMAR (Ministry of the Navy)	CAAAREM (Mexico's Confederation of Customs Brokers Associations)	
Copa Airlines	EMP (Presidential Bodyguards Unit)	CANAPAT (National Chamber of Auto transports for Passengers and Tourism)	
Iberia	Ministry of Health	ASA	
Lufthansa	Ministry of Foreign Affairs	Helicopter operators	
Avianca	Ministry of Economy		
Others: Freight and courier	Ministry of Tourism		

Source: Author's own workwith information provided by GACM.

Consultation with these actors is thought of as an ongoing process divided into three stages:

- *October 2014-June 2015:* It comprised 188 meetings to present the project to users and collect information regarding their operative requirements.
- *September 2015-March 2016:* It aims to incorporate specific requirements into the airport's design and business plan. Such requirements include dedicated areas, counter distribution, location of boarding gates, and remote gates, among others. For example, during this stage there will be talks with CANAERO and IATA to

analyse the procedures concerning customs, migration, and health, in order to review the regulatory framework to simplify them.

- *March 2016-Start of operations:* It aims to develop protocols to establish operation procedures for users. It implies a continuous follow-up process to validate different airport features.

The consultation carried out during the first stage was useful to validate the required capacity for the terminal, according to the operations anticipated by airlines, and the development phases for the other facilities; take measures to facilitate a functional and efficient operation for baggage and passengers; update forecasts regarding expansion plans of the airlines; and anticipate connectivity needs.

The third group of stakeholders is the wider public, which comprises a diverse set of communities, including the following:

- *Inhabitants of the area surrounding NAICM:* Their main interests are to preserve their assets and quality of life, including factors such as land value, the preservation of the environment, pollution (air and noise), access to their neighbourhoods, public safety, and economic opportunities. There are also political groups among the inhabitants who have interests in advocating in favour or against the construction of NAICM, but as mentioned before, those against are a minority.
- *Non-governmental organisations (NGOs)/academia:* Organisations in this group usually work around specific themes, such as the environment, mobility, competitiveness, transparency, and so on. Given their expertise, they can provide valuable analyses and information for the development of NAICM. In fact, in some cases, they have been hired by NAICM to perform specific studies. This is the case, for example, of the Engineering Institute of the National Autonomous University (*Instituto de Ingeniería de la UNAM*, II-UNAM). This group also includes, for example, the Mexican Academy of Engineering, the Environmental Law Mexican Centre (*Centro Mexicano de Derecho Ambiental*, CEMDA), and Mexico's Competitiveness Institute (*Instituto Mexicano para la Competitividad*, IMCO). Likewise, academic institutions such as the University Programme on the Environment and the Ecology Institute of UNAM, the Environmental Engineers Board (*Colegio de Ingenieros Ambientales de México*, CINAM), the Autonomous University of Mexico (UAM), and the Autonomous University of the State of Mexico (UAEM), were consulted on an honorary basis on mitigation measures of social impacts, planning, and public policies.
- *Businesses and business chambers:*Their interest is obviously economic; not only in terms of direct contracts, they can obtain work in the NAICM project, but also related to the economic dynamism the region would gain as a result of the construction and eventual operation of NAICM.[18] This group includes, for example, the Mexican Chamber of the Construction Industry (*Cámara Mexicana de la Industria de la Construcción,* CMIC).

There are many other and more disperse social groups, but the ones referenced above are those with the highest stake in NAICM.

The social consultation and engagement process has been prudent, as it was influenced by the previous experience in which the new airport project was cancelled as a result of social opposition. The social consultation strategy has been based mainly on individual and group meetings, with the participation of GACM. Group meetings are used to communicate relevant information to interest groups. These can be focused on specific chambers or associations or general for a wider public. Individual meetings aim at collecting feedback and identifying specific needs of individual entities or enterprises, as well as at answering questions. Some examples include GACM participation in the CANAERO Freight Committee to feed the planning process of the freight terminal and an informative public meeting dealing with environmental issues, which gathered around 580 participants including inhabitants of the areas surrounding NAICM, academics, and representatives of social groups. During the event, there were 21 interventions/presentations and more than 50 questions were asked about the potential environmental impact of NAICM. GACM also plans to organise "roadshows" in the near future to communicate strategic elements, such as the packaging strategy for procurement.[19]

Despite the previous initiatives, social consultation has not been as extensive as that carried out with airport users. GACM developed a strategy to comply with the Equator Principles, particularly Principle 5 on social consultation, but the strategy still needs to be rolled out.[20] The main exceptions to are the consultation on the Environmental Impact Assessment (Box 2.5), the advice requested from academic institutions, and the establishment of a website with an email address for complaints and suggestions. However, the strategy anticipates informative meetings, focus groups, community workshops, and fora, among others.

Box 2.5. **Environmental mitigation measures**

Compliance with the Equator Principles concerning environmental issues is linked to fulfilling the mitigation measures recommended in the resolution to the Environmental Impact Assessment. The following actions have already been undertaken:

- MXN 11.2 million were deposited to Mexico's Forests Fund to ensure reforestation initiatives.
- A compliance guarantee for environmental compensation for approximately MXN 770 million was contracted.
- More than 20 plans and programmes were developed and delivered on time to address the conditions established in the resolution to the Environmental Impact Assessment.
- A Committee for Environmental Surveillance was created.
- An Environmental Comptroller was hired to comply with Condition 10 of the resolution to the Environmental Impact Assessment.

Source: Presentation "*Sustentabilidad y Restauración Ambiental*", www.aeropuerto.gob.mx/documentos/05092014-ambiental.pdf, consulted on 20 September 2015.

In addition to those engagement plans led by GACM, specific NGOs have mobilised to provide feedback and oversight to the NAICM project. A notable example is that of the National Citizen Observatory of NAICM (*Observatorio Nacional Ciudadano*, ONC), organised by IMCO, CEMDA, and CTS Embarq Mexico. The ONC aims at being an open and transparent forum to make sure that NAICM maximises the economic, social, and environmental well-being in Mexico and to assess government policies and proposals regarding the project. To this end, the ONC organised a series of fora concerning environmental, competitiveness, urban development and mobility, and social inclusiveness issues in November-December 2014. In April 2015, the ONC presented a report with the conclusions of the fora (IMCO et al., 2015) (Box 2.6). GACM reacted by offering a reply to the report and establishing working groups to address the concerns expressed by the ONC.

Box 2.6. **Conclusions of the report by the National Citizen Observatory (*Observatorio Nacional Ciudadano,* ONC)**

The ONC report acknowledges the need for a new airport but highlights that, if not managed properly, the project may lead to important and long-lasting negative consequences. Hence, the need for the NAICM project to be part of an integral development strategy for the city and the country, anticipating direct and indirect effects on the economy, the environment, and society in general. ONC calls for transparency not only related to the main features of the project, but also its decision-making processes. Recommendations to the Government include the following:

- Environment
  - providing access to all the studies carried out to define mitigation measures to address environmental impacts
  - establishing an air quality monitoring system from the construction phases of NAICM
  - promoting an integral management system for water resources.
- Competitiveness
  - preparing a contingency plan for financing the NAICM considering different scenarios and funding alternatives
  - engaging COFECE in the oversight of strategic procurement procedures
  - establishing mechanisms to disclose conflict of interests of decision makers.
- Urban development and mobility
  - developing an urban development and environmental plan incorporating a regional and megalopolis approach
  - developing an integral mobility programme providing alternatives to connect NAICM with the metropolitan area of Mexico City and neighbouring cities
  - establishing collective public transport systems ("shuttle" type) to the areas of departure and final destination of passengers, with little stations connected strategically to the public transport networks.
- Social inclusiveness
  - developing a communications strategy to keep informed the inhabitants of the area where NAICM will be constructed about the main positive and negative impacts

Box 2.6. **Conclusions of the report by the National Citizen Observatory (*Observatorio Nacional Ciudadano*, ONC) *(continued)***

- carrying out public consultation sessions, including local inhabitants and experts, to discuss mitigation measures and other specific topics
- developing a compensation strategy to address negative effects on the inhabitants of the area where NAICM will be constructed.

Source: IMCO et al. (2015), *Observatorio Ciudadano del Nuevo Aeropuerto de la Ciudad de México*, available at http://imco.org.mx/wp-content/uploads/2015/04/2015_NAICM_Ejes_de_monitoreo_Documento_completo.pdf, consulted on 5 October 2015.

Proposals for action

1. The governance model of the project needs to be strengthened to allow timely decision making, accountability, and inclusiveness, as well as to effectively allocate risks

Governance is an element that runs through the veins of all aspects of successful project delivery. According to the UK Office of Government Commerce (OGC) five out of the eight causes of project failure identified in 2005 were attributable to weak governance. In contrast, OGC found that seven out of the ten common causes of confidence identified in 2010 were attributable to good governance. Similarly, PwC's 2012 *Global Study on Project Management Trends* identified that weak governance was the main contributor to project failure. Likewise, the Infrastructure UK *Cost Review Report 2010* and the UK National Audit Office's *Guide to Initiating Successful Projects* stress the importance of good governance by highlighting the need for a greater focus on the early stages of projects to ensure that they are set up to succeed, establishing the right delivery environment and capability to match the complexity of the project (Infrastructure UK, HM Treasury and Lord Deighton, 2014) (Box 2.7).

Weak governance at each stage of the preparation of construction projects for public investment can result in mismanagement and a risk of corruption and delays. Accordingly, a key to protecting investment in publicly funded construction is to strengthen governance. Since corruption can thrive where governance is weak, strengthening governance processes throughout the project cycle should lessen the opportunities for misbehaviour (Wells, 2015).

As the GACM risk matrix recognises, its organisational structure is not adequate for such a megaproject as NAICM. There are gaps in the definition of responsibilities among corporate directorates, including decision making. For example, no one is responsible for following up the mitigation measures mandated by the Environmental Impact Assessment and there have been delays in contract payments due to uncertainty on the procedures to follow. These delays could become a major problem once the pace of the works accelerates, not only to the credibility of the project and its timely progress, but this can also be a source of corruption (since contractors may then be tempted to pay bribes to secure their payments). If unresolved, slow decision making will likely end up consuming management time, leading to project delays.

Box 2.7. **Characteristics of good governance of infrastructure projects according to the United Kingdom's HM Treasury**

For infrastructure projects, good governance is about a balance between the natural desire of the sponsor to retain control and the need for the delivery team to have sufficient freedom to allow it to manage the risk to meet the project objectives. It is characterised by the following features:

- A clear statement of the objectives and parameters for delivery between the sponsor and the execution team, including arrangements for remedy in the event of difficulty.
- The project being sufficiently autonomous with a single controlling mind.
- A clear system of delegation and determined process for timely decisions that fall outside the limits of delegation.
- A determined process for controlling change.
- A determined process for reporting and other communications between the sponsor and the execution team.
- A collaborative culture and working relationship between the sponsor and the execution team.
- Board members have sufficient understanding of the project context to make reasonable timely decisions (or seek advice to help them).
- A defined system for assurance at all levels.

Source: Infrastructure UK, HM Treasury and Lord Deighton (2014), "Improving infrastructure delivery, project initiation routemap", October, www.gov.uk/government/publications/improving-infrastructure-delivery-project-initiation-routemap.

One reason why these gaps have appeared is that outsourced personnel and consultants are not public servants and therefore are not empowered to make decisions. Since the GACM structure is quite limited, many functions have been outsourced, but without enough control, creating redundancies and overlaps. In fact, in the international experience the weakness of project appraisal must in large part be attributed to weak capacity on the part of public sector clients (U4 Anti-corruption Centre). One solution is to outsource to private consulting companies, but this also creates risks that should be monitored and mitigated (Wells, 2015). In this sense, GACM should develop a policy on outsourcing, indicating clearly what criteria to consider when thinking about outsourcing and what protocols will be used to control outsourced activities. For the moment, a mapping of the services outsourced would help identify where overlaps are and avoid them in the future. These mapping should also include an accountability mechanism, so that there are specific GACM areas and staff following up their work. The risks of hiring consultants without proper accountability mechanisms include over-design to increase fees, incomplete design to leave room for changes that can later be manipulated, and collusion, among others. Such risks should be anticipated and mitigated when consultants need to be hired to bring in technical expertise (Box 2.8).

Box 2.8. **The governance of outsourcing**

Support functions such as information technology and human resource management may be outsourced to provide organisational benefits. Companies frequently point to the cost savings for labour and training, but also cite the benefits of releasing corporate resources for alternative uses and allowing the business to focus on its core competencies. Outsourcing support functions is not simple, though, and companies should manage the related risk factors.

With every outsourced task comes a new responsibility to govern that task properly. The burden of carrying out a support function may be outsourced, but the responsibility for managing the supplier and for ensuring quality and accountability does not disappear. Tasks that are hard or costly to outsource require an extra dose of management or should be carried out internally. The worst solution is to outsource them and then under-manage the transaction.

Source: Gomes-Casseres, B. (2009), "Outsourcing: Where will you draw the line?", *Harvard Business Review*, https://hbr.org/2009/08/outsourcing-where-will-you-dra; and Raiborn, C.A., J. Butler and M.F. Massoud (2009), "Outsourcing support functions: Identifying and managing the good, the bad, and the ugly", *Harvard Business Review*, https://hbr.org/product/outsourcing-support-functions-identifying-and-managing-the-good-the-bad-and-the-ugly/an/BH337-PDF-ENG.

The same effective accountability mechanisms need to be developed for GACM staff. Changes to the critical route of the project should be avoided and justified when this has to be done. As illustrated in Box 2.9, the lack of accountability mechanisms was part of the recipe for disaster during the construction of BBI. There should also be a detailed project corruption risk assessment that maps corruption risks throughout the project cycle and assesses whether existing controls are sufficient to manage those risks. The risk assessment should be an evolving document that is periodically reviewed and updated as the project moves on. A regularly revised risk assessment would support GACM's ability to adapt to the evolving environment of the project.

Outsourced services are just one example of gaps in the governance model. GACM needs to develop a wider governance map (see Figure 2.4) that goes beyond the structure of the Federal Government and identifies the relationships and functions of the three groups of stakeholders identified in this report, namely government institutions, airport users, and the wider public, which can be further disaggregated into community groups, control authorities (i.e. SFP, ASF), and strategic partnerships (i.e. COFECE, INAI, OECD), among others. For example, several government institutions influence NAICM through their policy formulation function. This is the case, for instance, of SCT, which is responsible for air transport policy (i.e. open skies) and SEMARNAT, which is in charge of environmental policies. Indeed, when one looks at Figure 2.4, the governance structure looks more complex.

Box 2.9. Governance failures in the management of the Berlin-Brandenburg International Airport

Inexperienced and non-specialist management and supervision

In 2003, the political leadership of the project decided to fire the consortium of private companies initially set up to finance, build, and operate the airport and to make the construction of the airport a fully public project, arguing that the private sector should not benefit at the expense of the public sector. This was intended to save money, promote the local construction industry, and keep the project on schedule. None of the members of the political leadership had any actual experience with such large construction projects. Supervision ended up almost exclusively in the hands of politicians, civil servants, and union officials. The lack of expertise and technical knowledge of the supervisory board prevented proper and rigorous oversight of the planning and progress, resulting in delays, confusion, and major cost overruns.

Inaccuracy of budget estimation

A number of experts have pointed to the fact that the initial cost previsions of the airport were significantly underestimated, causing management problems all the way through execution. It was important for the political leadership to keep the estimated costs of the construction of the new airport low in order to strengthen political support.

Experts have identified this as a common feature in major infrastructure projects. The literature suggests that there is a similar pattern in democratic societies, where politicians have a tendency to deceive the public about the actual costs of these projects. In consequence, cost overruns rarely come as a surprise. Politicians often try to calculate the price to be as low as possible in order to obtain support for the projects, deliberately veiling the potential risks. Often those at the political helm take a calculated risk by assuming they will not be held personally responsible if costs start to explode. Danish researcher Bent Flyvbjerg of Oxford University argued that it often is not the best projects that are completed, but those that "are made to look best on paper (and that also) are the projects that amass the highest cost overruns and benefit shortfalls in reality." This phenomenon is called "survival of the unfittest".

Poor planning and procurement

The modification of the governance structure at the very beginning of the project made the preparation team lose substantial time. In 2007, new plans had to be drawn up and invitations to bid had to be prepared. The main construction contracts were only awarded in early 2009, and yet the airport was supposed to open in October 2011. The European Court of Auditors noted weaknesses in project preparation in the airport infrastructure project: planning documents were not ready and had to be modified during the tendering process, leading to significant cost overruns.

The poor planning process led to the operating agency directly awarding several additional contracts without a bidding process. This meant that the airport company systematically violated EU public procurement directives. The additional work covered by those contracts, the auditors noted, was foreseeable to management and should thus have been awarded via a bidding process.

The comptrollers from the European Court of Auditors found several eyebrow-raising items, such as a plan to create elevated parking spaces for Berlin Mayor and his VIP guests, so they could have easier access to gates, with a cost of EUR 567 000.

Changes and variations

A number of significant (and allegedly unnecessary) changes were integrated in the project along the way, increasing costs and time resources. For example, the board devoted considerable attention to the question of whether and where a two-story jet way for the Airbus A380 was to be built, and just before construction was slated to begin, the board decided to move the costly jet way from the main terminal, where all airlines can dock, to the Air Berlin departure area. Such variations or change orders contributed to blurring the execution of the project, creating opportunities for abuse and increasing overall costs.

Box 2.9. **Governance failures in the management of the Berlin-Brandenburg International Airport *(continued)***

Lack of internal communication

The lines of information and communication between the governance and management entities were allegedly uneven, particularly with regards to the potential opening date. This is to be linked to the poor supervision of the project, due to a lack of technical expertise. The asymmetry of information between the different bodies led both to management difficulties as well as to public communication issues.

Source: www.spiegel.de/international/germany/spiegel-investigation-how-the-new-berlin-airport-project-fell-apart-a-868283.html; www.spiegel.de/international/business/disastrous-public-works-projects-in-germany-a-876856.html; www.spiegel.de/international/germany/new-berlin-airport-faces-major-funding-difficulties-a-975863.html; www.spiegel.de/international/germany/how-berlin-s-new-international-airport-opening-was-delayed-a-833122.html.

Figure 2.4. **Governance map**

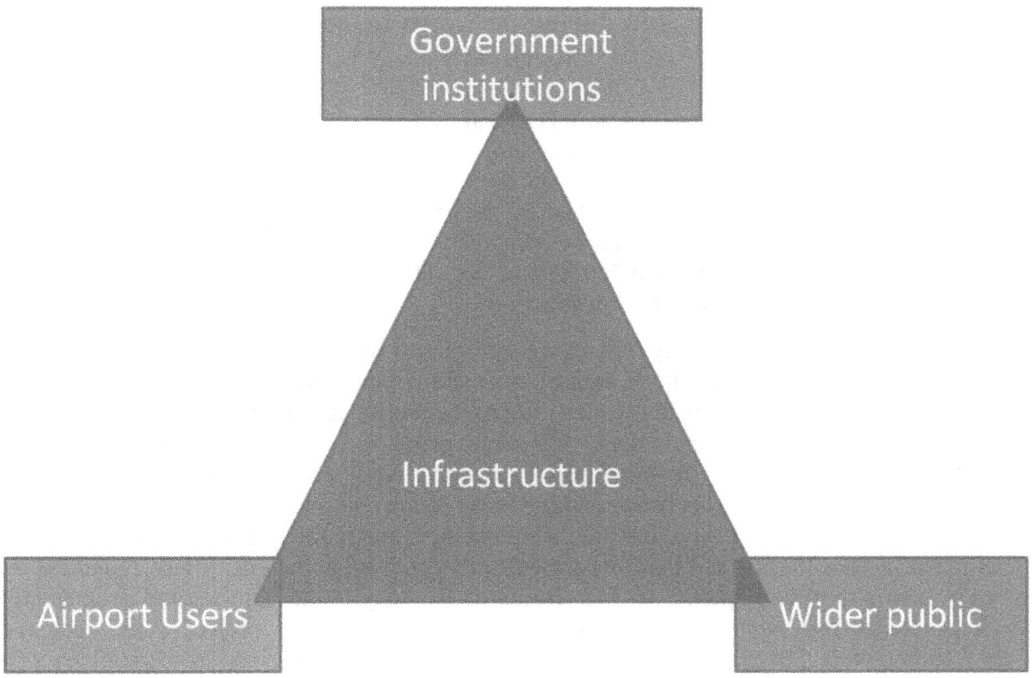

Source: Author's own work.

In addition to the mapping of outsourced services, formalising two advisory groups would support the inclusiveness of the project. First, a monitoring group, composed not only of control authorities but also of NGOs (i.e. the Mexican chapter of Transparency International) and academia (II-UNAM). In fact, independent project monitoring is critical. The inclusiveness of this group could be helpful to providing credibility to control and follow-up mechanisms. Second, strategic partnerships should be formalised with a clear definition of the objectives of each one. While an agreement with the OECD has already been formalised, GACM should pursue the partnership already in the pipeline with COFECE and assign a special unit in SFP, notably, to review tender documentation.

Reshuffling governance is a time-consuming endeavour; therefore, it is important to get it right early. In fact, ineffective governance and project management at the preliminary stages of a project can have repercussions beyond an inappropriate choice of projects, leading to corrupt acts during implementation (Wells, 2015). Governance pitfalls are some of the factors identified as catalysts for the BBI failure (see Box 2.9).

An additional issue that deserves review is the allocation of risks derived from public works. In the end, it is the project owner, GACM, who is ultimately accountable for time,, , quality, safety and costs. It is common that in megaprojects, the owner tries to transfer risks down the supply chain through the use of the procurement system. This is a motivation for contractors to price the risk within their tenders and in turn try to pass on the risk to their subcontractors. Alternatively, the owner may assume responsibility for risks while providing financial incentives for suppliers, rewarding successful performance. This approach proved to be successful during the construction of Heathrow Airport Terminal 5 (see Box 2.10).

Box 2.10. **Allocation of risks during the construction of Heathrow Airport Terminal 5**

The construction of Heathrow Airport Terminal 5 (T5) was the largest construction project in Europe in the early 2000s. The T5 project was an innovative and extremely complex multi-modal transport interchange designed to handle up to 30 million passengers a year. The scope of the T5 programme encompassed more than 60 contractors; 16 major integrated projects, e.g. buildings, air traffic control tower, earthworks, airfield, baggage handling system; 147 sub-projects; and 2 train extensions on a 260 ha site. By 2008, 50 000 people, employees, and key stakeholders had been involved in the construction.

The British Airports Authority (BAA), a major airport operator privatised in 1986, realised rapidly that if the projects were to be built on time and within budget a unique approach would be required. During the planning phase, just prior to the project construction phase in 2002, BAA carried out a two-year in-depth study of every major UK construction project of over GBP 1 billion conducted over the previous 10 years and every international airport that opened over the previous 15 years. This benchmarking study found that no such major UK construction project had successfully delivered on time, within budget, and to the quality standards originally determined in the contract, and that few projects had good safety records. It also found that no recently built airport had opened on time. Based on its study of 12 major airport programmes, BAA concluded that without a radically different approach the T5 project would cost over GBP 1 billion more than was affordable, would be two years late, and result in six fatalities.

BAA specifically identified two areas that contributed to the poor performance of megaprojects: the lack of collaboration among project partners and the client's reluctance to assume responsibility for project risk. BAA recognised that the only way it could achieve the desired outcome on a major project was to change the "rules of the game" by establishing a new type of partnership with its first tier suppliers.

The bedrock of BAA's project management approach was the T5 agreement, a relational contract between BAA and all the T5 first tier suppliers, including architects and engineering design consultants, general and specialised contractors and manufacturers, which junked the traditional concepts of construction contract. The BAA legal and commercial teams designed the contract aiming to minimise the conflicts that usually plagued major projects. Instead of spelling out a set of clauses accepting that things could go wrong, and seeking to pass the blame and

Box1.10. **Allocation of risks during the construction of Heathrow Airport Terminal 5 *(continued)***

recover money from suppliers, the T5 agreement aimed at creating incentives for positive problem-solving behaviours that would not allow things to go wrong in the first place. BAA deemed this stance fundamental for creating totally integrated project teams with the suppliers and enabling the latter to achieve exceptional performance.

The ethos of the T5 agreement was to move away from the traditional practice of infrastructure clients choosing suppliers who bid lowest. In this practice, clients often perceived suppliers as attempting to opportunistically exploit design errors and omissions for claiming payments for additional work, which offset the tight profit margins built in the bid. Due to disagreements between suppliers and clients about the legitimacy of these claims, costly litigation often followed causing work stoppages and delays. In contrast, the T5 agreement aimed to encourage suppliers to move into best practice and exceptional performance, and to actively seek and offer affordable and excellent solutions.

BAA took a different and unique approach to risk in T5 – it held all the risk - deciding it would be the best way to achieve price certainty. Subsequently, the contractors risk contingency was removed, lowering the overall tenders. Obviously with no risk placed on the contractor, incentives were required to encourage all to work to minimise the risk – the approach of "it doesn't matter, it is not my bill" had to be avoided for this scheme to be successful. The risk was managed through financial incentives for suppliers, rewarding successful performances. During the design stage the risk contingency was held within each project, however in 2004 it was decided that cost targets could be more challenging. This resulted in GBP 100 million taken from individual projects to a central pot that allowed the risk contingency to be allocated depending on where it was needed. This contingency allowed greater control of the financial implications of risk at a more global level and thus tighter overall budget control.

Arguably it was the formation of trust from contract mechanisms that enabled the success of T5; the formation of integrated teams and the application of a novel form of contract enabled trust between all parties. Experts suggest that the risk associated with large, complex projects can provide the motivation for clients to pursue and reward innovation by contractors and suppliers. By taking on and actively managing project risk, BAA was able to pursue a strategy of rewarding performance enhanced by innovations from all participants.

Source: www.designingbuildings.co.uk/wiki/Procurement_of_Heathrow_T5; www.airport-technology.com/projects/heathrow5/; Brady, T. and A. Davies (2010), "From hero to hubris – Reconsidering the project management of Heathrow's Terminal 5", *International Journal of Project Management* 28 (2010), pp. 151–157, www.itn.liu.se/mit/education/courses/tnfl05-risk-och-olycksanalys/vecka-47/1.304769/BradyochDavies2010.pdf

Finally, GACM should consider that project governance arrangements can, and indeed should, change over time as the sponsor, in this case SCT, gains more understanding of risks and arrangements for management, as the management team and processes mature and demonstrate competence, and as the NAICM project progresses through its lifecycle.

2. Corporate governance should be reviewed to align with good international practice defined in the OECD Guidelines on Corporate Governance of SOEs

A first recommendation would be for the Federal Government to communicate its expectations to GACM through a letter to the board. This has been a successful tool in other OECD countries, as these "letters of intent" serve as medium-term roadmaps and allow boards to resist ad hoc political pressures (see OECD, 2013b). Even though a letter of intent would require strengthened co-ordination and reconciliation of the interests of different ministries, it would be extremely useful to define the State's role as the owner of GACM.

In order to strengthen the vertical separation suggested by the OECD Guidelines on Corporate Governance of State-Owned Enterprises, the responsibilities of SCT (*vis-à-vis* GACM), the Board, and GACM's executive management need to be more clearly defined. For example, the GACM Board will only fulfil its duties of oversight if it is given the powers to appoint and remove the Director General, but that would contravene the contents of LFEP. Likewise, the Director General would need greater executive autonomy to fulfil his management duties.

The second recommendation has to do with board composition and nomination. A more transparent and merit-based nomination of board members supports the avoidance of politisation of the appointment procedures, which would not ensure that the best professionals get the job. A central recommendation of the OECD Guidelines is that boards should be composed to exercise "independent and objective judgment". In most OECD countries, SOE boards are composed of a mix of civil servants, other individuals tasked with pursuing the public interest and "independent" directors.[21] The trend, fuelled by a growing commercialisation of SOEs, is toward a greater reliance on independent board members – or persons with relevant commercial experience.

Given that the appointment process to GACM's Board is an attribution of the President through SCT, this ministry could put together a committee, consisting of representatives from different ministries, to make proposals to the President. This committee would be charged with identifying a pool of qualified candidates with experience in airport management, not only public officials, for the President to consider. Alternatively, the recruitment of suitable board members could be based on formal eligibility rules, processes to advice or vet ministerial candidates for board appointment, or actual or *de facto* nomination committees proposing candidates for the ultimate decision of the President. Since LFEP already considers the possibility of appointing non-public servants, there is no legal obstacle to give the board some diversity. In addition, training programmes should be established to facilitate the introduction of new board members. Practical training could include meetings with GACM managers and professional staff to improve the knowledge of the organisation.

That said, there is growing recognition that certain public sector representatives are not acceptable as SOE board members under any circumstance. OECD consensus holds that neither ministers, state secretaries, nor other direct representatives of, nor parties closely related to the executive powers should be represented on SOE boards. Scandinavian countries have gone further than most jurisdictions to formally limit the weight of politicians and bureaucrats in SOE boards. For example, active politicians, including members of parliament, ministers, state secretaries, as well as civil servants who within their remit exert regulatory or controlling authority over the company or deal with matters of substantial importance for the company, cannot be elected to the board of directors in Norway. Similar rules are in place in Germany, except regarding state secretaries who can be appointed in SOE boards if they are not members of the parliament. New Zealand (which also has an express process for vetting conflict of interest) has gone farthest in instituting an absolute ban on any serving politicians or civil servants sitting on SOE boards.

Moreover, many countries have restrictions concerning the nomination of civil servants as board members. In Finland, for instance, only one civil servant from the ownership function (and in some cases another from a relevant administration) can serve on an SOE board, but potential conflict issues are avoided by generally not allowing the politically appointed civil servants to serve on boards. A similar approach has been adopted by Australia where appointment of departmental officers can only be considered in exceptional circumstances, having regard to their ability to represent the interests of the government, their possession of business skills, and to any potential conflicts of interest that might arise. So, in general, good practice is to avoid officials directly linked with the executive powers from sitting on SOE boards (OECD, 2013c) (Box 2.11).

Box 2.11. **Board appointment process in the United Kingdom**

The General Office of the Commissioner of Public Appointments (OCPA) recruitment process is as follows (although this may vary slightly depending on the size of the SOE and the specific requirements of the post):

- The central ownership advisory unit, the Shareholder Executive (ShEx) and the SOE Chair agree on the mix of skills and experience required on the board, leading to agreement on a strategic plan of public appointments.
- A timetable for recruitment is then agreed between the SOE, the lead Director in ShEx, and an independent assessor (IA).
- A draft specification setting out the role and requirements for the board appointment is drafted and agreed with HR and the SOE. The role and person specification is then agreed with the body or minister making the final decision.
- A candidate search is undertaken with the vacant position being publicly announced (i.e. advertised) and often involving the use of recruitment agencies to ensure a more thorough search of potential candidates.
- On the basis of applications received, a long list of potential candidates is produced. An initial assessment involving ShEx, the IA, and the SOE is conducted to produce a short list of candidates to interview.
- An interview panel is established comprising the lead ShEx policy official, the IA, and the Chair of the SOE.
- The panel then reaches agreement on the preferred candidate and submits a panel report with recommendations to departmental ministers.
- Once ministers have agreed on the recommendation, the appointment can be made.
- An appointment is normally for a fixed period of three years at which point the position is subject to re-election.

Where the post is not OCPA regulated, the SOE runs the process, but follows the OCPA guidelines in most instances.

Source: OECD (2013c), *Boards of Directors of State-Owned Enterprises: An Overview of National Practices*, OECD Publishing, Paris, p. 41.

GACM's board members should then consider its participation as a personal duty and not as a function of the office they hold in the APF. Alternate members should not be considered interchangeable with the actual members and they should only attend board meetings instead of the regular members in extreme circumstances. This should be expressly regulated as experience illustrates that alternate members' participation can quickly become the rule, rather than the exception.

A third recommendation deals with the lack of GACM's internal audit function. An internal audit mechanism should be established to report directly to the GACM Board. This would strengthen the board's ability to perform its oversight functions and would complement other audit mechanisms, such as those exercised by SFP and ASF.

Finally, the GACM Board should establish an annual process of self-evaluation. Such assessment would analyse how efficiently the board has carried out its duties, as a collegial entity and as individual members. These evaluations could be based on self-reporting or involve external facilitators. The reports would have to be submitted to the Federal Executive.

By aligning with the OECD Guidelines, Mexico's authorities can enhance GACM's governance without losing control of the entity and without compromising its strategic objectives, but giving it the flexibility that such a megaproject such as NAICM requires, and the possibility to benefit from the advantages of a corporate design.

3. While co-ordination among central government stakeholders seems to be working well, there should be a continuous effort to improve it

Optimal co-ordination is not a one-off exercise, but rather a permanent effort to bring coherence to the activities of different entities towards a common objective. Continuous efforts must be pursued to improve and fill the co-ordination gaps that, without a doubt, are always present in megaprojects. The leadership of ministries and agencies of federal government institutions should make sure that the information "cascades down" to the public officials who actually execute the programmes and initiatives related to the NAICM.

As the project moves on, the need for co-ordination will be even greater. For example, the procurement packaging strategy requires co-ordination from the different entities participating in the tender packages, the PM, the suppliers, the competition and control authorities, among others. The choice for a packaging strategy, while having many advantages, also calls for strong co-ordination.

Co-ordination with sub-national governments was an opportunity identified by the OECD team. This is also going to be more necessary as the project enters into phases that will require urban infrastructure and mobility measures. Since the new airport will be in the territory of the State of Mexico and its area of impact of around 300 km^2 will cover 11 municipalities of the State of Mexico and 3 delegations of the Federal District, the need to involve these sub-national units is clear. In fact, the experience of OECD countries illustrates that multi-level co-ordination can be advanced around specific initiatives (i.e. mega-infrastructure projects, sports and cultural events, administrative reforms, and international affairs). Forming high-level councils or committees (i.e. a Metropolitan Council for the NAICM) could be a way to achieve coherence and speak with a single voice, improving efficiency, as well as avoiding public disagreements leading to tensions, such as the disagreement between the Federal Government and the Government of the Federal District on how to decide the destiny of the current airport.[22] It could also be the starting point for developing a collaborative culture (OECD, forthcoming).

Furthermore, there is value in pursuing the idea of a special relationship with autonomous bodies such as the one established with INAI. The point is not to have these bodies intervening in every step GACM takes (i.e. having COFECE reviewing every tender), but rather to concentrate their interventions with a sense of proportionality of where the main risks are. Still, the expertise of these institutions does not only provide value to GACM activities, but also builds on the credibility of the NAICM project, which is a precious asset that should be protected and grown. See Box 2.12 as a relevant example.

Box 2.12. **Multi-level co-ordination in the development of Milan-Malpensa Airport**

Malpensa, the main airport of Milan and the second largest Italian airport, was between 1998 and 2007 the main hub of Alitalia. It is located approximately 50 km northwest of Milan, at the western border of a wide and economically active area with 3.9 million inhabitants, being inversely cone-shaped between Milan and the Alps. The other airports in the metropolitan area are Linate, 7 kilometres east of Milan's centre, and Bergamo Orio al Serio, about 50 km east of Milan.

The airport was included in the 1983 regional transport planning (Regione Lombardia, 1983), although with a limited geographical role. In 1985, the airport franchisee, SEA, produced a new Master Plan for its development, based on traffic forecasts of 12 million passengers. On the basis of this, two national laws allocated resources for construction. In 1986 the General Transport Plan of Italy included the development of Malpensa to make it a ''large airport for Northern Italy''. The Malpensa 2000 project was approved by Lombardy Regional Council and later in 1987 by the Italian Ministry of Transport.

The success of Malpensa airport has been at least partially dependent on better surface access, in which sub-national governments had a significant contribution. From the beginning surface access was seen as a potential weakness and cause of constraint for the project development. Although basic rail and highway access from Milan was promptly improved, Malpensa is still seen as remote, particularly from the rest of the region.

The regional government managed the planning of surface access mainly through dedicated plans and agreements. The two main documents were the agreement signed in 1999 and the annual regional financial plan (Regione Lombardia, 1999), both signed after the opening of the airport. The plan included approximately 40 road and rail investments, to be completed over a 7-8 year period with funding shared between Regione Lombardia and the State. The cost included some investments not linked at all to airport accessibility.

Source: Beria, P. and A.B. Scholz (2010), "Strategies and pitfalls in the infrastructure development of airports: A comparison of Milan Malpensa and Berlin Brandenburg international airports", *Journal of Air Transport Management* 16(2010), pp. 65-73.

4. GACM capacities need to be proportionate to the magnitude and complexity of the project, and a collaborative working environment should be developed

The GACM faces serious capacity and human resource constraints, which becomes evident when benchmarking the project against other airport projects. Up to April 2015, GACM was operating with 65 members of staff with temporary, renewable three-month contracts, plus 65 additional staff from outsourced companies, for a total of approximately 130 individuals. The projects for the construction of the airports of Hong Kong and Abu Dhabi required approximately 800 and 1 800 officials respectively, just from the leading authorities.

Since it would not be realistic to consider an expansion of the staff to a similar magnitude, more than numbers, it is necessary for GACM to identify the functions and skills that need to be reinforced. There is an urgency to align the complexity of the project with GACM's capabilities. One example is the need to develop a communications department with professional skills and capable of implementing a proper communications strategy. Currently, communications regarding NAICM are managed from SCT and the Office of the President. Another example is the need to create a market intelligence team within the Deputy Direction for Procurement. The packaging strategy being developed requires market analyses to take good decisions concerning tender methodologies, timing, and sequencing. As of June 2015, it is not clear how GACM will proceed to gather market information. In this sense, the different government entities should recognise the extraordinary nature of the NAICM project, hence promoting a new vision for the GACM structure. In fact, the GACM organisational structure is governed by SHCP and SFP regulations. While dialogue between GACM and these ministries seems to be fluid, their timely interventions and decisions will be required to strengthen GACM capacities. This will not be an easy task considering the period of fiscal restrictions that Mexico is going through (partially due to low oil prices).

Capacity gaps can also be identified by benchmarking the organisational structure of GACM. It is necessary to analyse the responsibilities of the different corporate directorates and match them with the skill set. There are basically two alternative options for structuring the broader owner's team: the indicative function-based structure and the indicative package-based structure (see Figures 1.5 and 1.6).

Figure 2.5. **Indicative function-based structure**

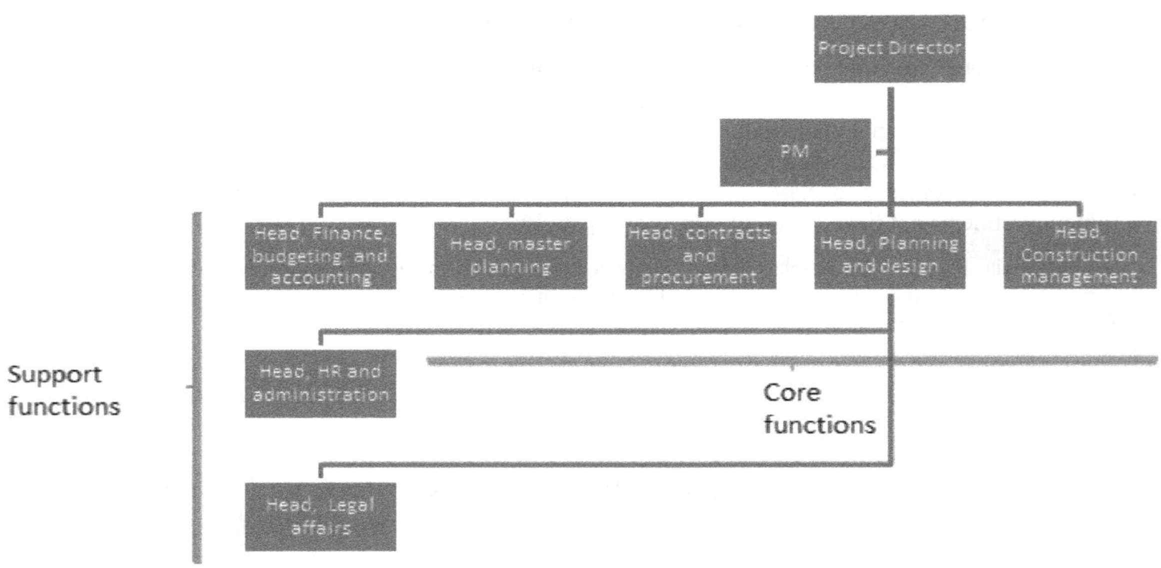

Source: Author's own work.

The indicative function-based structure is a traditional organisational structure with standard job descriptions, and for which it is relatively easier to recruit talent. However, it leads to functional silos and diluted accountability and co-ordination. As a consequence, end-to-end perspective is lost. This structure requires the PM and the project head to be strong integrators. This is the kind of structure GACM currently has with four core functions embodied in the four corporate directorates. However, a significant difference is that support functions in GACM are not directly subordinated to the Director General, but are inserted into the four corporate directorates. Legal affairs, for example, is within the Corporate Directorate for Administration and Real Estate Management, as is human resources. The transversal nature of such support functions is, therefore, not recognised in GACM's organisation. Another noticeable difference is that in GACM one single area deals with bulk procurement, small purchases, and contract management. The different sets of skills for each one of these activities have not been developed within GACM's structure. It is even plausible to enlarge and shrink the structures of the different areas as the project progresses and its needs vary. For example, during the most intensive construction phases, the structures of the corporate directorates for administration and infrastructure will need to grow, even if some functions are outsourced.

Figure 2.6. **Indicative package-based structure**

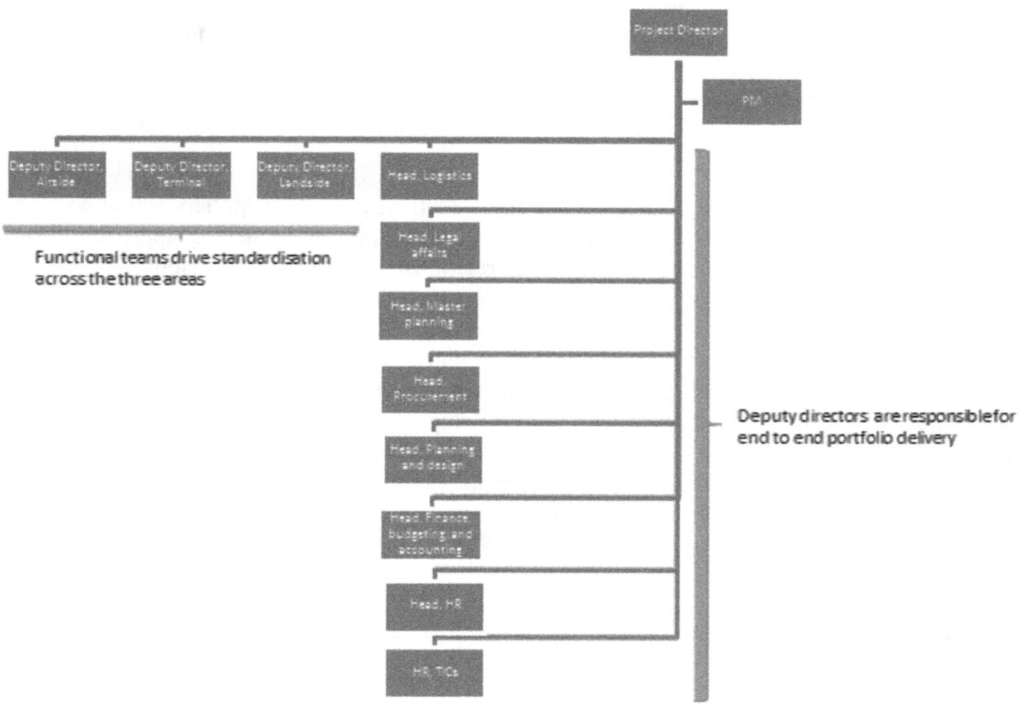

Source: Author's own work.

The indicative package-based structure is quite popular in megaprojects. It provides an end-to-end view and clearer accountability links. However, managing packages requires a specific set of skills that is not easy to find. Likewise, matrix reporting is confusing due to functional implants in packages. Migrating to such a structure would require first closing the capacity gaps identified earlier and a major reorganisation of the NAICM project around portfolios (i.e. runways, terminal).

In addition to strengthening the organisational structure and the capacities of GACM, its leadership should be aware that successful megaprojects are accompanied of strong teams with favourable working conditions. This is even more relevant given the reduced timeline for the NAICM project. Indeed, a high degree of turnover would result in learning curves and, therefore, wasted time. A favourable working environment not only contributes to internal co-ordination, but also to reducing incentives for corruption. Appropriate salary levels, employment stability, a high degree of professionalism, and pride among the staff, as well as an environment in which officials and businessmen caught bribing or trying to manipulate processes find difficult to obtain other business, making corruption a high-risk activity, are all elements that ensure an adequate working environment. See Box 2.13 as an exemplary case study to consider.

Box 2.13. **Positive work culture in the construction of Heathrow Airport Terminal 5**

One of the core values within T5 was teamwork. This was encouraged through the passing of a rock upon a completed milestone. This ceremonial handover may seem trivial, but was done with great pride and the teamwork culture within the project meant workers did not want to let the team down by passing the rock late. Within T5, the British Airports Authority (BAA) sought to create a new culture that encouraged people to: *i)* seek out, capture, and exploit the best practices of others; *ii)* remove the barriers and inhibitors to doing things differently; *iii)* motivate and support good ideas; and *iv)* leverage the commercial incentives to perform exceptionally. The procurement methods adopted in the T5 agreement created a different climate compared to that of traditional design and build methods, as the feeling of trust and co-operation is key to success.

The T5 agreement was a cost-plus contract (the client pays the suppliers actual cost plus a fixed fee which includes overheads and profit) based upon a partnering approach. The T5 agreement was based upon behaviours and relationships, allowing "bespoke" interactions between BAA and suppliers. Literature suggests that contractors involved in megaprojects usually "play games" with more traditional contracts, such as bidding low to win the project and then working to commercially protect their company. The approach adopted within T5 discouraged these methods by adopting fair payment practices and changing the culture within the project. BAA instilled a culture with reduced emphasis on contractual principles commonly observed in construction and promoted a behavioural focus. The reduction in contract focus allowed an informal approach, in turn reducing the contractual conflict commonly reported. A goal sharing rather than individual goal culture was adopted within T5.

Source: www.designingbuildings.co.uk/wiki/Procurement_of_Heathrow_T5.

5. Continuous and open dialogue with stakeholders, involving them in planning, decision making, and oversight, is a key feature of successful megaprojects

Even though GACM has already advanced an extensive strategy to consult airport users and more limited efforts of social consultation, there is a need for a more systematic approach that not only informs, but also involves social groups in planning, decision making, and oversight. The objective is not only to communicate information, but to empower and develop ownership of the project by the different communities. Achieving such a degree of involvement requires going beyond the typical *ex ante* approach to consultations to develop permanent engagement mechanisms and tools. In this way, social groups not only take ownership of the project, but also become advocates of their benefits and create incentives for good performance (Box 2.14). Indeed, it is widely accepted that a powerful catalyst for improved performance in megaprojects often comes from demands for accountability. Such demands may come from different sources such as the legislature, tax payers, voters, and civil society (Wells, 2015). Furthermore, a more inclusive approach would contribute to fulfilling the Equator Principles, an objective being pursued by GACM's management.

Box 2.14. **Stakeholder engagement during the construction of Heathrow Airport Terminal 5**

Construction of T5 was approved by the Secretary of State on 20 November 2001, after the longest public inquiry in British history (46 months). Construction of the new terminal started in September 2002. Phase 1 of the project was completed and opened in March 2008, with the second phase opening in June 2011. The project required an estimated investment (mostly from British Airport Authority) of more than GBP 4.2 billion.

As said, the construction of Heathrow's Terminal 5 holds the record of the longest public inquiry in the history of the United Kingdom, which lasted nearly four years. The public inquiry cost GBP 80 million, heard 700 witnesses, and generated 100 000 pages of transcripts. The Secretary of State gave his approval to the project after reviewing the public inquiry report, and a number of conditions and limitations were imposed to take into account the complaints of local communities regarding noise and pollution. Heathrow has since launched property and noise consultations to develop compensation packages and seek views on how that compensation fund should be used.

The London Chamber of Commerce became an advocate for the project as it launched a campaign, Business for T5, to promote the benefits of expanding the airport. It claimed that overseas visitors would spend an estimated 10 million fewer nights in Britain if Terminal 5 did not go ahead with a loss of about GBP 1 billion to the hotels sector and another GBP 500 million to the wider tourist industry.

Source: Butcher, L. (2014), *Aviation: London Heathrow Airport*, House of Commons.

In contrast, insufficient transparency in decision making may hurt confidence and trust in the project as stakeholders are not able to understand how, when, and by whom project decisions are made. International experience suggests different mechanisms to further citizen engagement in megaprojects and develop ownership, particularly in processes of planning and decision making, such as the following from OECD, 2014:

- *Public meetings/open houses held at project milestones:* This form of engagement opens opportunities for the public to participate in project development, not only previous to the launching of the project, but on a continuous basis. Members of the public are invited to provide written and/or oral comments on the scope of the project and to suggest reasonable alternatives for consideration. The public may also be invited to comment during the circulation of specific documents, such as the Environmental Impact Statement. Comments raised should be responded to in order to develop trust and keep the engagement of social actors, who otherwise may consider their efforts useless. Major meetings may be advertised in local newspapers to ensure maximum public participation.

- *Targeted meetings with stakeholders*: These kinds of meetings may include get-togethers with the villages and towns adjacent to the airport, briefings with elected officials, and meetings with representatives of municipal agencies such as the urban planning and transportation departments of the municipalities and delegations concerned, special interest groups, community groups, and with other interested parties as appropriate.
- *Mailing list:* A mailing list may include elected officials, public agency contacts, stakeholder and community groups, media, and individuals. The mailing list could be used to distribute meeting announcements and information about the project. An e-mail list could also be available for "e-mail blasts" that announce upcoming meetings and other information. These lists should be updated regularly to keep their relevance. A project mailing list, totalling more than 5 000 names and addresses, was compiled during the Tappan Zee Bridge/I-287 Corridor Project. Previous efforts also included the establishment of a Stakeholder Committee, five Stakeholders' Advisory Working Groups (on finance, environment, land use, traffic and transit, and bridge issues), an Inter-metropolitan Planning Organisation, and task forces.[23]
- *Informational materials:* These can be produced at key points during the project development process. Content could include written information on the project as well as visuals (photos, maps, and charts) and contact information. Presentations, meeting hand-outs, and other materials should be developed as appropriate to keep the public fully informed about project developments. Comment sheets should be made available at public meetings to encourage public input. In this sense, social media has also opened up new ways to interact with stakeholders and get their feedback efficiently.
- *Media outreach:* When appropriate, a media outreach effort should be conducted. This would involve contacting the media when there are new project developments to communicate, as well as issuing press releases at major milestones. This effort should include newspapers serving low-income and minority communities. GACM is going in the right direction as it has held press conferences to inform about the main features of NAICM and is planning others to, for example, describe the procurement packaging strategy. Nonetheless, this media outreach efforts need to be linked to a more holistic engagement strategy.
- *Repositories:* Local repositories throughout the project area would enable members of the public to examine project documents, including, for example, the Environmental Impact Assessment and the Infrastructure Master Plan. The repositories could include local libraries, town halls, and community centres.

Likewise, different tools can be promoted to motivate citizen engagement in the oversight of the project. The most common mechanisms include public information and complaints management, as well as third-party monitoring agreements (i.e. agreements with universities to monitor public works and enhance supervision).

There are, however, other mechanisms for more profound engagements, such as community monitors, social contracts, and social participation frameworks (OECD, 2014):

- Community monitors observe progress and the quality of megaprojects. They can be useful for creating trust among stakeholders, but need to be properly trained.

- Social contracts are designed to clarify and capture stakeholder commitments. These are co-signed by the leading agency and representatives of users, contractors, local governments, and congressmen during the implementation phase of the project. The contracts reflect the agreed roles that emerge from dialogue processes. They illustrate not only the adherence of the leading agency to social participation principles, but also the contributions of each stakeholder towards the project, as well as roles and behaviours of each party that contribute implicitly to fighting corruption and to enhancing the governance environment. Social contracts can also be complemented with bilateral agreements between the leading agency and the parties.
- A social participation framework (SPF), when applied, is set up from the outset of the project. The SPF is used during project preparation and continued throughout its cycle. The SPF contemplates three components: participation, communication, and transparency and accountability. The overall main objectives of the SPF are: *i)* guaranteeing a broad participation of the different stakeholders aiming at among other objectives, establishing their roles and responsibilities in realistic and fair terms; *ii)* creating awareness of the importance of expenditures and mechanisms for maintenance to preserve the project's condition; *iii)* disseminating the project's objectives and achievements; and *iv)* increasing the project's transparency and accountability throughout its cycle (see Box 2.15 for more on the use of SPFs by the World Bank).

All the mechanisms mentioned above are useful to break away from a common feature of megaprojects around the world: keeping citizens at a significant distance from decision making. NAICM is certainly an opportunity to become a benchmark for inclusiveness.

6. Periodic financial and procurement reviews must be undertaken to respond to evolving conditions

Recurrent and integrated financial management and procurement reviews should be performed to confirm the adequacy of contract management arrangements. In terms of financial management, these reviews are useful to analyse issues such as the scheduled spending and the response to changes in the financing conditions of the project (i.e. budget cuts as a result of falling oil prices and contraction of private funding markets). GACM has developed alternative scenarios and strategies to address potential (and likely) budget cuts. These anticipatory actions should continue responding to changes in the markets.

Regarding procurement, evaluation is necessary, for example, to assess the achievement of secondary policy objectives against value for money. Appropriate planning, baseline analysis, risk assessment, key performance indicators (KPIs), and target outcomes should be established as the basis for the development of action plans or guidelines for implementation. The results of any use of the public procurement system of GACM to support secondary policy objectives (i.e. training Mexican companies to participate in megaprojects abroad) should be measured against appropriate milestones to provide policy makers with the necessary information regarding the benefits and costs of such use (OECD, 2015).

Box 2.15. The use of social participation frameworks by the World Bank

The Road Maintenance Project for Paraguay is an initiative of the Republic of Paraguay that received financial support from the World Bank in the form of a Specific Investment Lending. The Road Maintenance Project for Paraguay established a sustainable road management strategy to ensure the upgrading and maintenance of the road network through a rational and balanced use of scarce resources.

A social participation framework resulted from a series of consultations with key stakeholders aimed at ascertaining the local existing experience in similar processes. As part of this framework, the project implemented the following measures: *i)* consolidating participation mechanisms with differentiated intervention strategies according to the needs and capacities of all relevant stakeholders, and mainly the more vulnerable beneficiary groups, developing a wealth of feasible mechanisms ranging from one-way communication, such as information meetings, to collaborative mechanisms (shared control over decision making) and empowerment towards sustainability of the project if possible (transfer of control over decisions and resources); *ii)* strengthening of the communication activities with public awareness campaigns and training of different stakeholders, according to their needs and cultural characteristics; *iii)* developing of transparency and accountability measures in a comprehensive *Improved Governance Framework and Project Action Plan* to ensure fluent flow of reliable information to relevant stakeholders, continued feedback, social oversight; and clear signs of accomplishment of obligation of power-holders to take responsibility for their actions; and *iv)* an institutional strengthening component aimed at facilitating the institutional arrangement for implementation of these measures.

Many activities of this framework were developed during project preparation, among them the selection of the Basic Rural Unpaved Road Network in the three departments to be supported by the project. This component was designed and prepared through a participatory process with local communities, local governments, and civil society, both for the definition of the basic road network to include in the project and also to define the contributions, in-kind or monetary that the community could make to the project. This approach has had the advantage of involving potential beneficiaries from the beginning, empowering them, encouraging them to participate in decisions that will influence final outcomes and also promoting transparency and commitment with the project.

Source: OECD (2014), "Good practices for the implementation of an integrity strategy in major infrastructure projects", working document.

Experience in OECD member and observer countries illustrates that most of them do not consider the opportunity costs and potential risks when using procurement to support socio-economic objectives. In fact, 43% of the countries surveyed to assess progress with the 2008 "Recommendation of the Council on Enhancing Integrity in Public Procurement"[24] did not systematically require written verification that public procurement is the best tool to achieve government objectives. The costs of achieving these goals should be considered and the trade-offs should be made explicit to determine whether procurement is a more cost-effective way to achieve socio-economic objectives than direct social policies (OECD, 2012).

The GACM governance structure allows for carrying out such evaluations, as there is one corporate directorate in charge of this task. However, other measures can be taken to make sure that such evaluations do occur, for example, the establishment of special units in SFP and SHCP to deal with issues related to NAICM (i.e. shortages of human resources, reviewing tender documentation and adapting the financing strategy).

Periodic reviews can also be useful to assess the relevance of the governance framework and the need for adjustment. The UK government developed the "Project Initiation Routemap", which provides questions to complete such assessment (see Box 2.16).

Box 2.16. **The Project Initiation Routemap**

The Project Initiation Routemap is a product of the UK Government that arose from working collaboratively with industry and the University of Leeds. It is an aid to strategic decision making and supports the alignment of the sponsor and client capabilities to meet the degree of challenge during initiation and delivery of a project. It provides an objective and structured approach to project initiation, founded on a set of assessment tools.

The governance module of the routemap provides the key questions that project leaders should ask themselves when defining and reviewing the governance framework:

- Does the governance framework cover concerns identified in a complexity-capability assessment?
- Does it formalise which parties are accountable for what?
- Does it ensure people have sufficient authority to discharge their accountabilities?
- Does it enable effective decisions to be made (i.e. decisions that will stick)?
- Does it enable efficient decisions to be made (i.e. decision routes that are not overly burdensome)?
- Does it give stakeholders confidence in project delivery?
- Does it ensure risk is allocated to participating organisations aligned with their ability and willingness to own the risks?

Source: Infrastructure UK, HM Treasury and Lord Deighton (2014), "Improving infrastructure delivery, project initiation routemap", October, www.gov.uk/government/publications/improving-infrastructure-delivery-project-initiation-routemap.

Notes

1. ASA is a decentralised body of the Federal Government, with its own assets and legal personality, that operates, manages, and builds airports, provides fuelling services, technical advice, and consulting, as well as training and research regarding aeronautics and airports, and collaborates with the SCT concerning airport regulation, verification, and surveillance.

2. As stated on the GACM website at www.aeropuerto.gob.mx/gacm/quienes-somos.php, consulted on 12 May 2015.

3. The revised Guidelines were approved by the OECD Council on 8 July 2015. More information can be found at www.oecd.org/daf/ca/guidelines-corporate-governance-soes.htm.

4. For the purpose of the Guidelines, any corporate entity in which the state exercises ownership should be considered as a state-owned enterprise (SOE).

5. Article 9 of LFEP mandates that the SHCP must be represented in the boards of enterprises with majority state participation.

6. Up to the appointment of GACM's own internal comptroller. audit and control functions were being performed temporarily by the OIC of SCT.

7. See the GACM Organisation Manual for more information.

8. See the GACM Organisation Manual for more information.

9. Many other primary laws apply to specific activities and functions of the GACM (i.e. budgeting and transparency) but, for practical purposes, only the main and more general ones are described in this section. GACM's Organisation Manual lists 72 primary laws, 10 codes, the budget decree of the corresponding years, 54 bylaws, 3 decrees, 39 treaties and international conventions, 30 agreements, 10 administrative manuals of general application, 8 bulletins (circulares), and 9 other regulatory instruments. Primary laws applicable to procurement will be discussed in length in the next chapter.

10. Preliminary results from the 2014 OECD Regulatory Management Indicators survey indicate that 61% of member countries have requirements for stakeholder engagement for all draft primary laws, 15% for only major regulations, 18% for some regulations, and only 6% never have such requirements. The numbers for secondary regulations are 52%, 20%, 17%, and 11%, respectively.

11. For more information, see the GACM website, at www.aeropuerto.gob.mx/gacm/estudios-y-documentos.php, consulted on 18 May 2015.

12. LEED is an international certification for sustainable design and construction. It is granted since 1998 by the Council of Green Buildings of the United States. Some

52 000 projects have been certified in the world, 1 700 in Latin America, and 320 in Mexico.

13. Information provided by GACM.

14. Information provided by GACM.

15. See http://archivo.eluniversal.com.mx/nacion-mexico/2014/encuesta-convence-construccion-de-aeropuerto--1036700.html#encuesta090914. The poll was taken by phone on 7-14 September 2014 and was applied to 1 000 individuals residing in the Federal District and its metropolitan area.

16. At the time of the interview (July 2015), the studies referenced had not yet been shared with GACM.

17. For more information, see the NAICM website at www.aeropuerto.gob.mx/fases-del-proyecto-del-nuevo-aeropuerto-de-mexico.php, consulted on 26 May 2015.

18. Research suggests links between centrality in airline networks and economic development. See Alberts, Bowen, Jr. and Cidell (2009).

19. As of July 2015, the exact dates and formats of the "roadshows" had not been defined.

20. More information about the Equator Principles can be found at www.equator-principles.com/.

21. Independent directors (subject to national definitions) are individuals who do not directly represent any particular stakeholder interest in the SOE, but who are sought to bring specific skills and competencies to the board.

22. The current Mexico City airport will be shut down upon the beginning of operations of NAICM. There is still no definition over what to do with those facilities. While the Federal Government argues for consulting experts to make a decision, the Government of the Federal District has been promoting the idea of a public consultation.

23. The Tappan Zee Bridge is located in the State of New York, crossing the Hudson River between the Village of South Nyack in Rockland County and the Village of Tarrytown in Westchester County. The project started in 2012-13 and the first span of the new twin-span bridge is scheduled to open in 2016. The new bridge should be complete in 2018.

24. The OECD "Recommendation of the Council on Public Procurement", adopted in 2015, replaced the 2008 Recommendation.

References

Alberts, H.C., J.T. Bowen, Jr. and J.L. Cidell (2009), "Missed opportunities: The restructuring of Berlin's airport system and the city's position in international airline networks", *Regional Studies* 43:5, p. 741.

Beria, P. and A.B. Scholz (2010), "Strategies and pitfalls in the infrastructure development of airports: A comparison of Milan Malpensa and Berlin Brandenburg international airports", *Journal of Air Transport Management* 16(2010), pp. 65-73.

Brady, T. and A. Davies (2010), "From hero to hubris – Reconsidering the project management of Heathrow's Terminal 5", *International Journal of Project Management* 28 (2010), pp. 151–157, www.itn.liu.se/mit/education/courses/tnfl05-risk-och-olycksanalys/vecka-47/1.304769/BradyochDavies2010.pdf.

Butcher, L. (2014), *Aviation: London Heathrow Airport*, House of Commons.

Gomes-Casseres, B. (2009), "Outsourcing: Where will you draw the line?", *Harvard Business Review*, https://hbr.org/2009/08/outsourcing-where-will-you-dra.

IMCO et al. (2015), *Observatorio Ciudadano del Nuevo Aeropuerto de la Ciudad de México*, available at http://imco.org.mx/wp-content/uploads/2015/04/2015_NAICM_Ejes_de_monitoreo_Documento_completo.pdf.

Infrastructure UK, HM Treasury and Lord Deighton (2014), "Improving infrastructure delivery, project initiation routemap", October, www.gov.uk/government/publications/improving-infrastructure-delivery-project-initiation-routemap.

OECD (2015), *OECD Territorial Reviews: Valle de México, Mexico*, OECD Publishing, Paris, http://dx.doi.org/10.1787/9789264245174-en.

OECD (2015), "Recommendation of the Council on Public Procurement", www.oecd.org/corruption/recommendation-on-public-procurement.htm.

OECD (2014), "Good practices for the implementation of an integrity strategy in major infrastructure projects", working document.

OECD (2013a), *Corporate Governance and Board Arrangements at* Petroleos Mexicanos, *Evaluation and Recommendations*, OECD Publishing, Paris.

OECD (2013b), "Balancing commercial and non-commercial priorities of state-owned enterprises", *Working Papers on Corporate Governance*, No. 6, http://dx.doi.org/10.1787/5k4dkhztkp9r-en.

OECD (2013c), *Boards of Directors of State-Owned Enterprises: An Overview of National Practices*, OECD Publishing, Paris, http://dx.doi.org/10.1787/9789264200425-en.

OECD (2012), *Progress Made in Implementing the OECD Recommendation on Enhancing Integrity in Public Procurement*, OECD Publishing, Paris.

Raiborn, C.A., J. Butler and M.F. Massoud (2009), "Outsourcing support functions: Identifying and managing the good, the bad, and the ugly", *Harvard Business Review*, https://hbr.org/product/outsourcing-support-functions-identifying-and-managing-the-good-the-bad-and-the-ugly/an/BH337-PDF-ENG.

Wells, J. (2015), "Corruption in the construction of public infrastructure: Critical issues in project preparation", *U4 Issue* No. 8, U4 Anti-corruption Resource Centre.

Chapter 3

Public procurement strategies and challenges relative to the NAICM project

*This chapter provides an overview of the public procurement framework surrounding the New International Airport of Mexico City (*Nuevo Aeropuerto Internacional de la Ciudad de México, *NAICM) project. It describes the interactions between various stakeholders in competitive procurement processes. The analysis focuses on procurement strategies and objectives defined by the Airport Group of Mexico City (GACM), and provides recommendations on adapting standard processes according to the magnitude and complexity of the project. It identifies challenges and opportunities in the critical phase of selecting suppliers who will be participating in the construction of the airport.*

As discussed in Chapter 2, GACM (*Grupo Aeroportuario de la Ciudad de México,* Airport Group of Mexico City) was established in 1998 through a governmental decree as an enterprise with state participation. As such, GACM is subject to the public procurement framework applicable to public entities.

Beyond being subject to public procurement regulations, the nature of the project also impacts its surrounding legislative environment. The construction of an airport, a major infrastructure asset, with several different components, including military facilities, shall also abide, yet in a more indirect way, by legislative frameworks relating to environmental policies and national security rules.

These different laws, although not directly framing the procurement processes carried out for the construction of the airport, have effects on some of their features from the type of procurement process used to the definition of award criteria.

However this regulatory framework does not prevent GACM from adapting standard public procurement processes for the provision of public works to the extraordinary nature and complexity of the project. GACM should then adapt its procurement strategy to its overarching ambition to deliver a new international airport in an exceptionally short timeframe and which will provide, throughout its different stages, the expected economic, social and environmental benefits.

The public procurement framework in Mexico: a constrained regulatory environment

A fragmented and detailed regulatory environment applicable to public procurement

In Mexico, all procurement entities are bound by various primary and secondary rules ranging from the Mexican Constitution (*Constitución Política de los Estados Unidos Mexicanos*, CPEUM) to a series of laws, regulations, codes, decrees, institutional agreements and manuals.

Article 134 of the Constitution establishes that the procurement of goods and services by the Federal Public Administration, states, municipalities and the Federal District is carried out through public tenders in order to achieve the best terms in price, quantity, financing arrangements, and convenience. As a consequence, public tender shall be the rule unless specific and justified circumstances prevent its being so.

When GACM carries out public procurement, one of the following federal statutes (and their associated regulations) is applicable: the Procurement Act, covering the public procurement of goods and services; the Public Works Act, covering the commissioning of public works and related services; and the Public-Private Partnerships Act. In accordance with the choice made by the Government and the nature of the project, the main set of laws and regulations where the applicable regulatory framework is to be found are the laws, regulations, codes, decrees, institutional agreements, and manuals governing public works and associated services.

The principles set out in the Constitution are then detailed in a set of normative instruments, some of which apply to the federal public administration as a whole, while others are specific to GACM.

The primary legislation that regulates public procurement in this area is the Law on Public Works and Associated Services (*Ley de Obras Públicas y Servicios Relacionados con las Mismas*, LOPSRM). This law was first implemented in January 2004 and since that time has been subject to further amendments, the latest occurring in November 2014.

Article 1, Section V specifies that it is applicable to private companies whose majority of shares are owned by the State. This is the case of GACM, which is owned in majority by the Federal Government through Airports and Auxiliary Services (*Aeropuertos y Servicios Auxiliares*, ASA) and the Ministry for Communication and Transport (*Secretaria de Comunicaciones y Transportes*, SCT).

Beyond strict public works, the Law also encompasses all related services. Article 4 of the Law on Public Works broadly defines related services that fall under this law, including preliminary studies of all sorts (structural, environmental, financial). All procurement operations in the New International Airport of Mexico City (*Nuevo Aeropuerto Internacional de la Ciudad de México*, NAICM) project shall thus be governed by its provisions and associated regulations, codes and manuals.

The Law details overarching principles governing public procurement for public works and associated services. It notably defines the major steps applicable to competitive procurement processes, from the procurement plan to contract management. It also provides the grounds for exception to public tender and provisions on the settlement of disputes arising during the competitive procurement process.

The Law on Public Works is directly complemented by the Regulation on Public Works and Associated Services (*Reglamento de Obras Públicas y Servicios Relacionados con las Mismas*, ROPSRM). These provisions depict administrative procedures and steps relating to the procurement of public works. It provides additional details on aspects of public procurement specific to the Law on Public Works such as the Works Committee (*Comité de Obras*) responsible for granting derogations to open public procurement, the prevalence of award criteria combining qualitative and quantitative aspects (*puntos y porcentajes*) and variations mechanisms to contracts during the execution phase.

In addition, every public institution designs and issues its own Policies, Ground Rules and Guidelines for Public Works and Associated Services (*Políticas, bases y lineamientos en materia de Obras Públicas y Servicios Relacionados con las Mismas*, POBALINES) to ensure that institutional procurement processes are aligned with the Law on Public Works and other applicable laws.

POBALINES must include administrative divisions within each public agency in charge of administering the public procurement acts and their implementing regulations. It should also detail the position and level of the procurement officials within each public agency responsible for supervising the different procedures during the tender processes and the manner in which each public agency complies with the terms and conditions of the laws and implementing regulations. The POBALINES issued by GACM detail all these elements.

Moreover, GACM is in the process of developing further practical guidance on various aspects relating to the construction of the NAICM such as the Manual for Planning, Contracting and Execution of Public Works and Associated Services (*Manual de Procedimientos para la Planeación, Contratación y Ejecución de Obra Pública y Servicios Relacionados con la Misma*). A first draft was issued in August 2014 and should be updated.

To further assist public procurement officials and describe the various procurement procedures, the Ministry of Public Administration (*Secretaría de la Función Pública*,

SFP) has released procurement manuals – the Administrative Manual for General Application concerning Acquisitions, Leasing and Services of the Public Sector (*Manual Administrativo de Aplicación General en Materia de Aquisiciones, Arrendamientos y Servicios del Sector Público*, MAAGMAASSP) and the Administrative Manual for General Application concerning Public Works and Associated Services (*Manual Administrativo de Aplicación General en Materia de Obra Públicas y Servicios Relacionados con las Mismas*, MAAGMOPSRM) commonly known as the General Procurement Manuals. Both detail procurement procedures step by step, supply general guidelines, and templates, and supersede any internal procurement document that may duplicate their content.

Increasingly complex within the regulatory environment applicable to airport infrastructure

In addition to the set of rules governing public procurement, the construction of airport infrastructure also has to comply with specific laws and regulations (notably the laws on civil aviation, national security, telecommunications, environmental policies and all their derived regulations).

While most of the specific provisions contained in these regulations have unsubstantial effects on public procurement activities relating to the NAICM, two components participate in framing the entire procurement strategy.

The first component is to be found in environmental regulatory framework. Article 20 of the Law on Public Works states that prior to conducting public works the procuring area shall conduct environmental impact assessments in accordance with the provisions set out in the General Law on Ecological Sustainability and Protection of the Environment (*Ley General del Equilibrio Ecológico y la Protección al Ambiente*).

Integrating environmental considerations into procurement processes related to infrastructure projects is relatively common in many OECD countries, e.g. Austria and France. Environmental objectives can be translated into procurement processes either by requiring environmental performance certificates from bidders or by assessing the relative environmental performance of proposals received. The Netherlands, for example, uses a mix of those two components (Box 3.1).

The second significant component that will influence the overall procurement strategy is to be found in legislation relating to national security since the airport should provide both civil and military aviation facilities.

The military component is subject to specific legislation, notably defining national or public security, which is broadly understood as any action causing prejudice to national strategic interests. The concept of national security, which could eventually be applied to some packages of the construction of NAICM, has one major consequence.

According to Article 42 Section IV of the LOPSRM, exception to public tendering is authorised when public works are being carried out for exclusive military purposes or if the open tender procedure would cause a significant prejudice to national security or public security according to their definitions in the corresponding laws. In this case, the oversight *ex ante* mechanism foreseen in the Law – the Committee on Public Works – is not mandatorily required to assess the justifications for derogation to open public tenders. The *ex post* oversight mechanism – the internal control body – is neither informed of the existence of the deriving contracts.

Box 3.1. **Green public procurement in the Netherlands**

Rijkswaterstaat (the Department of Public Works of the Ministry of Infrastructure and the Environment, RWS) developed a methodology for infrastructure projects whereby the functional specification of the tender, together with the quality input from the client, ensure an innovative and high-quality solution. The tenderer is also asked to respond to specific quality criteria. The RWS uses the most economically advantageous tender (MEAT) methodology, including specific sustainability criteria.

The RWS has decided to focus on two criteria when assessing the sustainability attributes of offers, work processes and associated products: CO_2 emissions and environmental impact. Two instruments have therefore been developed: the CO_2 performance ladder and "DuboCalc", respectively.

The CO_2 performance ladder is a certification system with which a tenderer can show the measures to be taken to limit CO_2 emissions within the company and in projects, as well as elsewhere in the supply chain. DuboCalc is a life-cycle analysis (LCA) based tool that calculates the sustainability value of a specific design based on the materials to be used. Bidders use DuboCalc to compare different design options for their submissions. The DuboCalc score of the preferred design is submitted with the tender price.

A tenderer can submit a CO_2 performance ladder certificate with their tender submission. The certificate obliges the tenderer to comply with a certain CO_2 reduction target according to its method of execution and working processes. Holders of the certificate have their submission price reduced by a value proportional to the effort made to reduce CO_2 emissions. The CO_2 performance ladder certificate can be provided as evidence at the tender submission stage, but this is not compulsory as long as the certificate is provided within one year of signing the contract.

CO_2 performance ladder

Contractors can apply for a CO_2 performance ladder certificate. In order to comply, contractors need to take steps towards reducing their carbon footprint. The first step (or "rung" on the ladder) is to measure the company's CO_2 emissions. In further steps, supply chain CO_2 emissions are also measured, and more importantly goals are set towards reducing emissions. The higher levels on the CO_2 ladder include steps towards CO_2 reduction in the supply chain.

The CO_2 performance ladder is used in the tendering procedure as follows: the bidder indicates at which of the five rungs (ambition levels) of the CO_2 performance ladder he/she intends to carry out the work; the higher the effort to reduce CO_2 emissions, the higher the rung. A commitment to a higher rung results in a greater deduction from the submission price, which increases the chance of winning the contract. Each CO_2 ambition level corresponds to a different percentage reduction of the submission price. The final amount assessed by the RWS using the CO_2 performance ladder is a deduction of 1% per rung of the submission price. The highest level is Rung 5, so the maximum deduction is 5%.

DuboCalc

To quantify the sustainability of material use, the RWS has developed a software tool that calculates the environmental impact of construction materials. This calculation is based on an LCA of the material. The software is called the Sustainable Building Calculator, or "DuboCalc". This tool can be used in tenders for works if the design phase is included in the tender. Dubocalc was developed as part of an overall trend towards performance-based tendering assessing the overall environmental impact of constructions rather than prescribing details.

With DuboCalc, all embedded environmental impacts of material use can be calculated, from raw material extraction and production up to and including demolition and recycling (the entire life cycle). DuboCalc also calculates the energy consumed by infrastructure works during the use phase.

For a DuboCalc calculation of infrastructure works, the programme requires input of the amounts of materials used for a particular design. Using LCA data from a built-in database, it calculates 11 environmental impact parameters. The software is based on an independent (national) dataset containing certified LCA information for each material.

Box 3.1. **Green public procurement in the Netherlands *(continued)***

DuboCalc calculates the value of these effects via the so-called "shadow price method" to arrive at a single figure, the Environmental Cost Indicator value (ECI value). The shadow price method is based on the costs of preventing emissions from arising. The ECI value indicates the environmental impact of a particular design for civil engineering works. A lower value indicates lower environmental impact. Designs that differ significantly from each other in terms of material use also differ in terms of environmental quality. DuboCalc enables designers to calculate ECI values of alternative designs to arrive at an optimally sustainable design.

The ECI value is used in the tendering procedure as follows: the contracting authority provides the tenderer with all the functional requirements and the latest version of the DuboCalc programme. The tenderer designs the infrastructure and calculates the price and the ECI value. The ECI value is transformed into a monetary value according to a formula that is prescribed by the tenderer (the ECI value and monetary value are inversely related and there is a minimum and a maximum). These two prices are offered to the contracting authority. The contracting authority selects the tenderer with the lowest price and ECI value combined to undertake the work.

Source: OECD (2014a), "Smart procurement: Best practices for green procurement", web page, www.oecd.org/gov/ethics/best-practices-for-green-procurement.htm (accessed on 30 September 2015).

While providing operational details on a number of aspects of public procurement, this regulatory environment is also significantly fragmented. Instructions, rules and guidance are provided by the Government, specific ministries and are also complemented by internal GACM policies. Still, this environment offers flexibility in a number of areas, which could be used to adapt standard public procurement processes to the extraordinary nature of this project.

Yet it provides opportunities to adapt procurement processes to the magnitude and complexity of the project

These laws, regulations, and manuals governing public procurement in Mexico, and more particularly in GACM, induce a series of operational consequences which together might somewhat affect the performance of public procurement processes. However, GACM could also take advantage of some of these consequences to align procurement operations with the scale of such an infrastructure project.

Supporting a sustainable financing architecture

Financial elements of infrastructure works also impact public procurement processes. Being the main method for spending public funds (OECD, 2015a), public procurement shall inherently follow government budget orientations or allocations of public funds. Considering the size and magnitude of public works, the Law on Public Works puts stronger emphasis on the surrounding budgetary preconditions to public procurement.

Figure 3.1 does not however do justice to procurement for public goods in Mexico. While Mexico ranks in the lower half of general government procurement as a percentage of GDP (gross domestic product) or share of total government expenditures, these data do not integrate procurement activities carried out by state-owned enterprises (SOEs). In Mexico, public procurement activities carried out by SOEs are extremely significant. As an example, one single SOE, the national oil company *Petróleos Mexicanos* (PEMEX), accounted for 26% of the total federal procurement expenditure in 2010.

Figure 3.1. **General government procurement as a percentage of GDP and as share of total government expenditures, 2013**

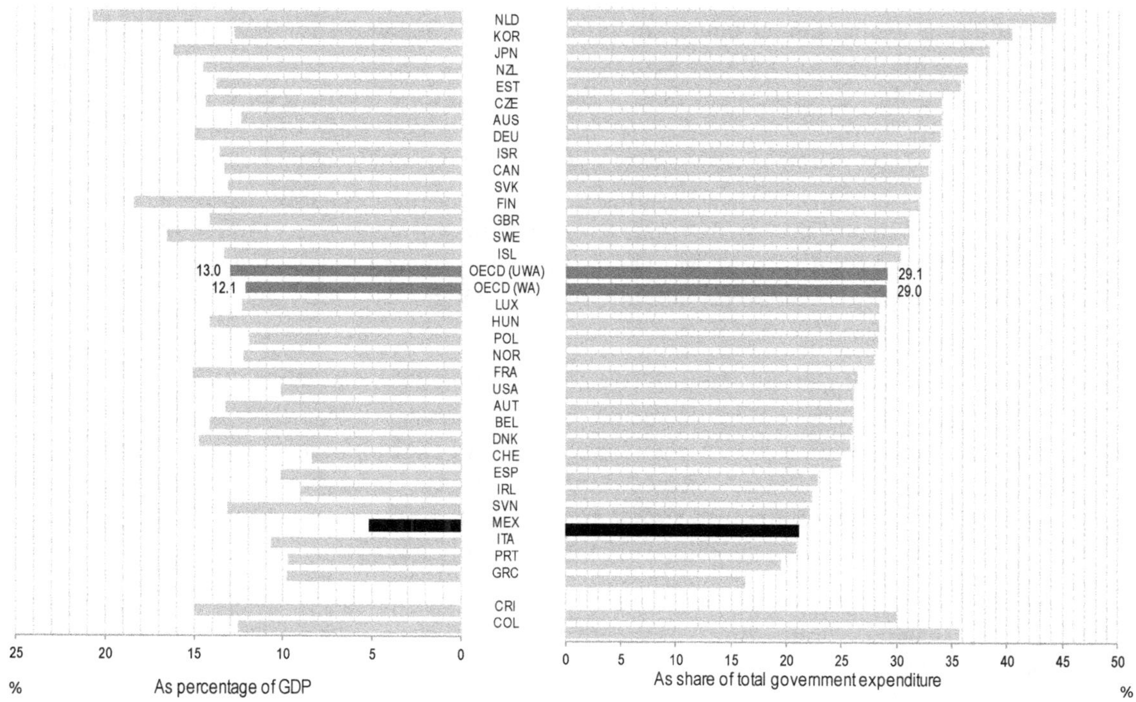

Note: Data for Australia are based on a combination of government finance statistics and National Accounts data provided by the Australian Bureau of Statistics.

Source: OECD (2015b), *OECD National Accounts Statistics* (database), http://dx.doi.org/10.1787/na-data-en (accessed on 30 September 2015).

Public procurement in Mexico, including for GACM, is subject to the prior availability of financial resources and the alignment of the projected public works with national strategic objectives. The laws relating to public financing comprise the National Development Plan (*Plan Nacional de Desarrollo*) and annual budget laws (*Ley Federal de Presupuesto y Responsabilidad Hacendaria*). Article 17 of the Public Works Law indicates that, before initiating any public works, federal entities shall ensure that planned operation fit within the objectives set out in the National Development Plan and corresponding resources are included in the annual budget law.

Building upon the general statements mentioned in the National Development Plan, the sectorial programme of the Ministry of Communications and Transport for 2013-18 further details the need to modernise airports infrastructures and to answer the increasing demand for airport services in Mexico City valley and in the centre of the country. NAICM, and the corresponding public works and associated services needed for its construction therefore fit with the requirement of Article 17 of the Law on Public Works. In addition, Article 18 indicates that public works relating to infrastructures shall be subject to feasibility studies, plan and development programmes in line with the National Development Plan.

GACM, as other entities subject to laws relating to public procurement, shall provide procurement plans for the fiscal year that shall be submitted to the Ministry of Public Administration. This is also the case for subsequent modifications.

In addition to the annual budget authorising the issuance of procurement processes, the nature of the project requires additional budgetary authorisation. For example, the construction of the terminal identified in the annual public works plan (GACM, 2015a) will last for more than a year. Article 50 of the Federal Law of Budget and Fiscal Responsibility (*Ley Federal de Presupuesto y Responsabilidad Hacendaria*, LFPRH) stipulates that public works entailing multi-year budget shall be duly justified and shall include a breakdown of budget by fiscal years. The proposal shall be approved in advance by the Director General of GACM. The relevant information, including the outcome of the procurement process, shall be submitted for information to the Ministry of Budget and Fiscal Responsibility.

The potential impact of these financial requirements is twofold. First, additional financial authorisations could influence the timeframe needed to carry out the corresponding competitive procurement procedures. In addition, the annual breakdown of works carried out in timeframes exceeding the fiscal year could require additional efforts on the structure of the technical specifications so that the execution of works and the level of investment required from suppliers are not negatively impacted.

While procurement procedures could be impacted by financial preconditions foreseen in the law, financial sustainability of the project might be influenced by the outcomes of competitive procurement processes, let alone a potential increase in the overall costs of construction. Indeed, a significant share of the construction costs will be financed via capital markets. According to public announcements, GACM intends to finance the initial phase of the construction of NAICM with up to 42% of private funding, including with long-term bonds.

Having recourse to private financing in infrastructure projects is not uncommon given scarce public resources and the financial significance of such projects. However this financing mechanism is dependent on the confidence of financial markets in the project and on the revenues it will be able to generate.

When investment decisions relate to infrastructure projects, securing private financing can be seriously affected, not only by a lack of planning in infrastructure projects, but also by the absence of demonstration of the capacity to prepare and execute projects successfully (OECD, 2015c). Delays or problems in the construction phase could therefore complicate the GACM's quest for private financing, which would in turn further delay the issuance of the following competitive procurement processes given the preconditions stated in the law. Alternatively, investors might require commensurate risk-adjusted compensation or insist on some form of minimum revenue guarantee to invest at all (OECD, 2015d). Deficient outcomes of procurement processes could therefore not only impact the timing of the construction of the airport or its direct costs, but also dramatically increase the total cost of ownership for the Mexican Government.

Identifying proposals which provide the best value for money

As in any other public procurement system, evaluation criteria set out in public procurement laws or in tender documentation is the main driver for identifying the submission that responds best to requirements put to tender. In Mexico, different evaluation methods exist, depending on the nature of the goods, services or works procured. Building on the duality of public procurement laws, the first consequence of the application of one normative instrument or the other relates to the method for evaluating responses to public tenders. The Procurement Act allows for two methods of evaluation: the points-based or the binary criterion. The Public Works Act favours, unless the area responsible decides not to do so, the utilisation of the points-based criterion for public works and related services and imposes the use of such criteria for infrastructure works.

The binary criterion awards the contract to the supplier that meets all of the qualifications conditions in the call for tender and offers the lowest price. This criterion is often used when standardised characteristics and specifications of the goods and services render those relatively interchangeable, thus giving financial attributes a decisive advantage.

The points-based criterion (*puntos y porcentajes*) provides a multidimensional assessment of goods, services and works presenting highly specialised or innovative characteristics and which require an expert evaluation. Under this evaluation mechanism, factors in addition to price are considered and a value is assigned for each factor to determine the most qualified bid (tenders are scored higher the more they satisfy the technical and qualitative requirements in the call for tender).

In these situations, purchasing entities face the challenge of designing tender processes which identify the optimal bid. This generally involves a trade-off between price and quality. A variety of awarding mechanisms have been used by governments in an attempt to account for quality, including: simultaneous bid evaluation of all attributes (price and non-price); two-stage evaluation procedures; over bids submitted on price and technical criteria; setting minimum quality standards for bidding participation; and private negotiations on all dimensions with a number of selected counterparts (OECD, 2015e). In public works, Mexico uses a two-stage approach where only qualified bids on the technical aspects are subject to a financial evaluation.

According to Article 31 Section XXII of the Law on Public Works, award criteria and their corresponding weightings shall be included in the tender documentation so as to duly inform potential bidders of the assessment mechanisms of their proposals. Article 38 further imposes that, among the criteria used to assess the overall value for money of proposals received, specific attention is given to the percentage of disabled workers employed by bidders. This requirement thus introduces social considerations into procurement processes.

In addition, Article 31 Section XX stipulates that the tender documentation, as the case may be, shall indicate the percentage of national content requested in the proposal. As opposed to the Law on Acquisitions, Leasing and Services of the Public Sector, the Law on Public Works does not impose a minimum threshold for such national content, except for labour workforce, which should equal at least 30% of the total labour workforce. The law merely refers to rules defined by the Ministry of Economy that provide additional guidance on formulas for evaluating the national content of public works. The percentage of national content requested in submissions from bidders is therefore mainly left to the discretion of the contracting authority.

In imposing points-based criteria for complex works, the Mexican legislative framework is aligned with best practices (for example the “Most Economically Advantageous Tender” in European countries, “Best Value” in the United States and Canada or the “Most Convenient Offer” in Costa Rica). Indeed, targeted evaluation criteria, relevant to the individual nature of the works put to tender and proportionate to their complexity, help identify solutions that best respond to the needs described in the technical specifications (OECD, 2014b). As an example, the terminal foundations for which works are planned to be put to tender in November 2015 are supposed to face technical challenges linked to land subsidence in the Mexico City valley (*El Debate*, 2015). The corresponding public tender could include specific evaluation criteria assessing the robustness of the proposals in addressing this issue.

The combination of qualitative and quantitative criteria, irrespective of the name given to this assessment method (cost/benefit ratio, value for money, most advantageous economically tender) is used in a large proportion of OECD countries, yet with differences in terms of coverage and on associated weightings (OECD, 2015e). Since the choice of the criteria and their corresponding weighting is often left to the discretion of the purchasing authority (except for disabled workers in the Law on Public Works), they are also often accompanied by detailed guidance based on the nature of goods, services or works put to tender.

This is not different in Mexico. Along with other practical documentation, the Ministry of Public Administration set out detailed guidance about criteria (SFP, 2010) to be used in procurement of public works and the range of percentages each criteria or sub-criteria could be assigned in the overall assessment of proposals received. This guidance however also allows for deviations from proposed evaluation criteria and weightings according to the nature of the project.

Yet, identification of the best-value-for-money proposal could not be achieved only by using multidimensional evaluation criteria; the assessment framework also needs to be tailored to tender specifics or to the objectives of the purchasing entity. The greater complexity of this assessment method providing evaluation of non-financial attributes entails higher scrutiny of the clarity and the structure of technical specifications, so responses provided by competitors could be seamlessly analysed against the criteria and the weighting defined in the tender documentation. Formulas used to score proposals received also significantly impact tender outcome (Box 3.2).

Taking advantage of CompraNet to alert markets and disseminate public procurement information

Various provisions of public procurement laws mandate contracting authorities (*unidades compradoras*) to disseminate procurement-related information via CompraNet, the electronic platform put in place by the Mexican Government. The SFP (Ministry of Public Administration) is in charge of administering this system, which includes information regarding the annual procurement and public works plans of public agencies, the registry of suppliers and contractors (including sanctioned suppliers), calls for tenders and their amendments, the minutes of "clarification meetings", the receipt and opening of proposals, the statements of "social witnesses", contract information and complaint resolutions. In 2014, 3 278 purchasing units from federal, state, and municipal governments utilised this system, representing a 42% increase compared to 2011.

While the first objective of the dissemination of procurement-related information on CompraNet is to increase the transparency of the public procurement system at all stages of the procurement cycle and promoting competition, it could also prove beneficial in alerting the market about future public procurement opportunities and help GACM finalise public tenders adapted to market capabilities.

Box 3.2. **Formulas for identifying the proposal that offers the best value for money**

Choosing the best bid is a significant step in any tendering process. If the award criterion is the economically most advantageous tender, this involves scoring bids on price and quality and ranking them. Scores are calculated using a bid evaluation formula that takes price and quality as inputs, and their respective weights. The choice of formula critically affects which bid wins.

A study of 38 formulas, against a sample of 382 real tenders, illustrates several aspects of these formulas and effects that derive from their application to real submissions.

- *Relative versus absolute scoring:* In the relative approach all bids are assessed against a formula which includes a component based on the characteristic of one bid or the average of bids (i.e. the highest or lowest price/quality or the average price/quality). Absolute formulas do not integrate information from the submitted bids as a reference point. The score calculated using an absolute formula depends only on the assessment of a given bid. While the former has been found to be used in the majority of the studied formulas, the second approach could support bidders' decisions to favour certain criteria.
- *Indifference curves*: Used in microeconomic theory, an indifference curve represents all combinations of price and quality that would receive the same overall scoring against a formula. This tool is useful to assess whether the substitution of one unit of quality by one unit of price has a constant effect (the curve is then straight) or if it evolves over time (the curve is either concave when consecutive units of quality are more and more valued or convex when consecutive units of quality are less and less valued).
- *Protection against an extremely high price*: Although a cautious balance in the corresponding weightings of price and quality components could protect purchasing entities from extremely high prices, tests where the price of the best bid in terms of quality has been multiplied by 50 show that some formulas provide rankings that are independent from price evolutions.
- *How a formula reflects the weights of price and quality*: Besides the mathematical method used to assess proposals, the weighting associated with each criterion plays a significant role in identifying the proposal offering the best value for money. The application of hypothetical scenarios (two proposals with low quality and significant price difference, two proposals different in quality and similar in price, etc.) allows for the definition of the tipping point, which is understood as the percentage weight of price above which the lower price-lower quality bid becomes the best bid.

While the definition of award criteria is commonly understood by purchasing entities, the choice of the formula itself often gets far less attention; formulas are often chosen without carefully analysing their properties and could have substantial effects on tender outcomes.

Source: Stilger, P.S., J. Siderius and E.M. van Raaij (2015), *A Comparative Study of Formulas for Choosing the Economically Most Advantageous Tender,* forthcoming in the Journal of Public Procurement http://dx.doi.org/10.2139/ssrn.2626934.

On the basis of Article 22 of LOPSRM, contracting authorities shall make publicly available, through CompraNet and its Internet website, no later than the 31st of January of every year, their Public Works and Related Services' Annual Programme, corresponding to the fiscal year in question, with the exception of the information that, in accordance with the applicable provisions, either of a reserved or confidential nature, under the established terms in the Federal Law of Transparency and Access to Governmental Public Information.

In accordance with Article 31 of LOPSRM for projects whose estimated value is above 10 000 times the minimum daily wage, the draft tender notice should be publicised on CompraNet for at least ten days before the issuance of the public tender. Below this threshold, any prior publication of the draft tender notice is optional. This disclosure is meant to allow interested parties to comment on the draft tender notice that includes detailed information about the modalities of the competition, the technical specifications or the duration of the works. The ROPSRM (Article 35) further indicates that comments and responses shall be duly documented, including justifications for not integrating comments into the final tender notice.

This information could help suppliers identify public procurement opportunities in which they could have interest. It could also provide additional time useful to form ad hoc alliances with other suppliers in case of tenders requiring distinct expertise or additional human resources which one supplier alone could not provide. It further offers GACM the opportunity to receive comments and feedback from the market on the tender documentation prior to the issuance of the open public tender.

Strengthening civil society's involvement in the project

Further engaging civil society in the project, and more specifically in procurement processes, is an objective which could be pursued in two ways. First, legislative requirements impose the integration of civil society in procurement processes above a certain threshold. However, these requirements provide for some flexibility and offer GACM the opportunity to further strengthen public engagement in the project.

Article 27b of LOPSRM stipulates that a social witness (*testigos sociales*) shall participate in all phases of open public tender procedures whose estimated value exceeds the equivalent of 10 million days of minimum wage in force in the Federal District where works shall be carried out, or upon decision of the Ministry of Public Administration as it sees fit. In financial terms, this means that participation of social witnesses is mandatory for procurement process whose estimated value exceeds approximately USD 46 million. The social witness could either be a natural person or a legal entity such as chambers of commerce or professional organisations. Social witnesses, selected by the Ministry of Public Administration (SFP), shall be honourable, possess an expertise related to the nature of services or works procurement and be independent from the parties involved in the process.

Below the threshold defined in the law, participation of social witnesses is optional. In addition to reinforcing citizen trust in public procurement by integrating social oversight in processes, social witnesses can also prove useful in providing non-binding advice in the process (OECD, 2013a). GACM could thus decide to make social witness participation mandatory in all procurement processes relating to the construction of the airport irrespective of the estimated amount of the packages put to tender.

Beyond including external scrutiny in public procurement processes, GACM also provides the procurement information related to NAICM to the general public via its website. This information includes procurement plans, latest major contracts awarded, and impact studies carried out before initiating the project. The integrity and communication chapters of this review assess the completeness of the information and address key recommendations to improve the overall transparency and accountability of the procurement process.

Ensuring transparency when granting derogations to open public procurement processes

Laws applicable to public procurement mandate purchasing entities, including GACM, to create oversight bodies responsible for assessing exceptions to open public tenders. The Committee on Public Works and Committee on Acquisition (*Comité de Obras y Comité de Adquisiciones*) are therefore responsible for granting derogations to open public procurement processes. In accordance with Article 26 of the ROPSRM, the Committee on Public Works shall be composed of:

- the General Director of GACM
- the Head of the Corporate Directorate for Real Estate Management and Administration
- the Head of the Corporate Directorate for Financing
- civil servants having recognised subject matter expertise and not affiliated to the Central Management Office (*Oficialía Mayor*).

The above composition ensures that this oversight body can function. However, the Law on Public Works also provides additional flexibility when stating that the Committee on Public Works could invite, but without the right to vote, any individual, bound by confidentiality obligations, whose clarifications are deemed necessary. This possibility could enhance transparency when a request for derogation is submitted to it and could ensure that the Committee makes an informed decision when deciding to grant a derogation to open public tender.

Derogation grounds are fully listed in Article 42 of the Law on Public Works and mostly find their origins in either technical (e.g. impossibility to precisely define the perimeter and amount of work needed) or legal matters (e.g. reserved intellectual property rights, force majeure, etc.). POBALINES indicate that technical justifications for the derogations submitted to the Committee on Public Works are provided by the Corporate Directorate for Infrastructure (*Dirección Corporativa de Infraestructura*).

The Public Works Committee is normally responsible for deciding whether to grant derogation from the obligation for public entities to award public contracts via an open tender procedure in advance of the process. However, based on Article 42 Section IV of the LOPSRM, exception to public tenders based on national security issues are not put forward before the Committee which is only informed by the purchasing entity after the contract is signed. Therefore, there is no *ex ante* control of this exception.

In addition, the internal control body (*Órgano Interno de Control*) shall be provided, in accordance with Article 41 of the LOPSRM, with a list of contracts signed by the entity in the preceding month and that were subject to derogations from the open public tender procedure. However, it is not necessary to report contracts based on derogations granted on the grounds of national security issues.

Infrastructure project requires the involvement of various stakeholders with distinct and uneven experience

Several directorates within GACM as well as other ministries have distinct, but interrelated, responsibilities in the procurement cycle

The POBALINES define the various areas responsible for the different stages of procurement processes.

The Corporate Directorate for Planning, Evaluation and Outreach is responsible for the overall co-ordination of GACM's activities and, more specifically, for the strategic planning for the development of the airport infrastructure of the Mexico Valley, its evaluation, and follow up.

The Corporate Directorate for Infrastructure is responsible for programming and managing the impact assessments, projects, works and related services, elaborating the terms of reference, managing the investment contracts, and supervising execution of the works.

The Corporate Directorate for Finance is responsible for planning, establishing and co-ordinating strategies and guidelines for carrying out the appropriate programming, budgeting and financial strategy.

Finally, the Corporate Directorate for Administration and Real Estate Management is responsible, among other things, for legally representing GACM and for carrying out the procurement processes necessary for public works acquisitions and related services.

Table 3.1 sets out a summary of the procurement-related responsibilities as they are carried out by each GACM corporate directorate.

Within these corporate directorates, entities are responsible for specific aspects embedded in the procurement process. While roles and responsibilities of the different areas are clearly spelled out in the POBALINES, the tight sequencing of activities required by the procurement strategy devised by GACM requires sound and efficient co-ordination.

From the initial procurement plan until the verification of the execution of the public works, a typical procurement process in GACM involves the four different directorates and no fewer than nine different sub-directorates or units. The most complex procurement processes, for example when social witnesses are required and contractual periods exceed a year, will involve other GACM directorates and other governmental entities, such as the SFP, the Ministry of Finance and Public Credit (*Secretaría de Hacienda y Crédito Público*, SHCP) and the Ministry of Environment and Natural Resources (*Secretaría de Medio Ambiente y Recursos Naturales*, SEMARNAT).

Table 3.1. **Procurement related responsibilities per GACM corporate directorate**

	Corporate Directorate for Planning	Corporate Directorate for Infrastructure	Corporate Directorate for Finance	Corporate Directorate for Administration and Real Estate Management
Responsibilities	• Overall co-ordination of GACM's activities • Strategic planning for the development of the airport infrastructure of the Mexico Valley • Evaluation • Follow up	• Planning and managing impact assessments, projects, works and related services • Elaborating terms of reference for the construction of NAICM • Management of investment contracts • Supervising execution of the works	• Planning, and establishing the necessary funding for the development of NAICM • Co-ordinating strategies and guidelines for carrying out the appropriate programming, budgeting and financial strategy	• Legally representing GACM • Ensuring compliance with the applicable regulatory frameworks • Carrying out the procurement processes necessary for public works acquisitions and related services, including market research • Real estate strategy • Planning, integration, direction, and management of human resources, real estate, buildings, and general services

Source: Author's own work.

GACM procurement activities, since GACM's inception, suggest limited experience in managing open competition procedures

Although formally created in 1998, GACM was only granted an organisational structure and the corresponding budget in late 2014 when the NAICM project was formally endorsed by the Mexican Government. Since then, GACM has been developing some internal practical guidance and notably procurement manuals to complement those published by the Ministry of Public Administration. Other manuals providing guidance on budgetary issues or on Committees on Public Works and on Acquisitions shall be further developed.

Its procurement activities only started the same year and are related to the NAICM project. Up to 12 August 2015, GACM carried out 36 distinct procurement processes directly relating to public works (Figure 3.2).

Figure 3.2. **Procurement processes related to public works and related services carried out by GACM since its inception**

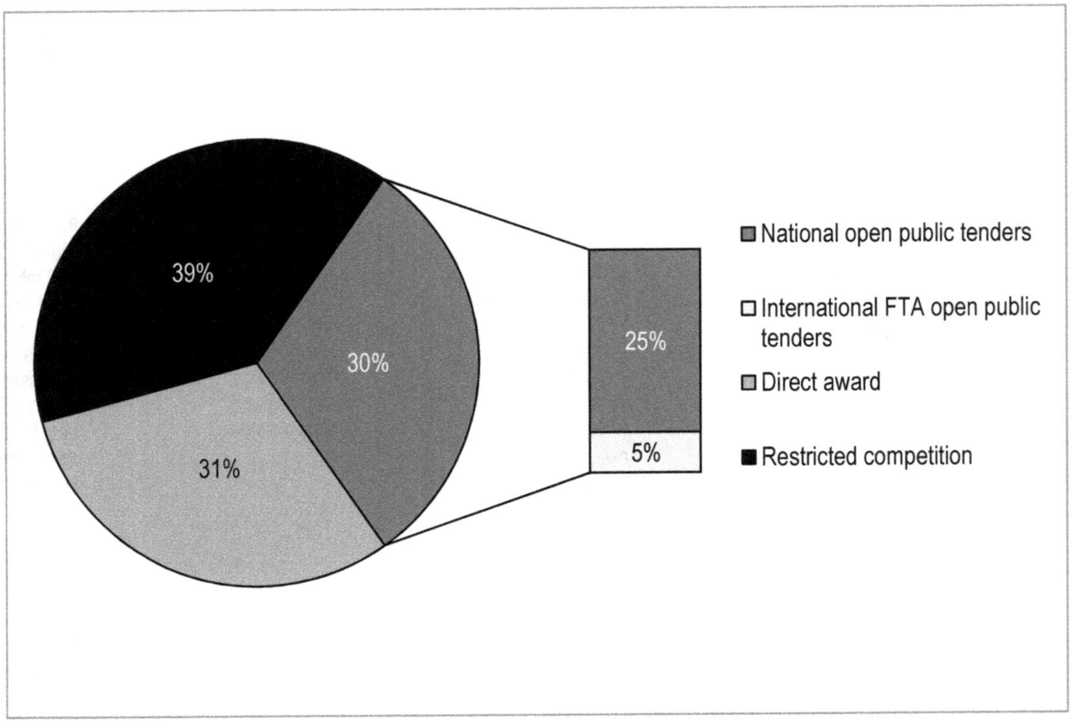

Source: Based on available information in CompraNet, (accessed on 12 August 2015).

Those procurement operations related almost exclusively to various impact assessments forming pre-conditions to the execution of public works relating to infrastructure (Articles 18 and 20 of the Law on Public Works). Considering the extraordinary character of infrastructure projects of this scale and size and the uneven related experience of public officials involved in those procurement processes, GACM also sought assistance in the design of the terms of reference.

More than two-thirds of the procurement processes carried out by GACM since its inception were conducted under exceptions to open public tenders and most notably under restricted competition *(invitación a cuando menos tres personas)*. By limiting competition to invited bidders, GACM incurred the risk of receiving proposals that were not of sufficient quality, and therefore had to cancel and re-issue the corresponding process. This happened in 21% of the procurement processes carried out under restricted competition. In addition, it is worth noting that more than 90% of the procurement processes only allowed for the participation of national companies.

Based on the information provided by GACM on the main construction packages (see "The packages: From strategy to implementation", below), these trends, both in terms of competitive procurement process used, and in terms of openness, will drastically change according to the public statements made to conduct all procurement activities relating to the construction of the NAICM under open public tenders.

This limited experience is mitigated by external assistance throughout the procurement cycle

In addition to ad hoc, outsourced technical assistance and considering the nature of the project, GACM will co-ordinate inputs that will come from a wide range of governmental entities, the project manager (PM) and the master architect.

Ministries of Communications and Transport, Public Administration, Environment and Natural Resources, Defence and Budget and Fiscal Responsibility will all be directly involved at one stage in the project as detailed above. This is without taking into account other several governmental entities, a significant part of the Mexican Government, which will be indirectly impacted.

Since the beginning of OECD support of the project, GACM has indicated that it has received technical assistance from specialised companies, notably for the PM. The company awarded with the responsibility to conduct the project management is Parsons, a US-based company with extensive know-how in large infrastructure constructions projects, and comprehensive experience in airports. Parsons provides inputs on the global design of the NAICM project, the structure of the packaging strategy, the outsourcing model in accordance with the legislative framework detailed above. They also participate in the drafting of the technical specifications that form the basis of the procurement processes and the rationale for the type of procedure used. As a project manager, Parsons will also play a lead role in the monitoring of the execution of the work, the co-ordination of the different lots and the reception of the work. As a project management office (PMO), they will design the work programme; plan and manage the project, including execution projects, equipment and systems; control all required actions for obtaining licensing; identify and monitor risks during the development of the project; monitor the quality systems; manage the allocated budget; and prepare the transfer of the current airport to the new one.

The adjudication of Parsons was managed by ASA in 2014 as GACM was not active by then. The process was concluded in May 2014 and signed in October 2014. Comprehensive market research was conducted first at the national level with no results, and then at the international level to identify the most qualified firms available to provide the wide range of services for the PM. The top seven firms in the world, plus the one responsible for the initial studies of the NAICM, were invited to present a quote for their services, following the Mexican Law of Public Works and Related Services, but limited responses were received. Parsons is the world leader in this type of service. The price presented by Parsons was compared with the civil engineers' unit personnel costs table in Mexico. An independent assessment of the total PM costs relative to the total amount of the project was conducted by the Mexican Consultants Chamber and the result was 2-5% of total project value. With this information, ASA studied Parsons' proposal and concluded that it was below market price. The market research concluded also that there was no significant number of competitors available in the global market, besides the ones invited.

One step of the procurement process where Parsons' participation is less clear is the phase relating to the analysis of the proposals received. Considering their technical expertise and experience in procurement of public works for large infrastructure projects, GACM officials would benefit from Parsons' inputs in identifying the strength and weaknesses of the proposals received in response to public tenders. This would be particularly true when several criteria form the basis for awarding public contracts.

The packages: From strategy to implementation

The Minister of Transport and Communications (SCT) stated his vision of the public procurement operations necessary for the construction of the NAICM in a press conference held on 8 June 2015. Mr. Ruiz Esparza indicated that tenders are aimed at encouraging the participation of Mexican companies; establish clear rules from the start; identify the largest number of qualified participants; and ensure transparency.

The growing recognition of public procurement in participating in services delivery for governments has been evidenced in a great number of countries and led to the "Recommendation of the Council on Public Procurement" (OECD, 2015f). Strategic use of procurement also advocates for smart implementation, which ensures that public procurement operations are effective, sustainable and deliver the best value for money from a whole-of-government perspective.

Achieving the strategic objectives defined by GACM and more largely by the Mexican authorities in the construction of the NAICM will thus require aligning implementation decisions made throughout the project with these objectives in mind.

Both the delivery model and the overall structure and openness of procurement processes are strategic choices that lead to a series of consequences. They are meant to bring certain benefits, but also come with associated challenges.

Balancing the allocation of responsibilities and risks between the public and private sectors in the project

The first and foremost strategic choice made by the Mexican Government relates to the outsourcing mode of the construction work. In infrastructure projects, three main processes are used: public procurement, concessions and public-private partnerships (PPPs). One commonality of concessions and PPPs is their inherent long-term approach, since the deriving contracts offset initial investment costs with long-term operation revenues. In sharp contrast, public procurement adopts a more phased approach (Burger and Hawkesworth, 2011).

Some analysis suggests that PPPs and long-term concessions may prove more adapted to the design, construction and operation of large infrastructure projects since these contractual schemes might transfer a great share of the risks to economic operators, if designed properly. Yet, they also open the door to drastic renegotiations of contracts if initial projections or assumptions are not met. A recent study shows that in Chile, Colombia and Peru between 1993 and 2010, 50 road concessions contracts out of 61 were renegotiated at least once (OECD, 2013b).

While putting most of the financial burden on the government upfront, public procurement, often limited to construction activities, also limits the risk of unsustainable long-term relationships with economic operators based on initial assumptions or projections that could prove overly optimistic. In line with this choice, GACM decided to phase the different construction activities into a series of sequential 21 procurement processes (GACM, 2015b).

Beyond the strategic choice of the global delivery method, another important factor is defining the allocation of risks in the project between the public and private sectors. Considering the complexity of large infrastructure projects such as the *Nuevo Aeropuerto Internacional de la Ciudad de Mexico* (NAICM), tender design strategy play a crucial role in the delivery of the project. The strategy defined by GACM as it pertains to the procurement of public works adopts a sequenced approach to the construction of the NAICM with a mix of Design-Bid-Build and Design-Build models.

These two models have several advantages, but also come with inherent challenges that should not be underestimated. The Design–Bid-Build model distinguishes the design phase from the construction phase, the latter being provided in the tender documentation with the plans and concepts elaborated by the design team. This traditional approach to public procurement for infrastructure projects differs from the Design-Build approach where all responsibilities, from architectural concepts to construction works, are granted to one contractor.

The major differences between these models, which are only two options amongst the different delivery models for infrastructure projects (Table 3.2), lie with the allocation of risks and the control over the construction of the infrastructure.

Table 3.2. **Different types of infrastructure delivery models**

Model	Responsibilities and risks
Design–bid –build	• Contracting authority has completed the majority of design work (sometimes with the assistance of specialised consultants). • Government engages contractor to build, based on supplied design. • Risks associated with design faults, changing requirements and adverse site conditions are typically borne by the contracting authority.
Design–build	• Contracting authority only provides a project brief in the tender documentation, sometimes with only performance-based requirements. • Contractor engages design consultants. • Contractors bid on their developed design and lump sum construction price. • Risks associated with errors or omissions in final design, and latent conditions typically borne by contractors and design consultants. • Costs of directed variation typically borne by the contracting authority.
Construction management or general contractor	• Contractor undertakes significant part of project management role, including: o obtaining development approvals o undertaking onsite investigations o finalisation of design o developing construction, commissioning and maintenance programme. • Assumes the risk for construction performance as the equivalent of a general contractor holding all subcontracts during the construction phase. • Contractors given incentives to manage project costs by sharing cost savings.
Alliance contracting	• Contracting authority and other alliance partners jointly develop design and share risks. • Other alliance partners may include designers, consultants, management service providers, suppliers, construction contractors. • Often considered to be of greatest value where the contracting authority has had limited experience with the risks for the project.
Public-private partnership (PPP) and concessions	• Contract between the public and private sector, which can reflect a number of different partnership models. • Private sector delivers infrastructure and services over the long term. • Some level of private financing for the project. • Project may be funded by government, user payments or a combination of the two.

Source: Author's work based on Australian Government Productivity Commission (2014), *Public Infrastructure: Productivity Commission Inquiry Report*, Volume I, No. 71, www.pc.gov.au/__data/assets/pdf_file/0003/137280/infrastructure-volume1.pdf.

The Design-Bid-Build model could imply several advantages, such as diversifying the pool of suppliers working on the project, ensuring that detailed technical specifications are included in the tender documentation for construction works or assisting GACM in estimating the amounts of the different packages, thus maintaining strong financial oversight. Yet, it also comes with difficulties, most notably the risks linked to design changes or inconsistencies that require precisely defining the roles, responsibilities and contractual obligations of the various consultants and companies.

Conversely, the Design-Build approach assigns all activities to one contractor. In terms of liability, it offers more certainty to the contracting authority since risks associated with design defaults are typically borne by the contractor. However, it also carries risks linked to reduced control by the contracting authority on the different phases of the project and reduced visibility of the overall value for money of the project, since design decisions made by the contractor will directly affect deriving construction costs (CMAA, 2012).

Fostering competition while safeguarding efficiency: A strategic assessment

Following strategies employed in other airport construction projects, the overall construction effort is divided into several packages. The Washington Dulles airport and the International Airport in Doha, among others, followed the same rationale. For example, the construction of the Doha International Airport initiated in 2004 was initially divided into 19 distinct lots that expanded to 21 different lots during the construction phase (GACM, 2014).

While other projects have been designed in a similar way to NAICM, alternative scenarios also exist, such as for the expansion of the Abu Dhabi airport where one main contractor, with several subcontractors, was appointed (GACM, 2014). Although this limits the diversity of suppliers that have direct contractual relationships with the entity responsible for the infrastructure project, this option also inherently contains the dilution of responsibilities deriving from multiple and interconnected contracts.

Construction works related to NAICM and carried out by GACM are divided into 21 different main lots, the so-called packages. In addition, the National Commission on Water (CONAGUA) will be responsible for the issuance of competitive procurement processes of public works relating to the drainage system in the Mexico valley and soil decontamination. Since the NAICM will provide infrastructures both for civil and military aviation, the Secretariat of National Defence (SEDENA) should also be directly responsible for undertaking and monitoring public works that affect national security.

The 21 main packages represent almost 75% (MXN 95 million) of the MXN 127 million allocated to the airport infrastructure. According to GACM statements, the remainder should finance various additional works, such as airlines and tenant facilities or information technology (IT) systems. They are not, however, integrated into the global strategy defined for the main 21 packages.

The overarching principle of the packaging strategy for the 21 main packages (hereafter referred to as the "packaging strategy"), as announced on 8 July 2015 during a press conference, is to have recourse to open public tenders for all packages, contrasting with previous GACM experience as evidenced by information available in CompraNet (see Figure 3.2).

According to Article 134 of the Constitution, open public tender is the norm. However, based on specific circumstances, derogations can be granted to use either direct award or restricted competition procedures. Derogations should be duly justified and works should be carried out under the same overarching principles of transparency, efficiency and financial soundness of the operation.

In fact, more than imposing open competition, the Constitution promotes the use of the procurement method, which best achieves the above-mentioned principles since the underlying rationale for granting exceptions is that these objectives would not be ideally pursued using open public tenders. Therefore, in accordance with the Constitution, GACM decisions concerning purchasing methods (open competition, direct award, and restricted competition) should first and foremost assess their relative merits in attaining these objectives.

Promoting competition is often found to result in better outcomes in public procurement and notably in infrastructure projects. On the basis of 200 infrastructure works put to tender in developing countries, fostering competition has been estimated to generate an 8.2% savings (Estache and Iimi, 2008). However, favouring competition should not be understood as just carrying out procurement processes under open public tenders.

Some analyses indeed suggest that fostered competition is dependent on three main factors: the complexity of the project and the level of details included in the tender documentation, the number of potential suppliers in the market and the costs of bidding (Tadelis and Bajari, 2006). In complex projects, competition opened to all interested suppliers, which requires significant investment from bidders in preparing a response may not provide sufficient incentives to bidders to submit a response, thus harming the competitiveness of proposals received. Worse, it may primarily influence the decisions of the most qualified bidders, since they might have higher confidence in their ability and greater experience in winning competitive procurement processes in other markets. Choices on the nature of the procurement process often imply a trade-off between competition and efficiency (OECD, 2015e).

Based on the information provided by GACM, the exact structure and content of packages is however still subject to further aggregation/disaggregation discussions on several components, such as the different phases of the terminal construction work. Decisions regarding the size and scope of packages inherently affect the outcome of the deriving competitive procurement processes.

Beyond identifying the main 21 packages and committing to carrying them out under open public tenders, the strategy details the timeline and main milestones for rolling out each procurement process, the level of openness (national vs. international) and the corresponding estimated amount for each package. This packaging strategy should provide GACM with a procurement dashboard useful for translating the objectives and strategies mentioned above into practical decisions and monitoring implementation.

However given the complexity and magnitude of infrastructure projects, further complicated by the phased approach chosen by GACM, the packaging strategy should be regularly updated and reviewed to assess whether it continues to deliver the objectives defined at the beginning of the project. Box 3.3 sets out a checklist that may be useful to GACM to this end.

Box 3.3. **Checklist for a periodic assessment of a procurement strategy in infrastructure projects**

Strategic consideration	Questions for purchasing entity
1. Is there a clear statement of the outputs to be purchased?	Have all elements of the output been clearly specified? Do you have a good understanding of the expected price that you will have to pay for the outputs?
2. Is there clear alignment to the objectives as stated in the procurement strategy?	Does your approach to this procurement activity still align with your strategic priorities? Is your proposed approach to aggregation and bundling (where relevant) consistent with your procurement strategy? Is there any reason why this procurement activity should no longer proceed? Are the identified economic, environmental and social considerations still relevant?
3. Is there appropriate procurement capability (either internal or external) to undertake the activity?	Do you have the capability to undertake the procurement activity? If not, where are the gaps and how is the required capability to be resourced? Do you have the necessary resources to deliver and monitor the contract? Are the risks associated with the procurement activity understood and quantified? Who is best placed to manage this risk?
4. What is the status of the supplier market?	Have there been any significant and relevant changes to the supplier market (i.e. number of suppliers, competitiveness of the market) that will affect your intended approach to the procurement activity? Are any other approved organisations purchasing similar goods and services? Is the proposed timing of your procurement activity able to be accommodated by the supplier market?
5. What are the risks and opportunities?	Are the identified risks and opportunities still relevant?

Source: NZ Transport Agency (2009), "Procurement manual", updated 2 August 2014, www.nzta.govt.nz/resources/procurement-manual/.

The draft tender notice released on 10 September 2015 provides different elements. First, the tender is reserved to Mexican companies. Second, the timeframe for carrying out the procurement process is reduced to 69 days. Major milestones affected by this reduction relate to the deadline for submission of bids (reduced by approximately 37%) and identification of the proposal offering the best value for money (reduced by approximately 57%). As discussed in this chapter, these two phases prove crucial in fostering competition and generating best value for money.

Promoting local content, which provides expected benefits to society, while maintaining competition

As stated by the Minister of Transport and Communication (SCT), tenders are meant to benefit Mexican companies. GACM employs two different options to pursue this objective. Considering the potential impact on local employment of such an infrastructure project (estimated to represent 160 000 jobs during the construction phase), Mexico, like many other countries, actively promotes requirements that favour local content in public procurement. These requirements could however impact competitiveness if not adapted to the context of the national market and expertise.

Article 30 of the Law on Public Works stipulates that open public tenders could either be national and thus limited to suppliers established in Mexico; international under the umbrella of free trade agreements where only suppliers originating from one party of the agreement could participate; or international with no limitation. The last procedure is only carried out when the previous two could not be carried out due to lack of national capacity following investigation or when a prior national procedure has not yielded a response.

Last paragraph of Article 30 also foresees another possibility, which is to introduce in open public tenders a "local content requirement". This requires bidders to submit proposals with a certain percentage of the total value of the public works set apart for national raw materials, machineries or equipment. Besides national products, open public tenders should, without prejudice of international treaties, comprise at least 30% of the workforce of Mexican nationality.

Based on the information provided by GACM, 42 % of its open public tenders are intended to be limited to national suppliers, translating into approximately 47 % of the total estimated value of the 21 packages. However, this figure does not capture the local content requirement that will supposedly be embedded into international open public tenders. If this requirement is set by GACM at 30% of the international public tenders, the overall national dimension of the packages would amount to approximately 60% of the total project (Figure 3.3).

Figure 3.3. **Size of packages against level of competition foreseen over time**

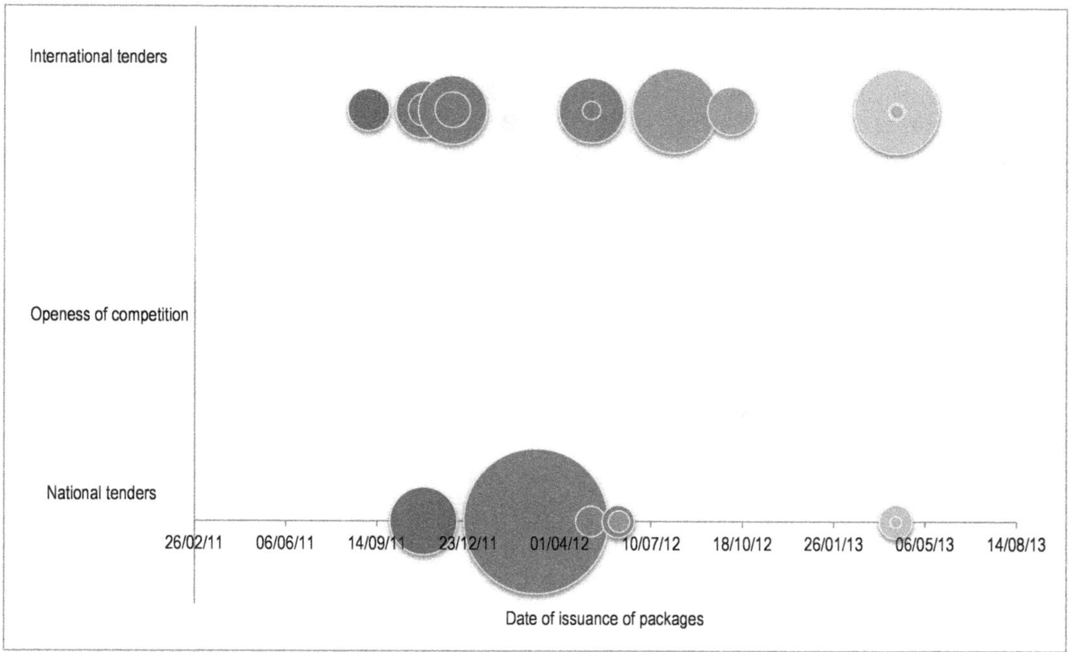

Note: The first package relating to land levelling will be subject to a national public tender, according to the draft tender notice released on 10 September 2015.

Source: Analysis based on GACM (2015b), "Packaging strategy", issued 24 July 2015.

Arguably, these various requirements could directly frame the involvement of the national private sector into this project and thus yield economic benefits for Mexico. Yet, an infrastructure project of this magnitude also advocates for a cautious assessment and implementation of procedures that are understandably designed for more day-to-day government procurement activities. Those requirements could indeed prove detrimental not only to competition, but also to national welfare if not adequately used.

It could first have a perverse impact on the competitiveness of the processes if internal market capacity is not able to respond to the needs put out to national public tenders. The market investigation phase, mandatory prior to each open public tender, should play a crucial role here in assessing the likely competitiveness of internal markets against each package. Failing to do so may result in additional delays due to unsuccessful tenders. Internal markets that are too constrained could also open the door to bid-rigging and notably to cover-bidding or market allocation (OECD, 2011) (Box 3.4).

Box 3.4. **Bid rigging and cartels during tendering in the European Union**

2014 - Power cable cartel: In 2014, the European Commission fined producers of high voltage power cables EUR 302 million for operating a cartel in violation of the EC Treaty's ban on restrictive business practices (Article 81). Such cables are typically used to connect generation capacity to the electricity grid or to interconnect power grids in different countries. The EC press release stated: "From 1999 onwards and for almost ten years, these companies shared markets and allocated customers between themselves on an almost worldwide scale. Part of this plan was to allocate important high voltage power cable projects in the European Economic Area (EEA), including large infrastructure and renewable energy projects such as offshore wind farms. Most of the world´s largest high voltage power cable producers, namely ABB, Nexans, Prysmian (previously Pirelli), J-Power Systems (previously Sumitomo Electric and Hitachi Metals), VISCAS (previously Furukawa Electric and Fujikura), EXSYM (previously SWCC Showa and Mitsubishi Cable), Brugg, NKT, Silec (previously Safran), LS Cable and Taihan, participated in the illegal agreements. ABB received full immunity from fines under the Commission's 2006 Leniency Notice as it was the first to reveal the cartel to the Commission."

2007 - Switchgear cartel: In 2007, the European Commission fined members of a gas insulated switchgear cartel over EUR 750 million. The companies fined were ABB, Alstom, Areva, Fuji Electric, Hitachi Japan AE Power Systems, Mitsubishi Electric Corporation, Schneider, Siemens, Toshiba and VA Tech. The EC press release stated: "Between 1988 and 2004, the companies rigged bids for procurement contracts, fixed prices, allocated projects to each other, shared markets and exchanged commercially important and confidential information. ABB received full immunity from fines under the Commission's leniency programme, as it was the first company to come forward with information about the cartel. The fine of EUR 396 million on Siemens, Germany constituted the largest ever fine imposed by the Commission on a single company for a single cartel infringement." The investigation started with surprise inspections in May 2004, which were prompted by an application for immunity lodged by ABB under a 2002 Leniency Notice.

2007 - Lifts and elevators cartel: In 2007, the European Commission fined members of lifts and escalators cartels over EUR 990 million for operating cartels for the installation and maintenance of lifts and escalators in Belgium, Germany, Luxembourg and the Netherlands. The companies fined were Otis, Kone, Schindler and ThyssenKrupp groups. The EC press release stated: "Between at least 1995 and 2004, these companies rigged bids for procurement contracts, fixed prices and allocated projects to each other, shared markets and exchanged commercially important and confidential information. The effects of this cartel may continue for twenty to fifty years as maintenance was often done by the companies that installed the equipment in the first place; by cartelising the installation, the companies had distorted the markets for years to come. Kone subsidiaries received full immunity from fines under the Commission's leniency programme in respect of the cartels in Belgium and Luxembourg, as they were first to provide information about these cartels. Similarly, Otis Netherlands received full immunity in respect of the Netherlands cartel. The fines imposed on the ThyssenKrupp companies were increased by 50%, as it was a repeat offender."

Source: EC Press Release, 2 April 2014: http://europa.eu/rapid/press-release_IP-14-358_en.htm; EC Press Release, 24 January 2007: http://europa.eu/rapid/press-release_IP-07-80_en.htm?locale=en; EC Press Release, 21 February 2007: http://europa.eu/rapid/press-release_IP-07-209_en.htm?locale=en.

Although not distorting competition, open public tenders limited to national suppliers could merely lead to a sub-optimal outcome and not provide GACM with the assurance to generate the overall best value for money from public tenders. Without an open international competition, purchasing entities limit *de facto* the scope of suppliers able to answer public procurement demand. See Box 3.5 for a case study from Australia that speaks to the benefits of international competition.

Box 3.5. **International competition in infrastructure projects in Australia**

Trade Minister Andrew Robb has hailed the emergence of new international competition in the local construction industry as an opportunity to get AUD 125 billion of infrastructure built cheaper and faster than it could have five years ago.

Mr. Robb said the arrival of six Spanish construction firms in Australia to compete for greenfields infrastructure had broken down the duopoly that had dominated the Australian market and highlighted the benefits of freer global trade.

Wrapping up weekend talks with trade ministers from the G20 meeting of the world's biggest economies, Mr. Robb said the competition had been drawn to Australia by the prospect of infrastructure investment being reinvigorated by asset sales to fund new developments.

"It is a huge opportunity to do it and have some of the best construction companies in the world bringing state-of-the-art expertise and innovation to all of this rollout of infrastructure,'' Mr. Robb told The Australian.

"What was seen as a duopoly in Australia with major projects has now become highly competitive in the space of five years,'' Mr. Robb said. He highlighted the east-west road development in Melbourne where there were Spanish companies in each of three short-listed consortia bidding for the project.

Infrastructure investment is one of the major themes for the G20 under Australia's presidency this year, in line with domestic efforts to encourage states to sell assets and recycle the money back into new projects.

Treasurer Joe Hockey has offered the states AUD 5 billion in top-up payments if they sell assets such as ports and electricity transmission and distribution networks and use the proceeds to build new roads, rail and hospitals.

Mr. Robb said the apparent certainty of funding for the projects from asset sales, combined with low financing costs and a shortfall of work elsewhere in the world had drawn international players to Australia.

Source: White, A. (2014), "More competition in building 'good for infrastructure'", *The Australian*, 21 July.

Local content requirements in international open public tenders should also be carefully used and adapted to the nature of the project. The Law on Public Works only mandates bidders to provide a declaration on oath stating that they comply with local content conditions set out in the call for tender, making this condition a requirement rather than a qualitative component of proposals received. Rather than being seen as a concrete policy objective, it could thus be perceived by suppliers as an administrative requirement.

Traditionally, large infrastructure projects are extremely labour intensive and therefore generate jobs. As a consequence, requiring bidders to commit to employing a certain percentage of local workers may offer a unique opportunity for the construction sector in Mexico. While the proportion of local content in terms of machineries, equipment and raw materials is left to the discretion of the purchasing entity, the share of local workforce should equal at least 30% of the total workforce employed for the works.

However statistics show that the construction sector, together with agriculture, is the sector with the largest percentage of low-qualified employees (76.7% of workers have only attained primary or secondary education) (Figure 3.4).

Figure 3.4. **Employee educational attainment, by economic sector, Mexico**

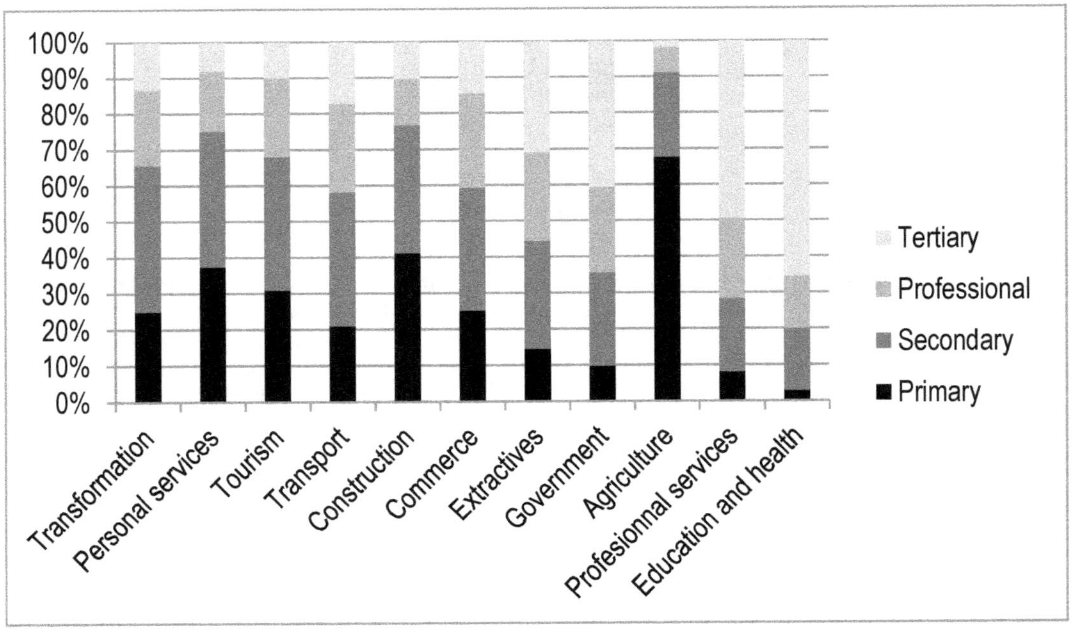

Source: Portal del Empleo (2015), "Panorama de ocupación por sector económico", accessed 10 August 2015.

Without additional guidance in the tender documentation, the local content requirement could thus incentivise foreign suppliers to recruit low-skilled workers of Mexican origin. Those low-skilled workers would likely be paid according to the minimum wage published by the National Commission on Minimum Salary (*Comisión Nacional de los Salarios Mínimos*, CONASMI). The minimum wage in the Mexico City valley is set at MXN 70.10 per day of work. According to OECD statistics on employment, the average wage paid to Mexican workers accounts for the lower average wage of OECD countries based on purchasing power parity (OECD, 2015g). Mexico is also the most unequal OECD country with the ten richest individuals in Mexico earning 30 times that of the poorest 10% workers.

Although creating jobs, requiring bidders to include a certain threshold of the local (Mexican) labour force without comprehensively assessing their working conditions, including salaries and benefits, could therefore lead to greater inequality. Conversely, embedding this element into the overall qualitative components of the proposals received could help evaluate the relative merits of each proposal, assess its influence on other factors, such as price, and purposely serve secondary policy objectives.

This would align this commendable objective with the OECD Recommendation on Public Procurement which indicates in Principle IV that "any use of a public procurement system to pursue secondary policy objectives should be balanced against the primary procurement objective." To this end, countries are encouraged to employ appropriate impact assessment methodology to measure the effectiveness of procurement in achieving secondary policy objectives. When trying to promote the development of the national market and local employment, such impact assessment should also be used to decide whether it is desirable and effective to leverage on public procurement to achieve such an objective.

Designing sustainable tender processes to roll out the project efficiently

Based on the information provided by GACM, the entire procurement cycle for construction works of the NAICM spans two years (from August 2015 until August 2017). Figure 3.5 illustrates the sequencing of the competition processes carried out by GACM.

Figure 3.5. **Sequencing of the competition processes carried out by GACM**

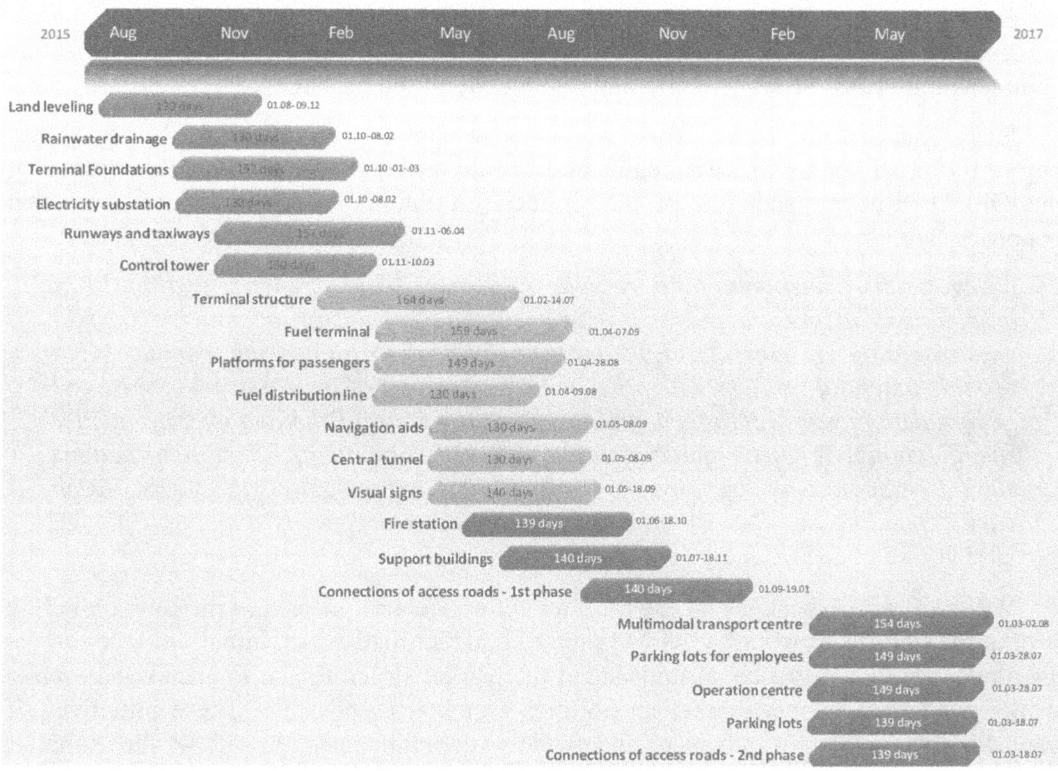

Source: Analysis based on GACM (2015b), "Packaging strategy", issued 24 July 2015.

The packaging strategy and the sequencing of procurement processes should allow some work to advance in parallel, which could help GACM meet the global timeline. Construction activities for the first phase of the airport should be finalised in 2018, in order to allow for two years of tests and certifications before opening to the public in 2020.

Other examples suggest that the global timeframe for the construction of NAICM is extremely ambitious. The expansion of the Abu Dhabi airport with the construction of a new terminal handling 30 million passengers – significantly less than the projected 50 million of passengers per year of NAICM – started in early 2012 with a construction phase of four years and will not be opened before 2017 (Abu Dhabi Airports, 2011).

This sequencing also presupposes that no major delays will occur in the procurement processes. Indeed, some packages are highly dependent on the successful completion of previous works. This implies that delays in specific areas will not only impact the timely conclusion of these works, but might also influence others.

Figure 3.5 illustrates the overall articulation of the different packages. It is worth noting that one-third of the procurement processes will be issued within approximately a three-month period (from March 2016 until June 2016). Information provided by GACM suggests that preparatory phases of two-thirds of the 21 packages will be carried out simultaneously with at least one other package.

As an example, the market analysis and finalisation of the tender documentation for the rainwater drainage system will be performed concurrently with the same for the terminal foundations. These decisions will undoubtedly impact resources allocated to the different processes. This phase proves crucial in the successful outcomes of public tenders processes (OECD, forthcoming-a), so timing and attention devoted to it should be commensurate with the relative size and complexity of the packages.

Early engagement with potential suppliers is vital to understanding the key issues before the procurement process begins and can be critical to its success. Principle V of the OECD "Recommendation of the Council on Public Procurement" provides that countries should:

> *...engage in transparent and regular dialogues with suppliers and business associations to present public procurement objectives and to assure a correct understanding of markets. Effective communication should be conducted to provide potential vendors with a better understanding of the country's needs, and government buyers with information to develop more realistic and effective tender specifications by better understanding market capabilities. Such interactions should be subject to due fairness, transparency and integrity safeguards, which vary depending on whether an active procurement process is ongoing.* (OECD, 2015f)

While *ex ante* exchanges on the draft tender notice are foreseen in the Law on Public Works for significant works, GACM opted to conduct roadshows, either via face-to-face meetings or remotely, to better understand the market structure and to ensure that public works put to tender met market capabilities as much as possible. These initiatives, if planned sufficiently in advance and widely communicated to allow the supplier community to mobilise, should help reduce asymmetry of information often evidenced in complex procurement projects (Saussier and Tirole, 2015).

Article 30 Section III of the Law on Public Works states that international open tenders can be carried out should previous market investigations reveal that national suppliers would not have the capacity to perform the works and it would not be desirable from a financial perspective. The role played by market analyses is therefore crucial in deciding the degree of openness of the procurement procedure.

Yet market analyses should not be limited to verifying the existence of similar works in CompraNet and assessing whether suppliers have previously responded to these types of works. Considering the scale of the project and the extent of resources needed to successfully carry out the construction work, GACM should not only assess the existence of Mexican suppliers in the different fields of expertise required but also their capacity to perform contracts of this magnitude. A recent decision of the Comptroller General of the United States highlights the necessity for purchasing entities to evaluate capabilities of the market against contractual requirements (Box 3.6).

Box 3.6. **Purchasing decisions guided by market analysis**

Protest is sustained where the agency's market research was insufficient to conclude that the agency would likely receive quotations from at least two responsible small business concerns that could meet the requirements in the RFQ at a fair market price, and therefore, the agency's decision to restrict the solicitation to small business concerns was unreasonable.

Under Federal Acquisition Regulation (FAR) § 19.502-2(b), a procurement with an anticipated dollar value of no more than USD 150 000, must be set aside for exclusive small business participation when there is a reasonable expectation that offers will be received from at least two responsible small business concerns, and award will be made at a fair market price.

On 2 April 2015, the Department of Veterans Affairs (VA) issued a RFQ for the manufacture and delivery of radiopharmaceutical and non-radiopharmaceutical items, as a small business set-aside, and designated North American Industry Classification System (NAICS) code 325412, Pharmaceutical Preparation Manufacturing, which has a corresponding size standard of 750 employees, as the size standard for small business participation in the procurement. The RFQ anticipates the issuance of a fixed-price contract, for a base year and four one-year options.

A contracting agency's investigation to determine the availability of responsible small business concerns for set-aside purposes, however, must address not only the existence of small businesses that might submit proposals, but also their capability to perform the contract; the fact that multiple small businesses are identified in the course of market research is not necessarily determinative.

The decision to set aside this procurement for small businesses resulted from market research conducted in November 2014 the result of which, "netted 14 companies". The market research also involved "[a] search of the SBA Dynamic Small Business Database (DSBD) which produced 676 vendors." The report explained that the Market Research was not limited by state or location, as it is common for pharmaceutical companies which produce radioisotopes to have facilities in other locations with their headquarters locations which show in DSBD." The market research report also noted the results of prior attempts to procure these items. Specifically, the report stated that a solicitation for the same requirement was posted on 9 September 2014, for isotope manufacture and delivery, with a performance period of four months.

In short, Triad contends that the VA has not reasonably shown that there is even one small business that can both meet the requirement that it manufacture its own radiopharmaceuticals and meet the brief delivery requirements set out in the solicitation.

VA's market research was insufficient to conclude that the agency would receive quotations from at least two responsible small business concerns that could meet the requirements in the RFQ at a fair market price. For this reason, the agency's decision to restrict the solicitation to small business concerns was unreasonable.

Source: Extracts from the Decision of the Comptroller General of the United States, United States Government Accountability Office, 16 July 2015, Triad Isotopes Inc. file B411360.

Beyond this initial phase, another area of particular attention is the assessment of proposals received to ensure that awarded bidders both represent the overall best-value-for-money option and effectively deliver the commitments taken into their proposals. This phase, starting with the receipt of proposals and ending on the award of the contract, is estimated to last either 30 or 40 calendar days, depending on the complexity of the works. On average, the time needed to carry out this phase lasts approximately 25% of a typical total duration of a procurement process.

While this proportion seems commensurate to the duration of each process, it should be noted that several processes will run concurrently according to the above analyses of the sequencing, therefore limiting the effective timeframe allocated to the assessment of proposals received for each package. In addition, the release of the first draft tender notice on 10 September 2015 demonstrates a significant decrease of the estimated time allotted to the assessment of proposals received and identification of the preferred bidder for the first package. In the draft tender notice, the phase starting with the opening of proposals and ending with the award of the contract decreased to 13 calendar days.

Considering the scale and complexity of infrastructure works which will be put to tenders, the timeframe allotted to review the submissions received, clarify with bidders their technical and financial proposals, analyse these against the predefined selection criteria and document the decision-making process supporting the entire procurement cycle should be cautiously factored in. Infrastructure Australia carried out a consultative study with stakeholders typically involved in infrastructure projects (government, procurement agencies, construction sector, etc.) to identify the optimal timeframe of each procurement phase to drive efficient outcomes in infrastructure projects varying in size and complexity of the contracting model (Table 3.3). This benchmark highlights significant differences with regard to the estimated timeframes set out in the GACM packaging strategy.

Ensuring an adequate degree of transparency and a thorough analysis of submissions received is crucial in both achieving efficient results and reinforcing citizen trust.

Infrastructure projects require inputs from various ministries and public agencies, and lack of co-ordination can be a major root for failure of sound implementation of infrastructure projects (OECD, 2015d). For example, the Ministry of Environment (SEMARNAT) will be responsible for assessing the environmental performance of proposals received. Likewise, the Ministry of National Defence should participate in procurement processes which, albeit not exclusively being for military purposes, could affect national security or public order.

These different interactions, crucial to abide by the anticipated sequencing and structure of the packages and the imposed recourse to complex evaluation criteria in infrastructure works should be cautiously factored in the timeframe devoted to each phase.

Table 3.3. **Benchmark of timeframes for main milestones of infrastructure procurement in Australia**

Procurement phase	Benchmark event	Measure	Time benchmarks (weeks or months)					
			Design and construct		PPP		Alliance	
			More complex	Less complex	More complex	Less complex	More complex	Less complex
Pre-procurement phase	Initial advance notice of project and market engagement	Months before issue of EOI	12	6	24	9	12	6
	Commence the market interaction with specific notice of likely scope, value, roles, contracts model and packaging	Months before issue of EOI	6	2	12	6	6	2
	Formal discussions, specific project details advised in terms of scope, contract models, risk, value, turnover, roles, timing	Months before issue of EOI	2	2	3	3	2	2
EOI phase	EOI preparation	Weeks from release of EOI document to submission of EOI responses	6*	4*	8*	6*	4*	3*
RFP phase	Duration of RFP period	Weeks from issue of RFP documents to submission of proposals	12 to 16	8 to 12	24**	18**	12	8
Evaluation / finalisation phase	Duration of evaluation	Weeks from submission close to selection	6	4	12	8	4	2
	Duration of finalisation	Weeks (selection to final documentation) assuming all material issues are resolved	3	3	4	4	3	3

Note: * Assumes effective engagement during Pre-Procurement Phase.

** Maximum 34 weeks for unique complex PPP and subject to specific market feedback at the Pre-Procurement Phase.

Less complex projects are those infrastructure projects valued around AUD 200 million (approximately USD 143 million) or AUD 1 billion (USD 716 million) for PPPs that do not require international expertise.

More complex projects are valued in excess of AUD 1 billion (USD 716 million) or AUD 2 billion (USD 1.4 billion) and require international specialists participation.

Source: Infrastructure Australia (2012), "Benchmark for efficient procurement of major infrastructure in efficiencies in major project procurement".

Assessing the effectiveness of procurement processes in achieving their primary and secondary objectives, and adapting accordingly

Strategic decisions taken by GACM on the structure and content of procurement processes are meant to generate benefits in various areas ranging from a sound management of financial resources, deadlines for completing the project, to social and urban developments. Therefore, the outcomes of the public procurement processes shall be measured and assessed against these objectives. Tools for measuring the performance of public procurement generated a lot of attention in OECD countries and discussions highlighted the main challenges involved in evaluating the performance of a procurement system as a whole, and notably the scarcity of standardised data to showcase meaningful information and analyses (OECD, 2013c).

These challenges might however be overcome more easily at the micro-level of the NAICM project. Indeed, although various stakeholders participate in the project as a whole, procurement processes are relatively concentrated in the hands of GACM. It could therefore offer a unique opportunity to measure performance of procurement activities in the project. Key performance indicators (KPIs) not only measure aggregated procurement performance, but prove also extremely helpful in assessing specific procurement process performance and providing grounds for procurement officials to guide future procurement decisions (OECD, 2015f). In so doing, GACM would transform itself into an agile organisation able to adapt to changing environments and pursue government objectives.

Based on the experience of different public procurement systems in several OECD countries the OECD proposed a first set of key performance indicators aiming at measuring the performance of the procurement system as a whole. Although all identified KPIs could be of relevance to assessing the performance of procurement processes of the construction of NAICM as a whole, some are of direct interest to assessing the degree of achievements of the packaging strategy's underlying objectives.

The first and foremost policy objective pursued in the construction of the NAICM is to foster economic benefits for the region, and for Mexico at large. Indeed, the construction of this new airport aims primarily at further developing tourism in the country and making the site a hub for the entire region. In OECD countries, tourism directly contributes to almost 5% of GDP, 6% of employment, and 21% of exports of services. While public procurement operations in this project don't directly account for the development of tourism, one related area where the efficiency of procurement process is directly involved is the overall cost for building the airport. Constraining construction costs of the airport will make this investment more profitable, thus yielding economic benefits to the country. Therefore, savings in the procurement process need to be measured (Box 3.7).

Box 3.7. **Key performance indicators: Savings**

$$\textbf{Total savings} = \textbf{average \% of savings per package}$$

$$\%\text{ of savings per package} = \frac{\text{Historical price} - \text{price paid for each package}}{\text{Historical price}} x\ 100$$

$$Average\ \%\ of\ savings = \frac{\sum Historical\ prices - \sum prices\ paid\ for\ each\ package}{\sum Historical\ prices} x\ 100$$

and/or

$$\textbf{Total savings} = \sum \textbf{savings per package}$$

$$\text{Savings per goods or services} = \text{Historical price of goods or services} - \text{Price paid per goods or services}\ x\ Q$$

$$\text{Savings per package} = \sum \text{savings per goods or services}$$

Historical prices: In the first formula, historical price is the value of the package estimated by GACM at the start of the process. In the second formula, it can be calculated as an average of past procurement prices for similar goods or services. If the good/service is not procured in the same year, the inflation impact should be calculated and removed.

Quantity (Q) is the number of each goods or services purchased for the package in question.

Source: Adapted from OECD (2014c), "Towards procurement performance indicators: First set of indicators", www.oecd.org/officialdocuments/publicdisplaydocumentpdf/?cote=gov/pgc(2015)12&doclanguage=en.

KPIs on savings tailored to the specificities of the project could provide meaningful results to assess the performance of procurement processes in constraining construction costs and achieving best value for money. Since GACM requests from bidders both lump prices and a detailed breakdown by unit price, it could assess both the overall performance of procurement in generating savings and obtain disaggregated information on prices, which could guide future procurement decisions.

Fostering competition also generates, albeit more indirectly, savings (Estache and Iimi, 2008). One of the key arguments put forward by GACM to support the decision to divide construction works into a series of distinct packages is the possibility of attracting more bidders and favouring new entrants in the market. GACM could develop a multidimensional assessment of competition that could help assess the efficiency of procurement processes in achieving these desired outcomes (Box 3.8).

Box 3.8. **Key performance indicators: Promoting competition**

$$\textbf{Attractiveness of competition} = \textbf{Ratio of bids received}$$

$$\text{Ratio of bids received} = \frac{Bids\ received\ per\ package}{Bidders\ consulted\ per\ package}$$

and/or

$$\textbf{Efficiency of competition} = \textbf{Ratio of qualified bids received}$$

$$\text{Ratio of qualified bids received} = \frac{Qualified\ bids}{Bids\ received\ per\ package}$$

Bids received per package: This indicates the number of proposals received by the deadline of the public tender.

Bidders consulted per package: This could indicate the number of potential bidders that participated in the clarification meetings.

Qualified bidders: This indicates bidders that have been assessed and judged of sufficient technical quality to warrant the assessment of their financial proposal.

Source: Adapted from OECD (2014c), "Towards procurement performance indicators: First set of indicators", www.oecd.org/officialdocuments/publicdisplaydocumentpdf/?cote=gov/pgc(2015)12&doclanguage=en.

When using points-based criteria GACM employs a two-stage assessment procedure that requires a first evaluation on whether the bid meets a minimum threshold of points on quality components to qualify for the assessment of its financial components. This assessment mechanism could be particularly useful to assess market capabilities and adapt future procurement procedures should previous processes fail to meet an acceptable quantity of bids of sufficient quality.

Another crucial element of the strategy whose evolution would inevitably affect the successfulness of the project is the sequencing of competitive procurement processes. Delays in carrying out these processes could have several consequences, ranging from accelerating procurement procedures that would somehow affect competition to postpone the planned date for the opening of the airport, thus delaying potential revenues generated by its operation. Delays in carrying out procurement processes could be either caused by delays in accomplishing certain mandatory steps or by unsuccessful procurement processes leading to reissuance of the package (Box 3.9).

Box 3.9. **Key performance indicators: Timely conclusion of procurement processes**

$$\textbf{Sequencing effectiveness} = \textbf{Level of unsuccessful processes}$$

$$= \frac{\text{Number of unsuccessful processes}}{\text{Total number of awarded contracts} + \text{total number of unsuccessful processes}} \times 100$$

and/or

$$\textbf{Planning effectiveness} = \textbf{Award time for packages}$$

$$\frac{\text{Total number of contracts awarded by GACM according to time guidelines}}{\text{Total number of contracts awarded} + \text{total number of unsuccessful processes}} \times 100$$

Time guidelines: This indicates the planned start and end date of each procurement process. Additional analysis could be performed when comparing the planned and effective date for each milestone within each package.

Source: Adapted from OECD (2014c), "Towards procurement performance indicators: First set of indicators", www.oecd.org/officialdocuments/publicdisplaydocumentpdf/?cote=gov/pgc(2015)12&doclanguage=en.

These indicators could obviously be complemented by others measuring the performance of procurement processes in achieving the local content objectives identified above or contract performance management. Yet, using this first set of indicators for the first packages to be released could provide GACM with detailed insights in procurement performance and allow for a swift adaption of the strategy should the first procurement processes not meet the desired objectives.

Procurement carries risks which could affect the project

The packaging strategy designed by GACM is supposed to yield several advantages, such as:

- diversifying risks
- fostering competition by providing wide access and transparency to suppliers to the tender processes
- simultaneous progress in several works to best meet timing constraints
- reaching out to more diverse expertise sources
- opening opportunities to national companies and small and medium-sized enterprises (SMEs).

However, this strategy also implies risks that must be considered beforehand to anticipate mitigation measures. In line with Principle XI of the OECD "Recommendation of the Council on Public Procurement", GACM implemented a risk management strategy to map, detect and mitigate risks throughout the procurement cycle. While some are identified, others risks linked to the procurement strategy are absent and should be integrated.

Risk management strategy developed by GACM

GACM set up a risk register (GACM, 2015c) to identify and assess – in terms of severity, criticality and likelihood – major risks to the successful completion of the project, probable causes and mitigation measures that could help reduce or alleviate those risks.

Lack of transparency

GACM identified risks linked to procurement processes relating to biased perception of civil society on the awarding procedures of contracts. Due to the lack of clarity on procurement processes, civil society could question the procedures, hence challenging the overall project.

This risk has been assessed as being high both in terms of severity and likelihood while the imminence of it is logically lower since this risk is more likely to arise towards the end of the procurement operations linked to the project. GACM considers that appropriate mitigation measures could derive from extensive disclosure of information related to all the steps of the procurement processes.

However, transparency does not only apply to the procurement process *stricto sensu* and could also be supported by additional measures demonstrating inclusive processes such as the broadcasting of the anticipated roadshows or the disclosure of detailed information on market consultations phases. This would provide civil society with a greater understanding of the different steps of the procurement processes.

Also, transparency should not end with the signature of the contract. While not disclosing information of a confidential nature that could be detrimental to the industrial secrets and business models of awarded suppliers, GACM could provide summaries of contracts' execution.

Inadequate or incomplete contractual design

This risk linked to the absence of adequate contractual expertise could lead to the signature of contracts which would prove unsustainable and result in disputes or renegotiations. This risk has the highest impact identified in the risk register and is also classified as high in terms of likelihood while being estimated to occur in the medium term.

To mitigate this risk, the Corporate Directorate of Real Estate Management and Administration, responsible for contract management, suggests relying on specialised external expertise such as specialised lawyers or the project manager and on internal co-ordination with other specialised entities, and notably the Corporate Directorate for Infrastructure.

Beyond the inherent complexity of infrastructure projects, the packaging strategy in itself, and the dilution of responsibilities implied by it, advocate for a cautious assessment of contractual robustness. Yet, exhaustive contracts are often found to be non-existent (Tirole, 2009).

Absence of internal co-ordination

GACM also identified risks linked to the absence of internal co-ordination. For example, issues such as the poor definition of responsibilities and the lack of empowered personnel to make decisions should be addressed to avoid bottlenecks that might delay tender decisions. While these issues pertain to GACM internal structure, they might be magnified by the participation of other stakeholders during the implementation of the packaging strategy.

The strategy imposes well thought-out co-ordination mechanisms and a shared understanding among stakeholders. While ownership of the project lies with GACM, the strategy calls for robust co-ordination between suppliers, consultants, the PM, control authorities (i.e. SFP), and GACM itself.

Risks linked to procurement processes and absent from the risk register

In addition to risks already identified by GACM, other factors directly associated with procurement processes could be detrimental to the successful completion of the project.

Sub-optimal performance of procurement processes

This risk is intimately linked and affected by the structure of the packaging strategy. The division of the construction into several packages could provide opportunities to attract more specialised companies otherwise not being able to respond to tenders, hence increasing competition and possibly further engaging with SMEs.

However, this strategy also runs the risk of inefficiently dividing some works, resulting in increased transaction costs both for GACM and for competitors who would have to mobilise resources and provide legal documentation on a number of different occasions. It could also induce an increase in management and co-ordination costs that should be factored in when defining the perimeter of each lot.

Overall transaction costs of procurement processes could also be mitigated by giving due consideration to possibilities to include post-construction activities in some tenders, such as periodic maintenance as a means to providing long-term opportunities to competitors, reinforcing attractiveness of public tenders.

Lack of engagement of suppliers

The project can only prove successful if the packages put to tender meet market capabilities and expectations, hence providing incentives to suppliers to respond. One major risk is the absence of response to a procurement process, or inadequacy of responses partially addressing GACM's needs, which would both have direct consequences on the timeframe of the project. This risk finds its roots in the various steps of procurement processes.

Firstly, considering the standard timeframes allocated to market consultation, insufficiently prepared suppliers could cause a significant drop in the number of submissions received in response to public procurement processes, which affects the level of competition.

GACM indicated it will allow at least two months between the public presentation of the packing strategy and the issuance of the first tenders. The period between the two should allow sufficient time for businesses to prepare their proposals, look for partners in case they are needed, and explore financing alternatives, in order to encourage as much competition as possible. Insufficient time between those two milestones might become a barrier for entry and hinder the reception of competitive offers or force GACM to carry out non-competitive procedures.

Secondly, the inadequacy between the nature of the procurement procedure and its requirements and the suppliers' capabilities could prove harmful to the attractiveness of the processes. For example, the proportion of national content requested in the proposal could negatively impact the level of competition if not aligned with national market capabilities. The type of procedure used for each package shall be proportionate to market size and structure, promote transparency and achieve value for money. Market analyses should help define the degree of openness of procurement processes.

According to the overarching principles set out in the Constitution, procurement procedures should first achieve the best possible outcome in terms of transparency, quality and efficiency. The choice of the procedure to be used (open public tenders, restricted competition or direct award) derives from this assessment. Considering the scale of this infrastructure and the duration of construction works, detailed market research shall be carried out by GACM and other stakeholders before deciding the exact type of procurement process, and considering both the national and international state of play in terms of competitors.

Insufficient or inadequate tools to generate best value for money

While constrained by the overall timeline of the project, the strategy should provide for specific timeframe for completion of each procurement process proportionate to its nature and complexity. Considering the infrastructure nature of the project and the technical dimensions of the packages, specialised expertise from stakeholders outside of GACM is likely to be required. One of the risks that could arise from excessive constraints on timeframes for completion of procurement process relates to inadequate award criteria. The greater complexity of points-based criteria necessitates close attention and strong expertise to appropriately design terms of reference and allow for a multidimensional assessment of proposals received, which would lead to identifying the submission offering the best value for money.

The timeframe allotted to review the submissions received, analyse these against the predefined selection criteria, and document the decision-making process supporting the entire procurement cycle should be defined on an ad hoc basis, considering at a minimum both the breadth of expertise required for evaluation proposals and the competitiveness of the market since those two elements have a direct impact on the time needed to evaluate responses. Ensuring an adequate degree of transparency and a thorough analysis of submissions received is crucial in both achieving efficient results and reinforcing citizen trust.

Grounded identification of proposals offering the best value for money has to translate into strong contract management ensuring that contractors' performance is periodically assessed against commitments spelled out in their proposals. Albeit not eliminated, contract management helps mitigate the risk of contract renegotiations increasing the overall cost of infrastructure.

Proposals for action

The successful construction of NAICM should represent a major achievement for the Mexican Government and for the development of Mexico. It should increase the country's competitiveness while demonstrating transparency and efficiency in its different development stages. Public procurement has been chosen to proceed with its construction as opposed to other delivery modes such as concession or public-private partnership.

This initial choice and the corresponding allocation of risks provide several advantages and most notably help to avoid long-term exploitation costs (either paid by governments or by taxpayers) based on overly optimistic projections which prove unsustainable, thus subject to renegotiations. Yet, this choice also implies challenges since it could prove less adapted to complex infrastructure projects, if not carefully prepared, and not deliver the best overall value for money.

Although not warranting success, strategic public procurement is a prerequisite to the completion of the project. Smart procurement demands an agile organisation able to reconcile regulatory environments, diversity of stakeholders, project structure, civil society requirements and government expectations to achieve the best possible value for money.

Adapting to the nature of the project

The very nature of the project, the construction of a major infrastructure asset, generates a series of consequences – from the nature of goods and services procured to the time needed to complete the project – that need to be integrated into the procurement strategy and governance.

Co-ordinating expertise allowing informed decisions

By creating a project-oriented advisory committee federating the different expertise, GACM could foster transparent and effective stakeholder direct participation to ensure a co-ordinated approach to the project.

While the ownership of the project lies with GACM, other stakeholders will be responsible for issuing specific packages.[1] Therefore, appropriate sequencing of actions and co-ordination between the different stakeholders is indispensable to the success of the project.

In addition, considering the nature of the works carried out, the surrounding regulatory environment imposes interactions both within GACM and with other public entities. Complementary efforts are needed from different areas of expertise in GACM and beyond in each step of the procurement process.

These inputs are not merely ad hoc advice or authorisations that would justify irregular interactions. As evidenced in some examples, interactions rather suggest stronger ties between public stakeholders. On environmental aspects, the authorisation of the Ministry of Environment and Natural Resources will be required for mandatory prior impact assessments in accordance with Article 20 of the Law on Public Works. However, the Ministry also has discretionary investigation powers to assess the effective compliance of the public works with environmental commitments.

Interactions with the Ministry of Public Administration will also be frequent, from developments of guidance material on public procurement processes to the use of social witnesses or participation in the Committee on Public Works.

The Cabinet Office of the United Kingdom identified the lack of effective engagement with stakeholders as one of the most common causes for project failure. To improve efficiency in infrastructure delivery, the Cabinet Office suggests that large-scale projects mobilising unprecedented experience where critical aspects of requirements or procurement are not yet fully set in stone should include a formalised governance structure allowing stakeholders to align their objectives (Infrastructure UK, HM Treasury and Lord Deighton, 2014) (Box 3.10).

Box 3.10. **The UK infrastructure procurement routemap**

The Government, through the Infrastructure Cost Review programme, has worked with leading infrastructure clients, industry and academics to develop an Infrastructure Procurement Routemap, a guide to improving delivery capability. It is aimed primarily at the sponsor and client organisations that deliver major projects and programmes, long-term capital investment plans and publicly procured megaprojects.

The key components and application of the routemap are based on:

- A suite of assessment tools developed as part of the routemap to enable sponsors, clients and the supply chain to align behaviours and identify capability gaps.
- The use of "complexity" assessment tools for establishing the nature of the delivery environment.
- Enabling the adoption of the common characteristics and behaviours associated with successful infrastructure project and programme delivery, including *inter alia*:
  - early visibility and commitment to the pipeline of programme opportunities or the specific project
  - clearly articulated sponsor requirements adopting whole life principles linked to service outcomes that define the project or programme requirement
  - effective governance, accountability and timely decision making
  - early supplier engagement that engages all tiers of the supply chain
  - effective use and structuring of standard contracts such as the NEC suite to align risk, reward and behaviours in an integrated supply chain
  - appropriate incentive-driven approaches that stimulate further integration of the supply chain
  - an environment that encourages innovation and departures from standards that embed cost and add no value to the outcome or safety.
- Pragmatic approaches to compliance with EU procurement legislation.
- An ongoing role for industry leaders and experts in the infrastructure sector to identify, develop and disseminate best practice.

Source: HM Treasury and Infrastructure UK (2013), "Infrastructure procurement routemap: A guide to improving delivery capability", January, www.gov.uk/government/uploads/system/uploads/attachment_data/file/329052/iuk_procurement_routemap_guide_to_improving_delivery_capability_280113.pdf.

The project imposes well thought-out co-ordination mechanisms and a shared understanding among stakeholders. GACM could consider creating a project-oriented advisory committee federating the different expertise required to successfully develop NAICM, either by setting up a new body or by expanding its existing administrative board to include all relevant public stakeholders.

Such a body would foster participation of all stakeholders in the procurement processes carried out for the completion of the project. Beyond general procurement governance of the project, the phased approach adopted by GACM to roll out the procurement processes in distinct packages could support the creation of multidisciplinary teams dedicated to each package. This would further strengthen decision-making processes.

Designing efficient award criteria

In designing appropriate award criteria and adequate frameworks proportionate to the need, GACM could facilitate access to procurement opportunities to competitors of all sizes and help identify proposals offering the best value for money.

The Law on Public Works imposes, considering their magnitude and complexity, the application of points-based evaluation criteria allowing for multidimensional assessment of proposals in competitive procurement processes for infrastructure works (Article 38 of the Law on Public Works and Article 63 of ROPSRM). The criteria and their corresponding weightings shall be publicised in the tender documentation (Article 39 of the Law on Public Works).

In April 2015, the OECD issued a survey (OECD, 2015e) to 56 jurisdictions in which questions about criteria for tender award were asked. Almost all respondents indicated using hybrid criteria for certain procurement processes to account for price and quality of submissions. The survey further evidences that the choice of non-price criteria and their corresponding weighting are often left to the discretion of the contracting authority.

Less flexibility is given to GACM in the selection and weights of relevant award criteria. The regulatory framework on Public Works imposes taking into account two secondary policy objectives when using points-based evaluation mechanisms. The percentage of disabled workers employed by the bidder and the share of subcontracting arrangements with SMEs shall be factored in the assessment. Yet, they do not count for stand-alone criteria, but rather for weighting factors of sub-criteria.

The Ministry of Public Administration provides practical guidance to identify and weight selection criteria (*Lineamientos para la aplicación del criterio de evaluación de proposiciones a través del mecanismo de punto o porcentajes en los procedimientos de contratación*). Although stating detailed guidance on the nature of the criteria and their minimum and maximum weightings, Section 1-7 allows for derogation to these guidelines when the specific characteristics of the works so require, subject to prior authorisation of the unit responsible for public contracts (*Unidad de Normatividad de Contrataciones Públicas*).

Using this flexibility will allow GACM to tailor award criteria to the specifics of each package, including secondary policy objectives. For example, public works could include specific award criteria when *i)* time for completion could be a competing factor because of possible alternative methodologies; or *ii)* where supply chain management of raw materials is of the essence considering the consequences a disruption of supplies would have; or *iii)* when prior market analysis suggests strong potential to develop local capacities.

Yet, designing strategic award criteria would only achieve partial results without efficient and unbiased assessments. Assessment frameworks need to be tailored to tender specifics or to the objectives of the purchasing entity. The greater complexity of this assessment method providing evaluation of non-financial attributes entails higher scrutiny on the clarity and the structure of technical specifications. Complex award criteria call for additional guidance provided to bidders. To ensure seamless and transparent assessment of proposals, bidders should be required to provide submissions in a standardised format, thus easing comparative analyses and ensuring that suppliers are on an equal footing.

GACM should mobilise the necessary expertise to design efficient award criteria and weightings in competitive procurement processes allowing for better identification of value for money and provide competitors with sound and standardised response frameworks so as to ensure streamlined, fair and transparent comparative assessments.

Effective procurement in infrastructure should lead to effective management of contracts

Sound contract design, including renegotiations mechanisms, and post-implementation contract management could allow GACM to drive efficiency throughout the entire procurement cycle.

Although extensive competition including efficient award criteria allows for identification of the proposal which represent the best value for money, the process in itself would have little relevance if not followed by solid contract execution and contract management.

GACM needs to ensure that contractors will effectively deliver what they committed to in their proposals. This presupposes both efficient contract design and effective contract management to periodically assess contractors' performance and verify that they are continuing to abide by their initial commitments (Box 3.11).

Box 3.11. **Delays and cost overruns in selected EU airports**

The EU auditors examined investment projects at 20 airports – in Estonia, Greece, Italy, Poland and Spain – which received more than EUR 600 million of EU funds from 2000 to 2013. The auditors found that only half of these airports could show the need for EU-funded investment and that funded infrastructure was often underused, with some EUR 38 million worth not being used at all.

The audit found that 17 of the 20 airports experienced delays. In 14 cases, the delay was more than a year with the average delay being 23 months. In 45% of the cases, airport construction experienced cost overruns of several million euros.

Only half of the airports audited increased passenger numbers, while, for more than half of them, air traffic forecasts significantly over-estimated increases. In Cordoba, for example, fewer than 7 000 passengers travelled in 2013, against the 179 000 forecast. In addition, for most airports there was little evidence of an improvement in customer service or of regional socio-economic benefits, such as the creation of additional jobs.

Seven of the airports, mostly those with fewer than 100 000 passengers per year, are not financially self-sustainable and will struggle to remain in operation without more public money. Some of the airports are no longer in operation.

Source: European Court of Auditors (2014), "EU-funded airport infrastructures: Poor value for money", press communiqué.

The regulatory environment surrounding the project puts a strong emphasis on the execution of the contracts deriving from public procurement of public works. It details supervision mechanisms of the execution of the works and also provides guidance on calculations methods for unforeseen extensions of the contracts.

The first significant factor shaping the outcomes of procurement processes is contract management. Once a supplier has been awarded a contract, detailed and thorough assessment of contractor's contract execution at regular intervals against pre-defined criteria or targets can create an environment conducive to performance (OECD, 2013a) (Box 3.12).

Box 3.12. **Fraud during construction: Short piling (Hong Kong, China)**

In 1997, Zen Pacific Civil Contractors Ltd. ("Zen Pacific") was the successful bidder for the piling works of all five buildings of the Yuen Chau Kok Home Ownership Scheme ("HOS") being built for the Hong Kong Housing Department ("HD"), an Hong Kong Government agency. The five buildings were to be two 41-storey buildings, three 33-storey buildings and one 4-storey facilities complex with a car park. Following the award of contract, and without informing the HD, Zen Pacific sub-contracted the piling works to Hui Hon Contractors Ltd., who was not on the HD's approved list of contractors. Throughout the entire construction period, Hui Hon's role as a subcontractor was concealed. Hui Hon staff were introduced as Zen Pacific staff and the Hui Hon site agent corresponded with the HD on Zen Pacific letterhead.

During 1998, Hui Hon carried out defective piling works for two of the apartment blocks. However, the subcontractor's directors took steps to ensure that these defects were concealed. During the subsequent investigation, some of the construction irregularities and deceptions included:

- driving the temporary casings to a depth of only 20–30m below ground, rather than to founding level.
- using Super Mud to stabilise the walls of excavated shafts without installing temporary casings.
- making the pile shafts shorter than specified so they could not hold the required amount of concrete.
- dropping temporary casings into the pile shafts instead of installing them properly.
- cleaning the pile shafts by running the pipes only halfway down the shaft, so guaranteeing that the flushing water from the shaft would run clear and give the impression that the cleaning process had been properly completed, when in fact it had not.
- faking core samples for core tests carried out to test the length of the piles and the integrity of the concrete.
- shortening the measuring tape that would be used to measure the actual length of the pile. This became known as the "magic measuring tape".
- arranging for concreting work to be completed well after 7:00 pm, thus ensuring that the concreting of 30 out of the 36 piles escaped the supervision of HD staff.

In 1999, the HD carried out an inspection of settlement conditions and found abnormal settlement conditions of two of the HOS buildings making it difficult to install lift shafts. An independent inquiry confirmed that the settlement of these two blocks was caused by short piling and was indeed severe. Out of 36 large diameter bored piles for two buildings, only four met the requirements. Twenty-one were shorter than the prescribed length by 2 m to 15 m, while 11 were resting on soft mud instead of bedrock. This meant that 90% or so of the bored piles in these two buildings failed to comply with standards and the already extensive superstructure was being supported by the only 10% of bored piles that were fully compliant. When the short piling was discovered, the two HOS buildings had already been constructed up to their 33rd and 34th floors respectively. Eventually on 16 March 2000, HD announced that the two buildings would be demolished in the interests of safety.

Box 3.12. **Fraud during construction: Short piling (Hong Kong, China)** ***(continued)***

The Hong Kong Independent Commission Against Corruption was called in to investigate. There were criminal and civil proceedings with the following outcomes:

- The two ex-directors and a site agent of Hui Hon were charged with dishonestly defrauding the HD. The site agent pleaded guilty and was sentenced to three and a half years in jail. Two ex-directors of Hui Hon were convicted and following an appeal were sentenced to ten years in jail.
- HD lodged a claim against Zen Pacific for losses amounting to HKD 650 million. These included the costs of demolishing the two buildings and the compensation paid to the superstructure contractor. After four years of arbitration lasting from 2000 to 2003, at legal costs of around HKD 40 million, HD reached an agreement with the Zen Pacific that Zen Pacific would pay compensation of HKD 80 million.
- Zen Pacific was permanently delisted from HD's list of approved contractors for constructing large diameter bored piles and demolition, and a Zen Pacific sister company was barred from undertaking any works for HD for two years.
- Nine HD staff members were held to have failed to perform their duties and three HD site officers to have turned a blind eye to the non-compliance of foundation works. It was found that they had approved the works without checking properly and failed to report progress to the project engineer. Disciplinary action was taken against these three by the Civil Service Bureau. The other six staff members were transferred to other posts.

The ICAC Report stated: "If the short piling had not come to light, as many as 656 households would have been placed in grave peril. The site was eventually turned into a leisure park."

Recommended preventive measures: The Corruption Prevention Department of the ICAC, in conjunction with HD and related Government departments, subsequently formulated corruption preventive measures including the following (as taken from the ICAC Report):

- **Strengthening of works supervision**: A works supervision plan should be formulated before the commencement of works under which professionals should be involved in monitoring major procedures and the frequency of inspections should be specified. All records relating to the works should be properly maintained.
- **Monitoring of works at night**: When it proved necessary to carry out any works at night, suitable supervisory staff should be appointed to stay at the site to monitor the quality of the works.
- **Specifying testing procedures**: Testing procedures, including how tests should be monitored, how frequent they should be, and the detailed nature of samples for testing, should be clearly specified. In particular, tight controls should be implemented over the extraction of samples and their secure storage and transport.
- **Preventing tampering with reports**: To prevent tampering, laboratories should be requested to deliver the reports directly to the consultancy companies. Consultancy companies should conduct independent random checks to verify the reliability of tests.
- **Monitoring subcontractors**: Contracts should include probity clauses covering such matters as codes of conduct and guidelines on conflicts of interest. The terms of the contracts should be so phrased as to deter main contractors and subcontractors from turning to corruption and malpractice.
- **Enhancing staff's awareness of corruption prevention**: Site supervisors' understanding of the Prevention of Bribery Ordinance should be improved and their ethical standards enhanced.

Box 3.12. **Fraud during construction: Short piling (Hong Kong, China)** ***(continued)***

Further investigation by the ICAC: To tackle the series of short piling scams that had come to light since 1999, the ICAC set up a 45-man task force on 1 February 2000 to investigate reports of corruption involving short piles and jerry-built construction works. The number of corruption reports received by the ICAC concerning the construction industry dropped since 2002, from a high of 295 reports in 2001 to 114 reports in 2007. This decline indicates that positive progress has been made in building a culture of integrity in the construction industry.

Source: Short Piling report by the ICAC: www.icac.org.hk/new_icac/eng/cases/piling/p03b.html.

The inherent nature of infrastructure works – scale and complexity of the works, interdependence of some packages and duration of contracts – opens the door to contract renegotiations. A study on Brazilian public works contracts awarded by the Federal Government between 2002 and 2007 estimates that nearly 30% of contracts were renegotiated and final prices were 40% higher on average than initial awarded prices (Fiuza and Rezende, 2012).

Most of the time contract renegotiations are caused by incomplete technical specifications in the tender documentation, which in turn influences bidders' strategies (Bajari, Houghton and Tadelis, 2014). The possibility of *ex post* renegotiations can incentivise bidders to submit abnormally low proposals, knowing that the playing field in case of renegotiations will be in their favour (OECD, 2015e). This possibility is further emphasised by the phased structure of the project since the packaging strategy might exponentially increase the costs for GACM in the case of disruption of activities.

As reported by some countries such as Sweden, putting a lower value on the financial component in the cost/benefit analysis helps mitigate bidders' incentives to submit abnormally low tenders which they know will be renegotiated. However, beyond intentional behaviour of competitors, renegotiations happen because of truly unforeseen circumstances.

As a first step, GACM could update its procurement guidelines and manuals to include more detailed guidance on the management of supplier's performance building upon the existing provisions in the ROPSRM. For example, additional guidance could be provided on regular assessments of ongoing work and introduce regular progress meetings to ensure works are carried out within the agreed timeframe.

More generally, GACM could introduce in the contracts service level agreements (SLAs) on key factors contributing to the successful completion of the works. Including an assessment framework of contractor's performance could also support objective evaluation of the necessity of contracts extensions.

To mitigate contractors' bargaining power, GACM could further develop in the contract governance mechanisms in situations allowing for renegotiations (*convenios modificatorios*). For example, roles and responsibilities of the parties and risks distribution mechanisms against various situations (natural disaster, changes in the design, etc.) that could lead to renegotiations could be detailed in the contract. This would frame the negotiation process.

Adapting to the environment of the project

Based on a sample of 200 infrastructure works put to tender in developing countries, the mere fact of promoting competition in infrastructure projects generates approximately 8.2% of savings (Estache and Iimi, 2008). The phased approach in the packaging strategy for the construction of the NAICM should create in a relatively short timeframe a large competitive environment for suppliers within Mexico and from abroad. However specific attention should be placed on measures that affect competitiveness and those that could foster this environment.

Incentivise competitor participation

Implementing procurement strategies proportionate to the magnitude of the project and aiming to facilitate access and increase attractiveness of public procurement operations while pursuing other policy objectives.

Competitor participation could be incentivised by removing barriers to entry into the competition and easing access to opportunities offered by the project. As an example, the purchasing entity might decide that the submission of proposals (Article 28 and 31 Section VIII LOPSRM, Article 34 Section VII ROPSRM) could be done remotely by electronic means or mailed in sealed envelopes, thus avoiding physical presence. This could ultimately encourage participation of competitors not reasonably close to GACM headquarters.

The national content requirement mentioned in the Law on Public Works and which could be included by the contracting authority as a qualification criterion in public tenders could also prove detrimental to competition and to its underlying objective. The Law on Public Works only mandates bidders to provide a declaration on oath stating that they comply with local content conditions set out in the call for tender, making this condition a requirement rather than a qualitative component of proposals received.

Close attention to market structure and diversity should be placed when defining this percentage since a high value could induce a series of consequences on the effectiveness of the procurement process. The national content requirement could affect the supply base by reducing, if not eliminating at all, competition. It could also negatively affect the financial element of the submissions. Finally it could prove counterproductive if not comprehensively assessed.

In addition to measures facilitating access to public opportunities for competitors of all sizes and origins, participation of suppliers could be incentivised by lowering transaction costs or increasing possible revenues.

While access to public tenders and submissions of proposals are free of charge, competitors incur costs linked to mobilising resources to answer needs detailed in the tender documentation and to provide the required legal documentation for each procurement process (for example tax payment and social security certificates). Diminishing the cost of procurement participation could prove useful to augment the level of competition and generate savings for both the public and private sectors (Box 3.13).

Box 3.13. **Reducing transaction costs for suppliers**

The Korean e-Procurement system (KONEPS) includes tools that reduce burden on suppliers by eliminating the need to submit duplicative certificates and other records, helping to ensure that the extent and complexity of information required in tender documentation and the time allotted for suppliers to respond is proportionate to the size and complexity of the procurement.

Companies that previously had to register individually for each public procurement bidding could now register only once with the Public Procurement Service and participate in all biddings from central government entities, local government entities, and public enterprises.

Through the shared use of government data through data interchange between KONEPS and other database owned by public authorities, KONEPS enabled the elimination of paper submission of business registration certificate and tax payment certificate. For public construction tenders, bidders become no longer required to submit certificates on past experiences, as such information was electronically collected through data interchange with construction industry associations.

According to a study conducted in 2009, annual transaction cost savings enabled through KONEPS amounts to KRW 9.5 trillion. Of this, the saving of KRW 1.6 trillion occurs in the public sector, from reduced labour and process time due to the streamlined and digitalised work process. KRW 7.9 trillion was saved in the private sector, mainly from reduced costs for visiting public entities and obtaining required certificates and proof documents. Reduced labour and time from streamlined and standardised process also contributed to the savings.

Source: OECD (forthcoming-b): *Public Procurement Review of the Public Procurement Service, Korea*, OECD Publishing, Paris.

Another means for lowering public competition costs for suppliers would reside in the grouping of public works that are of similar nature in the same tender process. This would avoid duplication of processes, which will reduce transaction costs both for suppliers and for GACM.

This exercise should not be done, however, at the expense of efficiency. Discussions in OECD countries on division of contracts into lots highlight that, while it could be a means to foster competition, this strategy could induce a trade-off between potential competition gains and efficiency losses. To avoid this situation, suppliers should be offered the possibility to submit bundle offers (OECD, 2015e).

As an example, open public tenders for the construction of the runways and taxiways are grouped into the same procurement process. To avoid harming competition, GACM could consider offering the option to suppliers to either submit a proposal on one of the two lots or on both. Should a supplier send an offer on both lots, it could be asked to demonstrate in its submission the extent of additional efficiencies which would derive from awarding the two lots to the same bidder. In doing so GACM would explore additional possibilities and synergies the market could possibly offer.

The packaging strategy seems to focus strictly on the construction phase for all lots. While this is understandable for most of the lots and the mandate given to GACM to render the new airport operational, some lots seem to include public works which would require further ongoing maintenance, whether to replace spare parts of the initial works or to maintain them in suitable operational working conditions.

For example, the visual signs allowing planes to take off and land *(ayudas visuales)* would require after their initial implementation, recurrent maintenance to ensure the constant safety of aviation operations. This deriving maintenance will obviously be subject to some sort of fees, whether recurring annual lump sums or fees paid based on unit prices. Including this work into the packaged tender could help foster competition by providing bidders with additional revenue sources. Should the implementation of the initial visual signs being based on proprietary techniques or materials, it will also avoid unnecessary future exception to public tender based on Article 42 Section I of the LOPSRM.

GACM could implement tailored procurement strategy for each package allowing both sides – demand and offer – to explore the different possibilities and scenarios for the construction of the NAICM project. GACM could therefore cautiously assess the existing barriers to entry into the competition which would diminish competition or affect the outcome of the procurement process.

Meeting market capabilities

Considering the crucial role played by the market consultation phase, GACM needs to engage in transparent and regular dialogues with suppliers, business associations and experts so as to decide the most efficient procurement process, its openness and design effective technical specifications and appropriate award criteria.

The type of procedure used for each package shall be proportionate to market size and structure, promote transparency and achieve value for money. As such, the main factor contributing to deciding which procedure to adopt should be the understanding of the market structure and capabilities. Similar assessment should be done on the national or international dimension of the process, including verifying its compliance with free trade agreements. As previously discussed, the national dimension of the packages could be no less than 60% of the total project based on the initial decision made by GACM.

Large constructions companies in Mexico capable of meeting the needs for the construction of the NAICM are scarce (GACM, 2014). Therefore, designing procurement processes capable of meeting market capabilities is essential. Sound and planned consultations are also an important factor in fostering competition and benefit from suppliers' expertise to reduce asymmetry of information before issuing tenders (Box 3.14).

Under the umbrella of the Corporate Directorate for Real Estate Management and Administration and in the presence of social witnesses nominated for the package, the Corporate Directorate for Infrastructure could meet with potential suppliers to better understand market capabilities.

As part of the effort to further publicise the construction of NAICM to increase private sector participation in procurement process, GACM could also consider advertising procurement opportunities beyond CompraNet and notably on specialised construction or civil engineering platforms.

Box 3.14. Early engagement in Canada

The Public Works and Government Services (PWGSC) in Canada encourages in its Supply Manual early engagement between client departments and potential suppliers to ensure that public tenders meet market capabilities.

Client departments are invited to engage with PWGSC contracting officers early in the process. This engagement may focus on different topics and may include various levels of engagement. It may be long before a signed requisition is received within PWGSC.

The early engagement with industry may also take many forms, such as issuing Letters of Interest (LOIs), Requests for Information (RFIs), one-on-one consultations with suppliers, the holding of industry days, etc. By engaging clients and suppliers through early and ongoing consultation and dialogue, contracting officers are better situated to identify the various complexities and risks associated with a client's requirement, enabling the development of mitigation strategies. Acquiring the knowledge of the requirement and its related complexities and risk better positions all stakeholders for a successful procurement that meets the client's needs.

Various tools are available to facilitate this early engagement. Some are listed below:

- the **Acquisitions Program Policy Suite**, which provides policy instruments on topics such as engagement and communications, governance, socio-economic objectives, risk management, etc.
- the **Procurement Library**, which includes the Complexity Assessment tools as well as copies of Risk Assessments for Complexity Levels 1 through 3 inclusive
- the **Procurement Nuggets**, which provide quick references on various procurement issues.

Source: Government of Canada (2014), "Early engagement with clients, suppliers and Public Works and Government Services Canada (PWGSC) contracting officers", https://buyandsell.gc.ca/policy-and-guidelines/supply-manual/section/2/26.

Considering the scale of this infrastructure and the duration of construction works, detailed market analyses must be carried out by GACM and other stakeholders before deciding the exact nature of the procurement process and considering both national and international state of play in terms of competitors.

Encouraging participation of SMEs

GACM should trigger all available means to foster participation of SMEs in the NAICM project.

The Law on Public Works foresees the possibility, as in many other countries such as the United States or China, to set aside a proportion of public procurement to SMEs. Yet, this share of public procurement reserved for SMEs is not to be found in infrastructure projects. Considering the nature, size and workforce necessary to perform public works related to the NAICM project, SME participation is likely to occur in subcontracting arrangements.

Article 63 Section II of the Regulations on Public Works encourages the integration of SME participation in the execution of public works by assigning a multiplication factor to proposals including subcontracting arrangements with SMEs in excess of the percentage indicated in the tender documentation..

The Ministry of Public Administration set out detailed guidance about award criteria (*Lineamientos para la aplicación del criterio de evaluación de proposiciones a través del mecanismo de puntos o porcentajes en los procedimientos de contratación*) and their corresponding weightings.

Yet, GACM has the possibility to derive from these instructions if deemed necessary. As a first step, GACM could then further increase in its tender procedures (whether open public tender or restricted competition) the multiplying factor for proposals committing to subcontract part of the work to SMEs. Unlike the traditional national content requirement, the additional points given to proposals including SMEs promote a positive approach towards the inclusion of the SMEs without prejudging market capabilities.

Such a strategy towards award criteria should then be widely disseminated to SME networks sufficiently in advance to leave them with sufficient time to explore consortia options or to negotiate subcontracting agreements. To do so, GACM could benefit from the existing specialised public entities.

Mapping and assessing the risks of the project

Risk management strategies commensurate to the magnitude and complexity of the NAICM should be an integral part of the procurement process and packaging strategy to ensure that threats of all sorts affecting the project are duly identified and mitigation measures are implemented.

Risks are inherent to an infrastructure project of this magnitude and they could evolve over time. Therefore their likelihood and criticality should be regularly assessed. The existence of mitigation measures and their effectiveness should also be reviewed at regular intervals (Table 3.4).

Table 3.4. **Risks and mitigation measures**

Risk	Mitigation measures
Co-ordination failures	• Address internal co-ordination and decision-making issues by updating the Organisation Manual and the procedures manuals. • Clear definition of roles, responsibilities, and decision-making powers considering all the stakeholders (GACM Corporate Directorates, PMO, etc.). • Mapping of consultants providing services to GACM on tender documentation, which will form the basis of technical specifications for the construction works. • Create a dedicated unit in SFP specifically devoted to review NAICM tender documents and preparations. Annex A details the case study of 2105 Expo Milano model set by the Italian Anti-Corruption Authority, ANAC.
Sub-optimal performance in process and outcomes	• Defining a clear critical route for each item in every package by assessing the procurement timeframe against planned completion dates and their interdependence with other packages. • Establishing an accountability scheme to require justification at the highest level for delays and adjustments to the critical route. • Defining relevant awarding criteria and corresponding weightings, proportionate to the nature of the works in each package. Avoid the trend to award contracts just based on the lowest price criterion. • Designing a control board with key performance indicators (KPIs). • Including post-construction activities in some tenders. • Balancing secondary objectives against achieving value for money by applying impact assessment methodologies to periodically measure effectiveness in the achievement of secondary objectives.
Limited use of competitive procedures	• Market research to gather information regarding the national and international state of play and be able to justify decisions. • Full transparency as to how decisions were taken, which implies full disclosure of procurement information on the GACM website. • Using social witnesses and social observers. • Documented use of exceptions to competitive tendering. • Periodically analysing the use of exceptions to competitive tendering to identify opportunities to minimise direct awards.
Insufficient time for potential suppliers to prepare their bids and for GACM to review submissions	• Early supplier engagement. • Consultation with key stakeholders (i.e. CMIC, the Architects Association, chambers of industries, etc.) regarding the time required for companies to get ready. • Estimation of time required to review submissions on the basis of other megaprojects (in Mexico and abroad).
Absence of suitable proposals	• Early supplier engagement discussing content and structure of technical specifications and awarding criteria. • Market research to allow for informed decisions. • Develop a market intelligence methodology and plan, assessing human and material resources required and including method variations according to complexity. • Strengthen the Deputy Direction for Procurement by formalising a market intelligence team. • Work with other institutions (i.e., Ministry of Economy, COFECE, ASA, AICM) to pool knowledge. • The goal of the market research is to collect information about the goods and services to be procured, at least: i) market size and the procurement volume in relation to market size; ii) market structure (percentage of SMEs in the market segment or concentration by big companies); iii) the most important suppliers in the market; iv) maturity of the products or services, pricing models, and different conditions offered by suppliers, and their commercial activities; and v) market development outlook for the coming years.
Poor design of tender documentation by consultants	• Accountability mechanisms by which GACM reviews and follows up the work of consultants. • Ensure that design and specification is written sufficiently broadly that a wide pool of contractors can bid (i.e. that the design or specification is not limited so as to favour one contractor). • Avoid naming specified products (or, if done for essential illustrative purposes, state "or equivalent").
Inadequate sequencing of operations	• Assess competitors' supply chain management and quality assurance processes to identify the least potential for disruption in construction activities. • Strong contract management. • Constantly reassessing the sequencing of procurement processes.

Notes

1. The Secretary of National Defence (SEDENA) will undertake and monitor the military components of public works which affect national security. The National Commission on Water (CONAGUA) will be responsible for the issuance of competitive procurement processes of public works relating to the drainage system and soil decontamination.

References

Abu Dhabi Airports (2011), "Abu Dhabi Airports releases the General Contractor Tender for the Midfield Terminal Building", 28 February 2011, www.adac.ae/english/mtp/MTP/latest-news/2011-02-2-abu-dhabi-airports-company-releases-the-general-contractor-tender-for-the-midfield-terminal-building.

Australian Government Productivity Commission (2014), *Public Infrastructure: Productivity Commission Inquiry Report*, Volume I, No. 71, www.pc.gov.au/__data/assets/pdf_file/0003/137280/infrastructure-volume1.pdf.

Bajari, Houghton and Tadelis (2014), "Bidding for incomplete contracts: An empirical analysis of adaptation costs", *American Economic Review* 2014.

Burger, P. and I. Hawkesworth (2011), "How to attain value for money: Comparing PPP and traditional infrastructure public procurement", *OECD Journal on Budgeting*, Vol. 11/1, http://dx.doi.org/10.1787/budget-11-5kg9zc0pvq6j.

CMAA (Construction Management Association of America) (2012), *An Owner's Guide to Project Delivery Methods*, CMAA, https://cmaanet.org/files/Owners%20Guide%20to%20Project%20Delivery%20Methods%20Final.pdf.

El Debate (2015), *NAICM: viene la tecnica de cimentacion*, 2 June, www.debate.com.mx/opinion/NAICM-viene-la-tecnica-de-cimentacion-20150601-0223.html.

Estache, A. and A. Iimi (2008), "Procurement efficiency for infrastructure development and financial needs reassessed", *Policy Research Working Paper* 4662, World Bank.

European Court of Auditors (2014), "EU-funded airport infrastructures: Poor value for money", press communiqué.

Fiuza, E. and L. Rezende (2012), "Renegotiation of public work contracts: An empirical assessment", www.webmeets.com/files/papers/earie/2012/651/FiuzaRezende%202012-03-15%20earie%20final.pdf.

GACM (*Grupo Aeroportuario de la Ciudad de México*) (2015a), "*Programa Anual de Obra*", www.aeropuerto.gob.mx/gacm/programas-anuales.php (accessed on 30 September 2015).

GACM (2015b), "Packaging strategy", issued 24 July 2015.

GACM (2015c), "*Registro de Riesgos NAICM*", issued 19 March 2015.

GACM (2014), "Contract packaging strategy", analysis based on data from "*Empresas de la construcción más grandes de México Obras, Julio 2014*".

Government of Canada (2014), "Early engagement with clients, suppliers and Public Works and Government Services Canada (PWGSC) contracting officers", https://buyandsell.gc.ca/policy-and-guidelines/supply-manual/section/2/26.

HM Treasury and Infrastructure UK (2013), "Infrastructure procurement routemap: A guide to improving delivery capability", January, www.gov.uk/government/uploads/system/uploads/attachment_data/file/329052/iuk_procurement_routemap_guide_to_improving_delivery_capability_280113.pdf.

Infrastructure Australia (2012), "Benchmark for efficient procurement of major infrastructure in efficiencies in major project procurement".

Infrastructure UK, HM Treasury and Lord Deighton (2014), "Improving infrastructure delivery, project initiation routemap", October, www.gov.uk/government/publications/improving-infrastructure-delivery-project-initiation-routemap.

NZ Transport Agency (2009), "Procurement manual", updated 2 August 2014, www.nzta.govt.nz/resources/procurement-manual/.

OECD (forthcoming-a), *Public Procurement Review of the Instituto de Seguridad y Servicios Sociales de los Trabajadores del Estado* (ISSSTE), OECD Publishing, Paris.

OECD (forthcoming-b): *Public Procurement Review of the Public Procurement Service, Korea*, OECD Publishing, Paris.

OECD (2015a), *Government at a Glance 2015*, OECD Publishing, Paris, http://dx.doi.org/10.1787/gov_glance-2015-en.

OECD (2015b), *OECD National Accounts Statistics* (database), http://dx.doi.org/10.1787/na-data-en (accessed on 30 September 2015).

OECD (2015c), "Updated report on G20/OECD checklist on long-term investment financing strategies and institutional investors", https://g20.org/wp-content/uploads/2015/05/G20-OECD-Report-on-Checklist-on-Long-Term-Investment-Financing-Strategies-and-Institutional-Investors-April-2015.pdf.

OECD (2015d), "Towards a framework for the governance and delivery of infrastructure", unclassified document, GOV/PGC/SBO(2015)6, www.oecd.org/officialdocuments/publicdisplaydocumentpdf/?cote=GOV/PGC/SBO(2015)6&docLanguage=En.

OECD (2015e), "Hearing on auctions and tenders: Further issues", unclassified document, DAF/COMP/WP2(2015)1, www.oecd.org/officialdocuments/publicdisplaydocumentpdf/?cote=daf/comp/wp2(2015)1&doclanguage=en.

OECD (2015f), "Recommendation of the Council on Public Procurement", www.oecd.org/corruption/recommendation-on-public-procurement.htm.

OECD (2015g), *OECD Employment Outlook 2015*, OECD Publishing, Paris, http://dx.doi.org/10.1787/empl_outlook-2015-en.

OECD (2014a), "Smart procurement: Best practices for green procurement", web page, www.oecd.org/gov/ethics/best-practices-for-green-procurement.htm.

OECD (2014b), "Hearing on the use of tenders and auctions", unclassified document, DAF/COMP/WP2(2014)15, www.oecd.org/officialdocuments/publicdisplaydocumentpdf/?cote=daf/comp/wp2(2014)15&doclanguage=en.

OECD (2014c), "Towards procurement performance indicators: First set of indicators", www.oecd.org/officialdocuments/publicdisplaydocumentpdf/?cote=gov/pgc(2015)12&doclanguage=en.

OECD (2013a), *Public Procurement Review of the Mexican Institute of Social Security: Enhancing Efficiency and Integrity for Better Health Care*, OECD Public Governance Reviews, OECD Publishing, Paris, http://dx.doi.org/10.1787/9789264197480-en.

OECD (2013b), "Opening the black box of contract renegotiations: An analysis of road concessions in Chile, Colombia and Peru", unclassified document, DEV/DOC(2013)2, www.oecd.org/officialdocuments/publicdisplaydocumentpdf/?cote=DEV/DOC(2013)2&docLanguage=En.

OECD (2013c), "Towards procurement performance indicators: Stocktaking report on procurement information collected in countries", declassified document, GOV/PGC/ETH(2013)9, www.oecd.org/officialdocuments/publicdisplaydocumentpdf/?cote=GOV/PGC/ETH(2013)9&docLanguage=En.

OECD (2011), "Competition and Procurement: Key Findings", www.oecd.org/regreform/sectors/competitionandprocurement-2011.htm.

Portal del Empleo (2015), "Panorama de ocupación por sector económico", accessed 10 August 2015.

SFP (*Secretaría de la Función Pública*) (2010), "*Lineamientos para la applicación del criterio de evaluación de proposiciones a través del mecanismo de puntos o porcentajes en los procedimientos de contratación*", DOF, 9 September.

Saussier, S. and J. Tirole (2015), "Renforcer l'efficacité de la commande publique", *Conseil d'analyse économique* 2015/3, No. 22, http://dx.doi.org/10.3917/ncae.022.0001.

Stilger, P.S., J. Siderius and E.M. van Raaij (2015), *A Comparative Study of Formulas for Choosing the Economically Most Advantageous Tender*, http://dx.doi.org/10.2139/ssrn.2626934.

Tadelis, S. and P. Bajari (2006), "Incentives and award procedures: Competitive tendering vs. negotiations in procurement", in Dimitri, Piga, and Spagnolo (eds.), *Handbook of Procurement*, Cambridge University Press.

Tirole, J. (2009), "Cognition and incomplete contracts", *American Economic Review*, Vol. 99, No. 1, March.

White, A. (2014), "More competition in building 'good for infrastructure'", *The Australian*, 21 July.

Chapter 4

Enhancing the integrity and transparency of the procurement process in the NAICM project

World experience has shown that infrastructure projects are particularly prone to corruption due in part to the large sums involved and the complexity of the sector. The construction of the new airport of Mexico is not exempt from this risk, yet no comprehensive strategy has been put in place by Mexico to prevent corruption in the construction of the airport.

Despite recent measures implemented by the Mexican Government to promote integrity in the public sector and reinforce the fight against corruption, much more needs to be done within Grupo Aeroportuario de la Ciudad de México S.A. de C.V. (GACM), the entity responsible for constructing the airport. This puts at high risk the credibility and effectiveness of the project.

This chapter assesses the vulnerability to corruption of the GACM and its procurement processes and provides policy options and good practices from OECD countries to mitigate risks and prevent corruption in the construction of the airport.

Awareness of corruption risks is essential for the success of the construction of the airport

Infrastructure projects are particularly prone to corruption and mismanagement

The infrastructure sector is particularly vulnerable to corruption and undue influence due to the extent of public officials' discretion over the investment decision, the multiple stages and the large sums of money and stakeholders involved, including elected and non-elected public officials, lobbyists, civil society organisations, trade unions, regulators, contractors, consultants, engineers and suppliers.

The public investment cycle is vulnerable to corruption in all its forms and at different phases, taking the form of undue influence or capture of the investment project by specific interests, conflict of interests or bribery. The needs assessment phase and the selection of the projects is a crucial step since it sets the tone for the whole construction project and can potentially open opportunities for corruption at later stages. It is particularly harmful because it can divert public funds towards projects with little social utility and with low return, and favours new constructions at the expense of maintenance (Kenny, 2009).

The project design phase and the implementation or execution phase often see corruption in the form of bribery (to influence the development of the bidding documents, to obtain a contract, etc.), favouritism towards certain bidders, conflicts of interest, fraud, collusion or cartels. In this context, public procurement is recognised as one of the government activities that is most vulnerable to corruption, given the close interactions between public and private agents with relatively high levels of discretion as well as important financial implications.

The steps following the actual contract award are as vulnerable to corruption as the previous phases of the cycle and it is essential to have mechanisms in place to make sure that the contract is implemented properly, without changes in costs or level of quality. Corruption during the project execution or implementation phase can result in poor quality infrastructure and substandard construction that will require extra maintenance costs at later stages, or in the near future, and hence significantly reduces the economic rate of return (Kenny, 2009).

Lastly, the evaluation phase can also be a fertile ground for corrupt practices to cover up any previous abuses and frauds. During this phase, contractors, evaluators and public officials can misrepresent activities and results through discrepancies in financial reporting; non-compliance with financial or non-financial standards and terms and substandard performance.

Corruption incurs high costs and has a significant impact on society

Corruption is difficult to measure and quantify and, similarly estimating the costs of such practices remains a challenge. Corruption in the construction sector is significant and costly; it has been estimated that the global average cost of corruption in infrastructure - solely due to bribery - ranges between 5% and 20% of the investment (Kenny, 2009). Transparency International, the OECD and the American Society of Civil Engineers estimate the costs of corruption to be between 10% and 30 % of investment in public infrastructure (Hawkins, 2013). According to another estimation, "annual losses in global construction through mismanagement, inefficiency and corruption could reach USD 2.5 trillion by 2020" (COST, 2012).

Corruption indeed comes at a high cost. Direct costs include bribe transfers, higher expenses, scarcity of essential services, lower quality and misallocations of public funds (OECD, 2015). When there are bribe payments involved in the investment process, those paying the bribes seek to recover the cost of the bribe through inflating prices, billing for work not performed, failing to meet contract standards, reducing quality of work or using inferior materials. One of the common consequences of corruption in the infrastructure sector is the purchase of lower quality material to compensate for the part of the budget used to bribe officials. In the most extreme situations, building infrastructure of lower quality can have fatal consequences, such as the collapse of a building or a bridge. Less dramatic consequences of low-quality infrastructure are the daily nuisance of a road that is too narrow. Poor-quality material comes with high costs in the long term, as maintenance will be required earlier and more regularly.

One of the most serious consequences of corruption in infrastructure is the selection of "white elephants" projects during the appraisal phase. "White elephants" serve to describe very costly infrastructure projects that have no particular social use and often come with negative return rates (Wells, 2015).

Furthermore, the costs of inefficient spending on public infrastructure are not only economic. Evidence of waste of public resources can cost governments dearly in terms of lost credibility and trust on the part of citizens. Governments are entrusted with spending taxpayers' money efficiently and allocating it for the economic and social welfare of the economy and society. Given the increasingly tight fiscal space faced by many governments, infrastructure spending decisions that are not based on strict need assessment and cost-benefit analysis could harm not only governments' budgets, but also the confidence of citizens in public institutions.

Promoting integrity in the procurement cycle thus contributes to reducing overall costs of construction and operation, and to encouraging efficient investment. Acknowledging these risks, Mexico has recently reinforced its legal framework to counter corruption, especially during the procurement process.

Recent efforts to counter corruption under the Mexican legal framework

The Mexican legal framework applicable to public procurement is based primarily on the Law on Acquisitions, Leasing and Services of the Public Sector (*Ley de Adquisiciones, Arrendamientos y Servicios del Sector Público*, LAASSP) and the Law on Public Works and Related Services (*Ley de Obras Públicas y Servicios relacionados con las Mismas*, LOPSRM). Although, both of them include various requirements and rules to structure and guide public procurement activities, they do not specifically address integrity and corruption risks.

The administrative sanction of public servants who take part in corrupt practices is covered mainly by the Federal Law on Administrative Responsibilities of Public Servants (*Ley Federal de Responsabilidades Administrativas de los Servidores Públicos*, LFRASP). The LFRASP aims to enhance the legality and integrity of public servants' performance of their administrative duties by establishing the administrative faults, the procedure for taking legal action, and the modality and degree of sanctioning to be applied to public servants. Specifically, the LFRASP prohibits procurement officials from:

- contracting with any person who performs a public function, or with any company in which such a person participates
- contracting with any person that has been prohibited from holding a job, position or commission in the public administration
- intervening in any situation which may create any personal or business-related conflict of interest
- participating in any act or procedure where integrity might be compromised
- exercising any form of influence peddling to former public servants, up to one year after they conclude their public function
- inhibiting whistleblowing or the filing of a complaint. (OECD, 2013a).

In addition, and related more specifically to the procurement process, Mexico adopted the Federal Anti-Corruption Law on Public Procurement (*Ley Federal Anticorrupción en Contrataciones Públicas, LFACP*), which directly addresses issues of corruption and fraud in public procurement (Box 4.1).

Furthermore, in early 2015, the President of Mexico issued a series of Executive Orders to strengthen public sector integrity focused primordially on preventing and managing conflict of interest, including the disclosure of potential conflict of interest of the public servant and his/her family member in their yearly asset declaration. The Executive Orders also require the issuances of a Code of Ethics for all public servants of the Federal Government (see Table 4.1 in the next section) and guidance[1] for public procurement officials when interacting with suppliers (*Protocolo de actuación de los servidores públicos en contrataciones públicas*); the creation of a classification and registry for procurement officials,[2] the certification of procurement officials, the online publication of sanctioned suppliers; increased collaboration with chambers of commerce; an online "one-stop shop" (*ventanilla única*) for transactions with government to reduce potential opportunities for bribery; and the creation of a Special Unit on Ethics and Conflict of Interests Prevention (*Unidad Especializada en Ética y Prevención de Conflictos de Interés*).

Box 4.1. **The Federal Anti-Corruption Law on Public Procurement (LFACP)**

The Federal Anti-Corruption Law on Public Procurement (*Ley Federal Anticorrupción en Contrataciones Públicas*, LFACP) was adopted in June 2012 and provides the following provisions to addresses issues of corruption and fraud in public procurement:

- Penalties and liabilities on both Mexican and foreign individuals and entities for infringing the law during their participation in any federal procurement process, applying to other related professions that may have an influence on the integrity of the public procurement process (including but not limited to public servants).
- Mexican individuals and entities involved in corruption in international business transactions are equally liable.
- Acts such as influence, bribery, collusion, shams, omission, evasion, filing false information, and forgery are considered infringements (Article 8).
- Penalties for violation of the law include fines and legal disqualification (*inhabilitación*) from the pertinent working sector for periods ranging from three months to eight years for individuals and three months to ten years for entities (Article 27).
- Pleading guilty and co-operating in the investigation reduces the sanctions up to 50%, if the plead takes place within 15 working days following the notification of the administrative disciplinary proceedings (Articles 20 and 31).
- Whistleblowers identities must remain confidential (Article 10).

Source: OECD (2013), *Public Procurement Review of the State's Employees' Social Security and Social Services Institute in Mexico*, OECD Public Governance Reviews, OECD Publishing. http://dx.doi.org/10.1787/9789264197305-en.

The governance of integrity policies in Mexico

The governance of integrity policies in Mexico is going through a period of significant change. This is mostly due to an Anti-corruption Decree entered into force in May 2015 (*Decreto por el que se reforman, adicionan y derogan diversas disposiciones de la Constitución Política de los Estados Unidos Mexicanos, en materia de combate a la corrupción*) which entailed a Constitutional reform.

Most notably, the revised version of its Article 113 introduces Mexico's National Anti-corruption System (*Sistema Nacional Anticorrupción*), which is framed as the co-ordination mechanism for all the authorities of any governmental level in charge of anti-corruption policies and the control of public funds.

The reform established two new institutional actors which will engage in the fight against corruption: firstly, the Anti-corruption Prosecutor Office (*Fiscalía Especializada en Combate a la Corrupción*), whose head will be nominated by the Senate; secondly, a Citizen Participation Committee (*Comité de Participación Ciudadana*) consisting of five citizens who have been distinguished for their contribution to transparency, auditing or the fight against corruption.

At the same time, the anti-corruption reform expands the mandate of two existing institutions, e.g. the Federal Administrative Justice Tribunal *(Tribunal Federal de Justicia*

Administrativa) and the Federal Supreme Audit Institution (*Auditoría Superior de la Federación or ASF*). The new Federal Administrative Justice Tribunal will be also in charge of settling disputes between the Public Administration and individuals, as well as of imposing sanctions on public officials for serious administrative responsibilities (Article 109[3]).

The reformed Article 113 of the Constitution also defines the organisation of the National Anti-corruption System, whereby a Co-ordination Committee (*Comité Coordinador*) will bring together the following actors: the Federal Supreme Audit Institution, the Federal Ministry of Public Administration (*Secretaría de la Función Pública*), the Federal Administrative Justice Tribunal, the Federal Judicial Council (*Consejo de la Judicatura Federal*), the Anticorruption Prosecutor Office, the National Institute of Transparency , Access to Information and Data Protection (INAI-*Instituto Nacional de Transparencia, Acceso a la Información y Protección de Datos*) and the Citizen Participation Committee. The Co-ordination Committee will be responsible for establishing co-ordination mechanisms, designing comprehensive policies, managing relevant information, and elaborating an annual report in relation to the overall activity on the fight against corruption and the control of public resources.

Promoting openness and a culture of integrity

The GACM needs to create a culture of integrity

A major public infrastructure project managed with integrity and efficiency can send a strong signal to the public that the Government spends taxpayers money efficiently, takes their concerns seriously and is committed to improve integrity standards. Yet, despite Mexico's ongoing reinforcement of its anti-corruption legal and policy framework, the GACM does not actively promote a culture of integrity and has not put in place specific anti-corruption and integrity measures and programmes in its procurement function beyond what is required by the Federal Law and federal dispositions. At interviews with GACM procurement officials they showed a strict focus on legal compliance with limited awareness of corruption risks and tools and mechanisms to mitigate such risks.

GACM would benefit greatly from raising awareness of corruption and promoting a culture of integrity particularly in its procurement processes. The benefits are threefold: economic, on the organisation's morale and externally with society.

Evidently, a strong organisational culture of integrity that successfully prevents corruption is beneficial from an economic perspective. It contributes to reducing the costs of operations since the potential costs incurred from engaging in corruption are multiple: *i)* the actual costs of bribery; *ii)* the staff-time required to maintain certain connections; *iii)* the risk of legal sanctions incurred; and *iv)* the risk of reputational damage that could dissuade future suppliers from collaborating with the organisation. Yet, corruption also has a negative effect on the personnel's well-being. Recent research finds that bribery's most significant impact on organisations is its negative effect on employee morale and other studies indicate that bribery affects employee morale even in cases where no-one outside of the organisation ever found out (Forbes, 2013). Conversely, clear ethical standards and practices improve employees satisfaction by fostering trust among employees who can feel confident that their organisation will quickly and consistently act upon verified or proven unethical behaviour, encourage team members to speak up about their concerns and commit to clear and fair standards applicable to all (CEB, 2015).

Recent research shows that a strong integrity culture reduces personnel misconduct by almost 70% (CEB, 2015).

Moreover, promoting a strong culture of integrity is not only beneficial internally; it can also have a significant impact on society as a whole. Major infrastructure projects, such as the new airport of Mexico, are highly visible and provide the opportunity for the Government to showcase an innovative and "clean" approach that benefits the public interest.

Setting common standards and norms

Corruption and wrongdoings can be the result of intentional dishonest behaviour, but it is often a consequence of ignorance of the laws and norms or the corollary of an institutional culture. Thus setting clear standards for the conduct expected by public officials is a necessary first step. Codes of conduct have proven to be instrumental in promoting integrity in any organisation as they provide a clear benchmark for acceptable behaviour and ethical standards against which personnel and the institution itself can be held accountable. A code of conduct can be seen as a sort of contract among employees within the organisation, as well as a statement to third parties about the ethical standards to expect and respect (CCAB, 2014).

In Mexico, according to the agreement which aims to issue the Code of Ethics for civil servants of the Federal Government, integrity rules for the exercise of public functions, and general guidelines to foster integrity of public servants and to implement permanent measures to encourage their ethical behaviour, through the Ethics Committees and the Prevention of Conflicts of Interest (*Acuerdo que tiene por objeto emitir el Código de Ética de los servidores públicos del Gobierno Federal, las Reglas de Integridad para el ejercicio de la función pública, y los Lineamientos generales para propiciar la integridad de los servidores públicos y para implementar acciones permanentes que favorezcan su comportamiento ético, a través de los Comités de Ética y de Prevención de Conflictos de Interés*, DOF: 20/08/2015[3]), every entity must apply to its public servants the Code of Ethics for Public Servants of the Federal Government (*Código de Ética de los servidores públicos del Gobierno Federal)* and have among others, a code of conduct and an Ethics Committee. Indeed, the GACM in its Organisation Manual included the 2012 Code of Ethics for Public Servants of the Federal Government and the GACM code of conduct. The GACM code of conduct was sent by email to all GACM personnel on the 1st July 2015, after its approval by the Ethics Committee. Yet, according to the guidelines mentioned above, the code of conduct should be published on line and printed. As of September 2015, the GACM Code of Conduct cannot be found on line. In addition, the GACM could not provide information on how the code of conduct was developed nor if GACM public officials participated in its creation.

In addition, the existing code of conduct remains extremely general, stating what is expected from public officials in general terms mentioning the organisation's values and standards (similar to the ones on the code of ethics) and does not address specific situations, for example, of conflict of interest, what to do in case of bribery. The code of conduct does not make a specific reference to public procurement or to regulate and/or limit the use of confidential information (Table 4.1).

Table 4.1. **Public servants of the Federal Government code of ethics and GACM code of conduct**

Code of ethics for public servants of the Federal Government	Code of conduct
Constitutional principles that all public servants must observe in the course of their job, office, commission or function:	In the performance of their duties, GACM public officials should behave in accordance with the following:
1) Legality Public servants do only what the rules expressly provide them and at all times they subject their actions to what the laws, regulations and other legal provisions attribute to their job, position or commission, so they know and comply with the provisions regulating the exercise of their functions, powers and duties.	1. Obligation to align his/her performance to the regulatory framework applicable to the mission and vision of the organisation, within a framework of social responsibility.
2) **Honesty** Public servants are conducted with honesty without using their job, office or commission to obtain or seek to obtain any benefit, advantage or personal gain or for third parties, or seek or accept compensation, benefits, grants, gifts or gifts of any person or organisation because they are aware that this compromises their duties and the exercise of any public office involves a high sense of austerity and commitment to service.	2. Provide assistance to citizens, guided by the principles of respect, effectiveness and dedication to service.
3) **Loyalty** Public servants respond to the confidence that the State has given them; They have an absolute commitment to serving society and satisfy the interests of the collective needs over individual, personal or outside the general interest and welfare interests.	3. Perform their duties efficiently and effectively to achieve the objectives that have been determined.
4) **Impartiality** Public servants give to citizens and the general population the same treatment, no privileges or preferences are granted to organizations or people, nor allow influences, interests or undue prejudice affect their commitment to make decisions and perform their duties objectively.	4. Frame their actions within the principles of transparency and accountability.
5) **Efficiency** Public servants act according to a service culture results-oriented, trying at all times better performance of its functions to achieve institutional goals according to their responsibilities and through responsible and clear use of public resources, eliminating any undue ostentation and discretion in their application.	5. They will manage with efficiency and honesty the resources that have been allocated exclusively to achieve the goals of the GACM.
Values that must precede all public servants in the performance of his/her job, office, commission or functions:	
1) **Public interest** Public servants act always seeking maximum attention to the needs and demands of society above interests and benefits, outside the collective satisfaction.	6. Perform his/her duties honestly, without using his/her position to have gratification, benefit, advantage or privileges.
2) **Respect** Public servants are conducted with austerity and without ostentation, and provide a dignified and cordial treatment to all people in general and their colleagues, superiors and subordinates, considering their rights, so that encourage civil dialogue and the co-ordinated implementation of instruments that lead to understanding, through efficiency and public interest.	7. Promote an environment of communication, respect and equality in which everyone can develop holistically, without being subject to discrimination.
3) **Respect human rights** Public servants respect human rights, and in the scope of their powers and competences, they guarantee, promote and protect them in accordance with the principles of: Universality which states that human rights belong to everyone; interdependence meaning that human rights are closely linked to each other; indivisibility meaning that human rights are complementary and inseparable, and progressivity providing that human rights are constantly evolving and under no circumstances justify a setback in their protection.	8. Continually seek innovation of processes and activities to provide better service and do his/her job more effectively.

Code of ethics for public servants of the Federal Government	Code of conduct
4) **Equality and non-discrimination** Public servants provide services to all persons without distinction, exclusion, restriction or preference based on national or ethnic origin, colour, culture, sex, gender, age, disability, social status economic, health or legal, religion, physical appearance, genetic characteristics, immigration status, pregnancy, language, opinions, sexual preference, identity or political affiliation, marital status, family status, family responsibilities, language, criminal or any other reason backgrounds.	
5) **Gender equality** Public servants, in the scope of their powers and competences, ensure that both women and men have access to the same conditions, possibilities and opportunities for public goods and services; programmes and institutional benefits, jobs, posts and government commissions.	
6) **Cultural and ecological environment** Civil servants in developing their activities prevent the involvement of the cultural heritage of any nation and the planet's ecosystems; take an iron will to respect, protection and preservation of culture and environment, and in the exercise of their functions and in accordance with its powers, promote in society the protection and conservation of culture and the environment, as the main legacy for future generations.	
7) **Integrity** Public servants always act in a consistent manner with the principles to be observed in the performance of an employment office, commission or function, convinced the commitment to adjust their behaviour to prevail in their performance, an ethic that responds to the public interest and generate full assurance of their behaviour towards everyone with whom it is linked or observe their actions.	
8) **Co-operation** Public servants work together and foster teamwork to achieve common objectives of government plans and programs , thus generating a total vocation of public service for the benefit of the community and citizens' trust in their institutions	
9) **Leadership** Public servants are guide, example and promoters of the Code of Ethics and Integrity Rules; they encourage and applied in the performance of their duties the principles that the Constitution and the law impose them, as well as those additional values that for their importance are intrinsic to the public service.	
10) **Transparency** Public servants in the exercise of their functions protect personal data under their custody; they favour the principle of maximum disclosure of public information, diligently attending access requirements and providing documentation that they generate, obtain, acquire, transform or preserve; and the scope of its competence, proactively disseminate government information, as an element that generates value to society and promotes open government	
11) **Accountability** Public servants assume fully their responsibility to society and its authorities that derives from the exercise of their job, office or commission, by informing, explaining and justifying their decisions and actions, and are subject to a system of penalties and evaluation and public scrutiny of their duties by the citizenship.	

Source: Code of Ethics for Public Servants of the Federal Government available at http://dof.gob.mx/nota_detalle.php?codigo=5404568&fecha=20/08/2015 and the *Manual de Organización de la Empresa de Participación Estatal Mayoritaria Denominada Grupo Aeroportuario de la Ciudad de México*, S.A. DE C.V.

The GACM could redraft its current code of conduct taking into account that it will need to: *i)* outline to GACM personnel and partners what is expected of them in terms of conduct; *ii)* contribute to reinforcing integrity in the organisational culture by setting new norms; and *iii)* provide a disciplinary framework to sanction deviant behaviour. For instance, a comprehensive code of conduct could include:

1. clear mission of the organisation, as well as its values and principles and the linkages with standards of professional conduct
2. visible guidelines on probity
3. clear definitions on what constitutes a corruption risk
4. guidelines on how public servants could deal with the ethical dilemmas, prejudices and grey areas that are encountered in everyday work
5. sanctions for integrity breaches, including administrative, disciplinary and criminal.

Furthermore, acknowledging that procurement officials bear an important responsibility in maintaining integrity and ensuring a proper use of public funds, the GACM could develop specific standards for procurement officials, for example through a specific code of conduct, as is practice in other OECD countries, such as Canada (Box 4.2) or Spain (Box 4.3).

Box 4.2. **Code of conduct for procurement in Canada**

The Government of Canada is responsible for maintaining the confidence of the vendor community and the Canadian public in the procurement system, by conducting procurement in an accountable, ethical and transparent manner.

The Code of Conduct for Procurement will aid the Government in fulfilling its commitment to reform procurement, ensuring greater transparency, accountability, and the highest standards of ethical conduct. The Code consolidates the Government's existing legal, regulatory and policy requirements into a concise and transparent statement of the expectations the Government has of its employees and its suppliers.

The Code of Conduct for Procurement provides all those involved in the procurement process – public servants and vendors alike – with a clear statement of mutual expectations to ensure a common basic understanding among all participants in procurement.

The Code reflects the policy of the Government of Canada and is framed by the principles set out in the Financial Administration Act and the Federal Accountability Act. It consolidates the Federal Government's measures on conflict of interest, post-employment measures and anti-corruption as well as other legislative and policy requirements relating specifically to procurement. This Code is intended to summarise existing law by providing a single point of reference to key responsibilities and obligations for both public servants and vendors. In addition, it describes vendor complaints and procedural safeguards.

The Government expects that all those involved in the procurement process will abide by the provisions of this Code.

Source: Public Works and Government Services Canada (PWGSC), *The Code of Conduct for Procurement*, www.tpsgc-pwgsc.gc.ca/app-acq/cndt-cndct/contexte-context-eng.html (accessed 17 June 2015).

Box 4.3. **Principles and code of conduct for procurement in Spain**

With the aim of contributing to excellence in administrative activities within the area of procurement, the Office for Supervision and Evaluation of Public Procurement has compiled in this code the basic principles and good practice that have already been integrated into the day-to-day activities of the ministries of the Administration of the *Generalitat of Catalonia* and the entities that form part of its public sector. New content for establishing the code of conduct and recommendations is also contained, contributed by the Working Group for the Promotion and Improvement of Procurement Processes, constituted within the Consultative Board on Administrative Procurement of the *Generalitat of Catalonia*, the Anti-Fraud Office of Catalonia, the Catalan Competition Authority, the Association of Secretaries, Mediators and Treasurers of the Catalan Local Administration, as well as business and trade union organisations. The aim of the Code is to consolidate the code of ethics in procurement as part of the culture and values of procurement bodies. The good procurement practice included in the Code is structured in the following sections:

1. the specifying of the basic principles and ethical values that must govern the procurement process
2. the identification of specific conduct of interest with a view to drawing up the guidelines to follow in a variety of possible real specific circumstances
3. the specifying of especially interesting contractual practices
4. the raising of awareness, training and the monitoring of the ethical commitment.

With the creation of the Ethics Committee in Procurement of the *Generalitat of Catalonia*, made up of representatives from the ministries and entities of the *Generalitat of Catalonia* and belonging to the Presidency Department, a follow up and a continuous updating of the Code in the Administration of the *Generalitat* and the entities of its public sector will be carried out.

Source: Principles and Code of Conduct for Procurement, Codi de principis i conductes recomanables en la contractació pública, http://transparencia.gencat.cat/en/indicadors/contractacions_serveis/contractacio/codi_de_principis_i_conductes_recomanables_en_la_contractacio_publica/ (accessed 17 June 2015).

Investing in training and guidance

Adopting a code of conduct has a communicational aspect as it sends a strong signal that the organisation is committed to observing the highest standards of integrity and that ethical behaviour is expected from all employees (Transparency International, 2014a). Yet, adopting a code of conduct and ethical standards is a necessary step but not a sufficient one. Without support and training, an organisation risks making its code an empty and largely useless tool. Ethics or integrity training for public officials, and procurement officials in particular, can raise awareness and develop knowledge of, and commitment to, the critical elements of a culture of integrity in public organisations.

Management's support for integrity training is key to its success and provides strong motivation for the staff. Such support should be demonstrated by the actions of the leadership that sets the example and allocates adequate resources to the training. Ethics training should be designed to fit the needs of the target audience and should be as practice-oriented as possible to help participants understand the principles, the values and the grey zones (OECD, 2013b).

As of September 2015, the GACM has not provided any training on the code of conduct or on ethical standards for its staff or its procurement officials. This creates a significant integrity knowledge gap in GACM. The GACM could thus provide specific training for procurement officials on integrity, ethics and anti-corruption tools following the practice in other OECD countries, such as Germany (Box 4.4) and France (Box 4.5).

Box 4.4. **Integrity training in Germany**

The Federal Procurement Agency is a government agency which manages purchasing for 26 different federal authorities, foundations and research institutions that fall under the responsibility of the Federal Ministry of the Interior. It is the second largest federal procurement agency after the Federal Office for Defence Technology and Procurement.

The Procurement Agency has taken several measures to promote integrity among its personnel, including support and advice by a corruption prevention officer ("Contact Person for the Prevention of Corruption"), the organisation of workshops and training on corruption and the rotation of its employees.

Since 2001, it is mandatory for new staff members to participate in a corruption-prevention workshop. They learn about the risks of getting involved in bribery and the briber's possible strategies. Another part of the training deals with how to behave when these situations occur; for example, by encouraging them to report it ("blow the whistle"). Workshops highlight the central role of employees whose ethical behaviour is an essential part of corruption prevention. About ten workshops took place with 190 persons who provided positive feedback concerning the content and the usefulness of the training. The involvement of the Agency's "Contact Person for the Prevention of Corruption" and the Head of the Department for Central Services in the workshops demonstrated to participants that corruption prevention is one of the priorities for the agency. In 2005 the target group of the workshops was enlarged to include not only induction training but also ongoing training for the entire personnel. Since then, six to seven workshops are being held per year at regular intervals, training approximately 70 new and existing employees per year.

Another key corruption prevention measure is the staff rotation after a period of five to eight years in order to avoid prolonged contact with suppliers, as well as improve motivation and make the job more attractive. However, the rotation of members of staff still meets difficulties in the Agency. Due to a high level of specialisation, many officials cannot change their organisational unit, their knowledge being indispensable for the work of the unit. In these cases alternative measures such as intensified (supervisory) control are being taken.

Source: Federal Procurement Agency, Germany.

Box 4.5. **Specialised training for public procurement in France**

The Central Service of Corruption Prevention, an inter-ministerial body attached to the Ministry of Justice in France has developed training material for public procurement to help officials identify irregularities and corruption in procurement. Below is a case study excerpted from the training material, which illustrates the challenges faced by various actors at different steps of the procedure. It also highlights the difficulty of gathering evidence on irregularities and corruption.

Issue at stake

Following an open invitation to bid, an unsuccessful bidder complains to the mayor of a commune accusing the bidding panel of irregularities because his bid was lower than that submitted by the winning bidder. How should the mayor deal with the problem?

Stage 1: Checking compliance with public procurement procedures

The firm making the complaint is well known and is not considered "litigious". The mayor therefore gives its claim his attention and requests the internal audit service to check the conditions of award of contract, particularly whether the procedure was in compliance with the regulations (the lowest bidder is not necessarily the best bidder) and with the notices published in the official journal. The mayor learns from the report prepared by the bidding committee that although the procedure was in accordance with the regulations, the bid by the firm in question had been revised upwards by the technical service responsible for comparing the offers. Apparently the firm had omitted certain cost headings which were added on to its initial bid.

Stage 2: Replying to the losing bidder

The mayor lets the losing bidder know exactly why its bid was unsuccessful. However, by return post, he receives a letter pointing out that no one had informed the company of the change made to its bid, which was in fact unjustified since the expenditure which had purportedly been omitted had in fact been included in the bid under another heading.

Stage 3: Suspicions

The internal audit service confirms the unsuccessful bidder's claim and points out that nothing in the report helps to establish any grounds for the change made by the technical service. It also points out that it would be difficult for an official with any experience, however little, not to see that the expenses had been accounted for under another heading. The mayor now requests the audit service to find out whether the technical service is in the habit of making such changes, whether it has already processed bids from the winning bidder and if contracts were frequently awarded to the latter. He also requests that it check out the background of the officials concerned by the audit. Do they have experience? Have they been trained? Do they have links with the successful contractor?

Could they have had links with them in their previous posts? What do their wives and children do? Examination of the personnel files of the officials and the shares of the company which won the contract fail to find anything conclusive: the only links between the officials or their families and the successful bidder are indirect.

Stage 4: Handing the case over to authorities of the Ministry of Justice

Having suspicions, but no proof, the mayor hands over information so that investigations can begin. The investigators now have to find proof that a criminal offence (favouritism, corruption, undue advantage, etc.) has been committed and will exercise their powers to examine bank accounts, conduct hearings, surveillance, etc. The case has now moved out of the domain of public procurement regulations and into the domain of criminal proceedings.

Box 4.5. **Specialised training for public procurement in France *(continued)***

Conclusion

Unable to gather any evidence and with no authority to conduct an in-depth investigation or question the parties concerned, the mayor makes the only decision that is within his power, which is to reorganise internally and change the duties of the two members of staff concerned. However, he must proceed cautiously when giving the reasons for his decision so as to avoid exposing innocent people to public condemnation or himself to accusations of defamation while the criminal investigation is in progress.

The mayor also decides that from then on the report by the technical services to the bidding committee should give a fuller explanation of its calculations and any changes it makes to the bids, as well as systematically inform bidders of any changes.

Source: OECD (2007), *Integrity in Public Procurement: Good Practice from A to Z*, OECD Publishing, Paris, http://dx.doi.org/10.1787/9789264027510-en.

Strengthening the governance of integrity within GACM

According to the General Guidelines for the Establishment of Permanent Actions to Ensure Integrity and Ethical Behaviour of Public Officials while Performing their Duties, both the code of ethics and the code of conduct should be developed between public officials and the GACM Ethics Committee.

The General Guidelines provides that each Mexican entity must create an Ethics Committee composed of the Director of Administration (*Oficial Mayor*) as the head of the Committee, an Executive Secretary, and public officials. These public officials should be elected by the employees and they must have at least a year of service at the moment of the election. The GACM General Director must determine the number of public officials to be elected and their hierarchical level depending on the entity's structure. The Ethics Committee is the body for consultation and advice in charge of assisting on the development, implementation and enforcement of the code of conduct. The Ethics Committee held its first session on 1St July 2015, where among other things the code of conduct was approved.

An ethics committee as in the United Kingdom (Box 4.6) would be an essential step towards strengthening the integrity architecture of GACM.

Having a group of employees or even a single identified member of personnel in charge of maintaining the standards, monitoring implementation, organising trainings, communicating about the code of conduct and about corruption risks is an additional safeguard against corruption and misconduct. The GACM could as quickly as possible increase the visibility and awareness the Ethics Committee to have a better dissemination and enforcement of the code of conduct and subsequent adaptation of norms to new risks.

Box 4.6. **Committee on Standards in Public Life, United Kingdom**

The Committee on Standards in Public Life is an advisory non-departmental public body (NDPB) sponsored by the Cabinet Office. The Chair and members are appointed by the Prime Minister. The Committee was established in October 1994, by the then Prime Minister, with the following terms of reference: "to examine current concerns about standards of conduct of all holders of public office, including arrangements relating to financial and commercial activities, and make recommendations as to any changes in present arrangements which might be required to ensure the highest standards of propriety in public life."

The Committee on Standards in Public Life (CSPL) advises the Prime Minister on ethical standards across the whole of public life in the United Kingdom. It monitors and reports on issues relating to the standards of conduct of all public office holders.

The Committee is a standing Committee. It can not only conduct inquiries into areas of concern about standards in public life, but can also revisit that area and monitor whether and how well its recommendations have been put into effect.

Source: Committee on Standards in Public Life, www.gov.uk/government/organisations/the-committee-on-standards-in-public-life (accessed 13 June 2015).

Establishing conflict of interest policies for public officials, bidders, and suppliers

Public infrastructure projects, such as the new airport of Mexico, need to serve the public interest and citizens expect individual public officials involved in such projects to perform their duties with integrity, in a fair and unbiased way. Thus, officials need to ensure that their private interests and affiliations to compromise their decision making, for example in the award of contracts.

The GACM has not developed any specific policy to identify and manage conflict of interests of its officials, which creates a significant risk of decisions being taken in the interest of individuals and not in the best interest of the project and the public interest. A comprehensive conflict of interest policy following, for example, the OECD Guidelines for Managing Conflict of Interest in the Public Service would be of great benefit.

Furthermore, the GACM could also develop a Procurement Management Framework that lists situations which would be considered as a conflict of interest, and provides guidance on the steps to follow (Box 4.7).

Box 4.7. **Conflict of interest management during tender evaluation in Australia**

The Government of South Australia's Department of Planning, Transport and Infrastructure (DPTI) addresses ways to address potential and material conflict of interest situations during the procurement process through the Procurement Management Framework. It states that the DPTI staff member should notify the evaluation Panel Chairperson as soon as they notice any apparent conflict of interest situation. Even though a potential conflict of interest will not necessarily preclude a person from being involved in the evaluation process, it is declared and can be independently assessed.

It also lists situations which would be considered as a material conflict of interest of a staff in relation to a company submitting a tender including: *i)* a significant shareholding in a small private company which is submitting a tender; *ii)* having an immediate relative (e.g. son, daughter, partner, sibling) employed by a company which is tendering, even though that person is not involved in the preparation of the tender and winning the tender would have a material impact on the company; *iii)* having a relative who is involved in the preparation of the tender to be submitted by a company; *iv)* exhibiting a bias or partiality for or against a tender (e.g. because of events that occurred during a previous contract); *v)* a person, engaged under a contract to assist DPTI with the assessment, assessing a direct competitor who is submitting a tender; *vi)* regularly socialising with an employee of tenderer who is involved with the preparation of the tender; *vii)* having received gifts, hospitality or similar benefits from a tenderer in the period leading up to the call of tenders; *viii)* having recently left the employment of a tenderer; or *ix)* considering an offer of future employment or some other inducement from a tenderer.

Source: Procurement Management Framework. Confidentiality and Conflict of Interest, PR115, http://dpti.sa.gov.au/__data/assets/pdf_file/0015/114351/PR115Confidentiality_and_Conflict_of_Interest.pdf, (accessed 16 June 2015).

Moreover, in the initial phase of the procurement process, conflict of interest verification could go beyond procurement officials, and can be applied to bidders as well. This will help to limit the risk of corruption and favouritism in the procurement process. The GACM could check any potential conflicts of interest before the procurement process begins and bidders could disclose any potential conflict of interest they may have with the contracting organisation or with the other bidders (Box 4.8).

Box 4.8. **Financial disclosures and conflicts of interest: State of Illinois, United States**

The Financial Disclosures and Conflicts of Interest form ("form") must be accurately completed and submitted by the vendor, parent entity(ies), and subcontractors. There are nine steps to this form and each must be completed as instructed in the step heading and within the step. A bid, offer, or proposal that does not include this form shall be considered non-responsive. The agency/university will consider this form when evaluating the bid, offer, or proposal or awarding the contract. The form is divided into eight steps as follows:

- Step 1. Supporting documentation submittal
- Step 2. Disclosure of Financial Interest or Board of Directors
- Step 3. Disclosure of lobbyist or agent

Box 4.8. **Financial disclosures and conflicts of interest: State of Illinois, United States *(continued)***

- Step 4. Prohibited conflicts of interest
- Step 5. Potential conflicts of interest relating to personal relationships
- Step 6. Explanation of affirmative responses
- Step 7. Potential conflicts of interest relating to debarment and legal proceedings
- Step 8. Disclosure of current and pending contracts.

The requirement of disclosure of financial interests and conflicts of interest is a continuing obligation. If circumstances change and the disclosure is no longer accurate, then disclosing entities must provide an updated form. Separate forms are required for the vendor, any parent entity(ies) and any subcontractors.

Source: Financial Disclosures and Conflicts of Interest, State of Illinois, **Error! Hyperlink reference not valid.** (accessed 13 June 2015).

In order to avoid conflict of interest and ensure the integrity of the GACM's procurement processes, the Minister of Transport and Communication (SCT) has developed the following template documents:

- *Declaration of possible conflict of interest*: This document must be presented and signed by the public official in charge of the procurement procedure.
- *Survey on anti-corruption practices for the contracts on public works*: This document needs to be completed and signed by the bidder. It includes questions on the knowledge on anti-corruption legal framework; if investigations and/or sanctions have been applied to the bidder; the existence of internal anti-corruption policy and if the bidder paid bribes to participate in the bid.
- *Template for the declaration of integrity*: This document must be signed by the bidder.

Although, these documents represent a step forward to promote integrity among public officials and businesses, as of September 2015, they are still under discussion and should be extended to all contracts, not only to public works. It is important that these documents are ready before the opening for proposals. They should become mandatory and be made publicly available.

Effective prevention of corruption is not only influenced by the controls and policies implemented in an organisation, but also by its culture and prevention efforts. Active involvement and commitment from public servants is imperative to maintain an environment that stimulates integrity and rejects wrongdoing.

An open organisational culture that can foster internal reporting and facilitate the detection of wrongdoing

Given the high risks involved in the construction of the airport, the GACM could benefit from maximising opportunities to detect wrongdoing. Encouraging internal reporting can prevent and deter corruption and avoid significant losses in the project. Experience has shown, however, that those who report wrongdoing are not welcome in most organisations and are subject to reprisals by managers and colleagues. The risk of reprisals following a disclosure can be high in organisations where a reporting environment is not encouraged.

Whistleblowers take on high personal risk and can be victims to a range of retaliatory measures, such as dismissal, professional marginalisation, demotion, medical testing or examination, and transfer or reassignment. Whistleblower protection should be provided to all who carry out activities relevant to an organisation's mission. To encourage whistleblowing, there should be availability of safe and clear reporting channels and well known through the organisation, along with clear rules and procedures as well as a description of the protection provided for reporting officials to facilitate disclosures. Importantly, in addition to raising awareness about the procedures and channels involved in the disclosure process, it is essential to establish what constitutes a protected disclosure and to maintain a high degree of confidentiality throughout (Box 4.9).

Box 4.9. **Disclosable conduct as defined by the Australian Public Interest Disclosure Act 2013**

The Australian Public Interest Disclosure Act 2013 defines disclosable conduct as conduct (in Australia or in a foreign country) that contravenes the law, that constitutes maladministration, that is an abuse of public trust, that results in wastage of public money, public property, money of a prescribed authority, property of a prescribed authority, or conduct that results in danger (or a risk of danger) to the health or safety of one or more persons or the environment. In addition, disclosable conduct also includes when a public official abuses his or her position as a public official and conduct engaged in by a public official that could, if proved, give reasonable grounds for disciplinary action against the public official.

Source: Australia's Public Interest Disclosure Act 2013 Part 2 Division 2 Section 29.

If the personnel feel comfortable speaking up and confident that management will act on their disclosures and not retaliate, the lines of communication can flow better, which in turn, can foster innovation and mitigate risk-management pitfalls (CEB, 2015) Mechanisms may consist of hotlines or electronic reporting systems that ensure confidentiality as established in Austria (Box 4.10). The GACM could assess the possibility of discussing with its public personnel which channels will provide confidence to report wrongdoing.

Box 4.10. **Whistleblower hotline in Austria**

In March 2013, the Ministry of Justice set up a whistleblower hotline on the homepage of the Public Prosecutor's Office against Corruption and White Collar Crime. As of September 2013, approximately 590 notifications were sent to the platform. Only 53 of those notifications were not relevant. The whistleblower hotline has a test phase of two years.

The Federal Ministry of Justice's whistleblowing website enables investigators from the Public Prosecutor's Office against Corruption and White Collar Crime (*Zentrale Staatsanwaltschaft zur Verfolgung von Wirtschaftsstrafsachen und Korruption*; WKStA) to get in direct contact with whistleblowers, with the anonymity of the latter being assured. In that event, the whisteblower is entitled to decide whether he/she would like to remain anonymous or to identify him/herself to the investigators.

Source: Transparency International (2013), "Whistleblowing in Europe", www.transparency.de/fileadmin/pdfs/Themen/Hinweisgebersysteme/EU_Whistleblower_Report_final_web.pdf, p. 25; Shoneherr (2013), *Austria: Whistleblower Hotline is Launched Online,* www.schoenherr.eu/knowledge/knowledge-detail/austria-whistleblower-hotline-is-launched-online/.

Protecting organisations from irresponsible and unethical whistleblowing – such as false reporting or reporting as a result of spite or competitiveness between colleagues – is equally essential, as the continuous misuse of reporting could damage the reputation and career of public servants. As such, the GACM could implement training and programmes education on the notion of integrity and the purpose of reporting to encourage the correct use of these mechanisms and prevent misuse.

The GACM Internal Control Office (OIC) is responsible for providing advice, guidance and protection to people who report wrongdoing or having witnessed conflict of interest situations and integrity breaches, yet, as explained further in the chapter, the GACM does not have its own OIC, which constitutes a major gap.

Empowering the Internal Control Office

A strong and strategic Internal Control Office is urgently needed

Internal control and auditing in infrastructure projects such as the construction of the airport of Mexico is essential because of the high corruption risks associated with these activities. Just as corruption risk mapping and management, internal control and audits contribute to the general understanding of the risk environment in which the project operates and provide the necessary tools to protect the project from those risks. Both preventive and detective controls can examine the financial situation, the performance of the entity and the compliance to laws and norms.

As other entities of the Mexican Federal Government, GACM's internal control functions are subject to the rules set by the Ministry of Public Administration (*Secretaría de la Función Pública*, SFP). SFP is responsible for defining the internal regulations of the Government, including federal entities' internal audit and control procedures, to ensure compliance with regulations on planning, budgeting, financing and investment. From this perspective, it organises and co-ordinates the governmental control and evaluation system to ensure that internal control methodologies are standardised and streamlined across federal entities and to designate the head of the OIC in each entity.

Despite the key role of the OIC to ensure transparency and integrity in the process and continuous improvements in the GACM, only at the beginning of October 2015 the GACM OIC was appointed. Previously, the GACM was under the OIC of the Ministry of Transport and Communications. During this time, the extent of its involvement was unclear and not significant. During the fact-finding mission, it was explained that for example, there was not a yearly audit plan defined. However, the GACM has been audited by the external auditor appointed by SFP on the financial statements and by ASF on the financial processes and the contracts carried out in 2014.

The OIC is important not only to ensure the integrity of the procurement process but also to guarantee that the GACM processes and procedures are adequately carried out and tailored to the specificity of the project. Due to this specificity, it is important that the OIC plays the role of an advisory body which supports GACMs procurement unit in striving for greater effectiveness and efficiency in their activities. Previous evidence from Reviews of the Mexican procurement systems in various entities suggests that the lack of communication and audits based on compliance rather than performance hinders the public official potential to innovate.

In this aspect, to move from compliance to performance and reduce the public officials' resistance to use allowed but no common procurement instruments, the GACM procurement units and the OIC could work closely with the SFP's *Mesa de acompañamiento*. SFP's *Mesa de acompañamiento* is carried out by the Regulatory Unit on Goods, Public Works, Services and Federal Assets (*Unidad de Normatividad de Adquisiciones, Obras Públicas, Servicios y Patrimonio Federal,* UNAOPSPF). The activity is intended as an interactive, preventive, multidisciplinary and specific consultancy process that takes place throughout the steps of a public procurement process (i.e. planning, programming, budgeting, negotiation, spending, and/or execution). The choice of the project is subject to the project's amount, strategic importance, presumption of lack of transparency and fairness, past discretion in similar processes, as well as its national and international impact. The objective is to review all the steps of the project's development and propose and implement improvements to strengthen the transparency, impartiality and legal provisions of every step of the procurement process. Although it was explained during the fact-finding mission the limited capacity of the SFP to carry out this type of activity, the GACM could explore a way of collaborating and working together with the SFP in order to carry out the activity for GACM's more complex procurements.

Integrity of the procurement process reduces corruption risks in all phases of the cycle

Integrity in public procurement is crucial to ensure that the construction project is adequately managed and meets the highest quality standards. A lack of integrity during the public procurement process is an obstacle to market competition, raises costs for the administration, directly affecting public expenditures and therefore taxpayers' resources (OECD, 2009). There is a number of corruption risks associated with the different stages of the procurement cycle (Table 4.2).

Table 4.2. **Corruption risks associated with the different stages of the procurement cycle**

Phase	Stage	Risks
Risks of the pre-tendering phase	Needs assessment	• Lack of adequate needs assessment • Influence of external actors on officials' decisions • Informal agreement on contract
	Planning and budgeting	• Poor procurement planning • Procurement not aligned with overall investment decision-making process • Failure to budget realistically or deficiency in the budget
	Development of specifications/ requirements	• Technical specifications are tailored for a specific company • Selection criteria is not objectively defined and no established in advance • Requesting samples of goods and services that can influence • Buying information on the project specifications.
Risks of the tendering phase	Choice of procurement procedure	• Lack of procurement integrity for the use of non-competitive procedures • Abuse of non-competitive procedures on the basis of legal exceptions: contract splitting, abuse of extreme urgency, non-supported modifications
	Request for proposal/bid	• Absence of public notice for the invitation to bid • Evaluation and award criteria are not announced • Procurement information is disclosed and made public
	Bid submission	• Lack of competition or cases of collusive bidding: – cover bidding – bid suppression – bid rotation – market allocation
	Bid evaluation	• Conflict of interest and corruption in the evaluation process through: – familiarity with bidders over time – personal interests such as gifts or future/additional employment – no effective implementation of the "four eyes-principle"
	Contract award	• Vendors fail to disclose accurate cost or pricing data in their price proposals, resulting in an increased contract price (i.e. invoice mark-ups, channel stuffing) • Conflict of interest and corruption in the approval process (i.e. no effective separation of financial, contractual and project authorities) • Lack access to records on the procedure
Risks of the post-award phase	Contract management/ performance	• Abuses of the supplier in performing the contract, in particular in relation to its quality, price and timing: – substantial change in contract conditions to allow more time and/ or higher prices for the bidder – product substitution or sub-standard work or service not meeting contract specifications – theft of new assets before delivery to end-user or before being recorded – deficient supervision from public officials and/or collusion between contractors and supervising officials – subcontractors and partners chosen in an on-transparent way or not kept accountable
	Order and payment	• Deficient separation of financial duties and/or lack of supervision of public officials leading to: – false accounting and cost misallocation or cost migration between contracts – late payments of invoices – false or duplicate invoicing for good and services not supplied and for interim payment in advance entitlement

Mapping and mitigating corruption risks in the procurement process

Assessing corruption risks is a preventive exercise that serves to identify weaknesses within the system that could create opportunities for corruption to occur. Corruption risk mapping serves to identify the level of potential risk, to inform anti-corruption strategies and to address weak areas in a governance system. Developing a corruption risk map at an early stage of a project can save both resources and time by allowing management to implement measures to protect the project from corruption and help employees respond quickly and efficiently to potential cases (Control Risks, 2011). Preventing corruption *a priori* is more cost-efficient and less time-consuming than having to handle corruption and misconduct *a posteriori*.

The risk map developed and provided by the GACM does not include corruption as a risk. The risk map does not identify or address corruption or other integrity breaches such as contract splitting, bid rigging, improper use of exceptions, inadequate bid evaluation or tailored specifications. As a consequence, the GACM has not put in place red flags or alert mechanisms that may help to timely detect wrongdoing.

The GACM has not conducted a mapping of corruption risks, thus it could develop a corruption risk map of the organisation and its processes in order to identify the positions of officials that are particularly vulnerable, the activities in the procurement cycle where risks can arise, and the specific projects at risk due to the value and complexity of the procurement. The GACM could base its risk map on the checklist of potential risks in the public works, goods and services procurement process carried out by the government of Tasmania in Australia (Box 4.11).

Box 4.11. **Tasmania's (Australia) checklist of potential risks in the goods and services procurement process**

The Tasmanian government developed a checklist of potential risks in the procurement cycle that is composed of 11 parts:

1. identifying the need and planning the purchase
2. developing the specification
3. selecting the purchasing method
4. purchasing documentation
5. inviting, clarifying and closing offers
6. evaluating offers
7. selecting the successful tenderer
8. negotiations
9. contract management
10. evaluating the procurement process
11. disposals.

Box 4.11. **Tasmania's (Australia) checklist of potential risks in the goods and services procurement process *(continued)***

For instance, these are the risks identified for the first phase:

Risk	Likely consequences	Action
Understatement of the need	Purchase of unsuitable product or service Money wasted Need not satisfied	Analyse need accurately
Overstatement of the need	Greater expense Poor competition	Analyse need accurately Use functional performance requirements
Misinterpretation of user needs	Totally unacceptable purchase or not most suitable product or service Time lost Increased costs Possible downtime	Improve consultation with users Obtain clear statement of work and definition of need
Insufficient funding	Delay in making the purchase Additional costs for re-tender	Obtain appropriate approvals before undertaking process Improve planning
Impractical timeframe	Inadequate responses from tenderers Reduced competition Delivery schedule not met	Improve forecasting, planning and consultation with users Improve communication with potential tenderers
Probity issues	Increased procurement costs Misuse of resources Most suitable product not obtained Unethical conduct	Implement best practice policies, guidelines and practices Maintain ethical environment Improve training of personnel Put suitable controls and reviews in place Consider using a probity adviser Improve communication with potential tenderers

Source: Tasmanian Government, "Checklist of potential risks in the goods and services procurement process", www.purchasing.tas.gov.au/buyingforgovernment/getpage.jsp?uid=07CC4222E4F10F00CA256C8D007F9FC6.

Once the risk map has been designed, the GACM could use a system of red flags. These are standardised warning signs that stretch over the whole procurement cycle and that assist in the detection of wrongdoing in a timely manner, avoiding significant delays between the time when the wrongdoing occurs and when it is noticed. The GACM could benefit from the red flags identified by the World Bank and by the Chartered Institute of Public Finance and Accountancy (Box 4.12).

Box 4.12. **Examples of red flags for procurement corruption**

World Bank red flags of fraud and corruption in procurement

1. Complaint from bidders or other parties
2. Multiple contracts below procurement threshold
3. Unusual bid patterns
4. Seemingly inflated agent fees
5. Suspicious bidder

Box 4.12. **Examples of red flags for procurement corruption *(continued)***

6. Lowest bidder not selected
7. Repeated awards to the same contractor
8. Changes in contract terms and value
9. Multiple contract change orders
10. Poor quality works and/or services

Chartered Institute of Public Finance and Accountancy red flags

- Physical losses
- Manipulation of data
- Incomplete management/audit trail
- Budget overspends
- Unusual invoices (e.g. format, numbers, address, phone, VAT number)
- Duplicate/photocopy invoice
- Round sum amounts invoiced
- Sequential invoice numbers over an extended period of time
- Non-declaration of interest/gifts/hospitality
- No process identifying risks (e.g. risk register)
- Unusual relationship with suppliers
- Photocopied documents
- IT-controls of audit logs disabled
- IT-login outside working hours
- Vague description of goods/services to be supplied
- High number of failed IT logins
- Favoured customer treatment
- Interest/ownership in external organisation
- Lack of supporting records
- Unusual increases/decreases

Source: World Bank, "Most common red flags of fraud and corruption in procurement", http://siteresources.worldbank.org/INTDOII/Resources/Red_flags_reader_friendly.pdf; OECD (2013), *Public Procurement Review of the State's Employees' Social Security and Social Services Institute in Mexico*, OECD Public Governance Reviews, OECD Publishing. http://dx.doi.org/10.1787/9789264197305-en.

Furthermore, the GACM could develop an integrity plan to facilitate the development of mitigation strategies following the mapping of specific corruption risks and thus ensure that all parties involved in the process are aware of existing integrity risks and mechanisms as well as their own responsibilities (Box 4.13).

Box 4.13. **Australia's procurement probity plans**

Australia's Procurement Transformation Division has developed a procurement guidance document that provides that a probity plan should be prepared before the commencement of each procurement process and forms part of procurement planning documentation. It should identify the probity risks and related management strategies for the procurement, including the role and responsibilities of each stakeholder in responding to those risks. Where the procurement is part of a broader project, the probity plan should be agreed with the project's governing body and management.

As part of the probity plan, a description should be provided of the probity services that are to be sourced, including whether a probity auditor and/or probity advisor is to be engaged, and the scope and nature of the probity services that will be delivered. All members involved in the procurement, or project, including the steering committee, advisors and other project stakeholders should be aware of arrangements put in place to preserve the probity of the process and should be provided with a copy of the probity plan.

Box 4.13. **Australia's procurement probity plans *(continued)***

In those procurement situations where more than one agency is involved in different elements of the procurement process, it is essential that the roles and responsibilities in relation to probity be addressed within the probity plan to ensure that accountabilities are clear and that governance practices are in place. The responsibility for probity remains with the agency to which funds have been appropriated. Where this agency engages service providers (Government or private) to engage in procurement activities on its behalf, it should require those providers to meet its (the agency's) responsibility and particular requirements regarding probity. However, this does not transfer the responsibility for probity to the service provider, which remains with the agency.

Source: Procurement Transformation Division (2014), "Procurement guidance - Use of probity auditors and advisors in procurement", www.hpw.qld.gov.au/SiteCollectionDocuments/ProcurementGuideProbityAuditorsAdvisors.pdf (accessed 19 June 2015).

The GACM could use additional tools to avoid integrity risks during the procurement process

Social witnesses and social observers

One way to face corruption risks is to create an interactive relationship with civil society through which they can take part in policy making and carry out a "direct social control" on government activities. In this context, Mexico is one of the first OECD countries to have introduced such controls through the involvement of so-called "social witnesses" in the procurement processes, who are legally required to participate in all stages of public tendering procedures above certain thresholds. In 2015, these thresholds are MXN 350 million (approximately USD 23 million) for goods and services and MXN 710 million (approximately USD 47 million) for public works.[5]

Social witnesses are elected by SFP through public tendering and when a federal entity requires the involvement of a social witness, SFP designates one from the preselected pool. Following their participation in procurement procedures, social witnesses issue a final report providing comments and recommendations on the process. These reports must subsequently be published on the Mexican federal e-procurement platform (CompraNet).

Social witnesses may also participate in public tendering procedures below the legal threshold, direct award procedures and restricted tendering if it is considered appropriate by SFP. During the field mission, GACM indicated that they were currently using social witnesses below the legal threshold - above MXN 100 million, approximately USD 6.5 million in the case of public works - as a way to promote public scrutiny and ensure the integrity of the process. However, this procedure is not institutionalised and is used on an ad hoc basis. The Public Works Procurement Manual of GACM only makes reference to the use of social witnesses in relation to the thresholds established by law. As of September 2015, the GACM has used 4 social witnesses for procedures ranging between USD 1.2 million and USD 6.6 million. This lack of institutionalisation may open the door to discretion in the decision as to whether to include or not a social witness in procurement procedures below the legal threshold. In addition, this initiative has only been applied to public works; it may be worthwhile to extend it to the procurement of goods and particularly services. The GACM could establish in its procurement manuals the mandatory involvement of social witnesses or clear rules to define whether or not it is necessary to include social witnesses below the legal thresholds.

Furthermore, along with the use of social witnesses as a way for civil society to participate, GACM has established other useful instruments such as the use of so-called "social observers" to participate in tender procedures. Higher education institutions, schools or professional institutes, are now invited by the GACM to participate in the elaboration of the tender documents independently of the participation of one or more social witnesses. For this, GACM has created a memorandum of agreement with different higher education institutions and industrial associations such as the Engineering Institute of the National Autonomous University of Mexico (*Instituto de Ingeniería de la UNAM*). GACM also reports that in the near future they will enter into a similar agreement with the Society of Alumni of the School of Engineering of the National Autonomous University of Mexico (*Sociedad de Egresados de la Facultad de Ingeniería de la UNAM*).

Involving the private sector

Wrongdoing and breaches of integrity are sometimes a two-way street where not only public officials are involved. The role of the private sector is critical to maintaining the integrity of the process. In this sense, the Mexican procurement law provides that bidders under public tendering procedures must sign a declaration of integrity and provide a written statement that they are not subject to any conditions under the law preventing them from being awarded a contract. However, the declaration is not made public. A simple way to reinforce this tool would be for the GACM to publish the signed declarations of bidders on its website. The SCT has recently developed a template Declaration of Integrity, however as of September 2015 the template has not yet been put in place.

Although the GACM does not have the leading role in Mexico in developing integrity and accountability standards for businesses, it could engage with certain suppliers to explore ways to encourage them to develop their own standards and programmes to enhance integrity in their relationship with GACM, e.g. through mechanisms similar to the US Construction Industry Ethics and Compliance Initiative (CIECI), (Box 4.14).

Box 4.14. **The Construction Industry Ethics and Compliance Initiative in the United States**

The Construction Industry Ethics and Compliance Initiative (CIECI) is a non-profit private association that brings together more than 50 companies in the US construction industry to establish a process for the industry to promote integrity and ethical conduct.

The construction industry is the United States' largest industry, ranging from building contractors who construct homes, schools, hospitals, sky scrapers and shopping centres to the heavy construction industry that builds power plants, highways, bridges, airports, dams, water treatment facilities and the like. Vast and diverse, the construction industry consists of architect/engineers, contractors and subcontractors who tend to specialise. The essential goals of the initiative are the advancement of organisational cultures that encourage and support ethical behaviour and compliance with the law, and the sharing of best ethical and compliance practices within the industry.

Box 4.14. **The Construction Industry Ethics and Compliance Initiative in the United States *(continued)***

The Initiative requires each signatory company to pledge to follow six core ethical principles, to adhere to these principles, and to participate in an Annual Best Practices Forum to discuss best ethical and business conduct practices among its members and with representatives from government and other organisations. The core principles are:

- Each member shall have and adhere to a written Code of Business Conduct. The Code shall establish high ethical values and compliance with the law applicable to the US construction industry.
- Each member shall train its personnel as to their personal responsibilities under the Code.
- Each member commits itself to work together toward maintaining open competition in the industry, free of conflicts of interest and undue influences.
- Each member shall be responsible for sharing best ethical and compliance practices in implementing the principles with others.
- Each member shall participate in the Annual Best Practices Forum.
- Each member, through participation in this Initiative, shall be accountable to the public.

Source: Construction Industry Ethics and Compliance Initiative, www.ciecinitiative.org/Faqs (accessed 18 June 2015).

Bidding documents standardisation

Another way to promote integrity in the procurement process is to standardise all bidding documents and procurement documentation to ensure predictability and systematic treatment. If non-standard bidding documents are used instead, it opens the door to manipulation and leads to opaque decision making (Transparency International, 2006). Considering that the tender documents cannot be standardised due to the complexity of the project and the specificity of works, goods and services that the GACM needs to procure, as far as possible other documents need to be standardised, such as bidding letters, template forms for the technical and economic proposals, statements of integrity as the ones currently being developed by SCT, etc.

The two-envelope approach

Furthermore, the GACM could implement the two-envelope approach to ensure that procurement decisions are taken according to the set criteria. During a bidding procedure using a two-envelope approach, bidders submit two sealed envelopes simultaneously, one with the technical proposal and the other with the economic proposal. Only the technical proposals are opened at the date and time indicated in the bidding document. The economic proposals remain sealed and are held in custody by the buyer (Asian Development Bank, 2015). The advantage of this approach is that the buyer can evaluate bids based solely on the technical requirements and proposals, without having any information about the cost. This excludes inadequate bids from the beginning, which contributes to ensuring good quality infrastructure and makes the competition fairer. This approach is used for example in the Slovak Republic (Box 4.15).

Box 4.15. **Two-envelope system used in the bids submission phase in the Slovak Republic**

Two substantial amendments to the Act No. 25/2006 Coll., on Public Procurement became effective in 2013. In the bids submission phase of the procurement cycle, the one-stage tender process has been replaced by a two-stage tender, involving a "two-envelope system".

Bids in the tenders are to be submitted in two parts: the "Criteria" part contains the offer with respect to the award criteria, i.e. in most cases only the price; while the "Other" part contains all other documentation and information related to the bid. The "Other" part is opened first and only after evaluation of whether the selection criteria (e.g. technical equipment) have been met can the "Criteria" part of all submitted bids be opened and evaluated. Generally, such a two-stage process should ensure that the price does not influence the technical evaluation of the bid.

Source: "Substantial changes in public procurement in Slovakia", www.schoenherr.eu/knowledge/knowledge-detail/slovakia-substantial-changes-in-public-procurement-every-detail-counts/ (accessed 18 June 2015).

The four-eyes principle

A standard practice to encourage collective decisions in the procurement process is the four-eyes principle, or the two-person rule. It requires that at least two people take part in any decision making. It should apply to all phases of the procurement cycle, and beyond, from the needs assessment to the design of projects and selection of bidders. The four-eyes principle limits public officials' discretionary power, ensures a certain level of deliberation and protects public officials from suspicion. The GACM could implement the four-eyes principle as carried out during the construction of the Tappan Zee Bridge Project, New York State, United States (Box 4.16).

Integrity monitor

Going beyond internal practices, there are initiatives that encourage all parties to a bidding process to make a mutual pledge under the oversight of an observer who would later monitor compliance. Guaranteeing oversight and preferably in the long term is an efficient way to prevent mismanagement and reassure the public that state funds are put to good use. Including an integrity monitor in a large infrastructure project allows for a comprehensive and constant oversight of the construction and management.

Box 4.16. **Four-eyes principle used in the Tappan Zee Bridge Project, New York State, United States**

The "four-eyes" principle is a requirement that two individuals review and approve some action before it can be taken. For the construction of the Tappan Zee Bridge in the State of New York, several teams were set up to ensure the respect of the four-eyes principle and the fairness of the selection process during the procurement phase:

- A Procurement Management Team, comprised of a team of public and private employees, responsible for directing the overall evaluation and selection process.
- A Legal Team, comprised of legal advisors, both public and private to conduct a legal pass/fail analysis of aspects of the proposals and provide guidance throughout the procurement process.
- A Financial Team to perform a financial pass/fail review and a net present value analysis of the price proposals.
- A Price Reasonableness Team to conduct reviews of each of the proposals and provide recommendations regarding the reasonableness of the pricing for each of the proposals.
- A Technical Evaluation Teams to evaluate the technical strengths and weaknesses of each proposal.
- A Value Assessment Team comprised of engineers and other professionals from both the public and private sectors, to assemble all of the reports for each proposer, and where feasible, use the accumulated reports to quantify the technical strengths and weaknesses of each proposal.
- A Blue Ribbon Selection Committee to present a non-binding recommendation to the Selection Executives. A Bridge Design Aesthetic Team, comprised of artists and architects, to review the proposed bridge designs and assist in the evaluation process.
- A group of Selection Executives comprised of the members of the Major Projects Committee of the Thruway Authority's Board, to review the selection and findings of the BRSC. The ultimate determination to award a contract was made by the full NYSTA Board.

Source: "Report of the Independent Procurement Integrity Monitor", www.newnybridge.com/documents/int-monitor-report.pdf (accessed 19 June 2015).

As opposed to social witnesses who concentrate on one phase of the cycle, the integrity monitor follows the entire process, including procurement, contract management, fiscal oversight, records compliance and onsite construction monitoring. Corruption and mismanagement can stem from lack of information and internal communication. An integrity monitor following the entire process would thus contribute to reducing such risks. The GACM could explore the possibility of designating an integrity monitor who can follow the entire procurement cycle, as used during the Tappan Zee Bridge Project (Box 4.17).

Box 4.17. **Integrity monitor, Tappan Zee Bridge Project, New York State, United States**

In order to counter the corruption risks associated with the Design-Build model of the Tappan Zee Bridge project, it was decided to retain an independent procurement integrity monitor for this project. The Governor's office and the NYSTA determined to address the tension between the need, on the one hand, for confidentiality in the evaluation of the proposals and negotiations with the proposers versus, on the other hand, the need for transparency in the decisions surrounding the expenditure of public funds, by having an independent firm, outside of the procurement process itself, monitor compliance with the controls governing that process.

The objectives of the integrity monitor included process evaluation, process enhancements and compliance monitoring. In order to achieve these ends, it was entitled to: *i)* obtain and review selected documentation relating to integrity and security of the procurement process; *ii)* make recommendations for enhancements of the process to appropriate personnel; *iii)* perform monitoring through: unannounced attendance at meetings selected on a random basis; review of documents produced by the procurement process; interview with those involved in process; physical observation of compliance with all critical security/integrity-related controls; communication with appropriate personnel as to any issues found so as to facilitate immediate remediation; and *iv)* prepare a final report.

Source: Thacher Associates, "Tappan Zee Hudson River Crossing Project: Report of the Independent Procurement Integrity Monitor", www.newnybridge.com/documents/int-monitor-report.pdf (accessed 19 June 2015).

Safeguarding the integrity of the whole procurement process including in outsourced services and subcontracting

When an organisation invests in its integrity framework, it is essential to develop mechanisms to ensure that the standards it has set for itself apply to all its contractors and subcontractors as well, so as to guarantee that the reputation and image of the organisation will not be tarnished by the behaviour of contracted partners.

Making sure that all partners involved in a project maintain high integrity, transparency and accountability standards is highly beneficial for the organisation and is essential to preventing corruption risks that would reflect badly on the public administration. Requiring contracted partners to apply the same norms and ethical standards creates a level playing field that allows for better and clearer collaboration and facilitates management.

Consultants and advisors might specifically face a number of ethical dilemmas in the course of their relationship with their clients. The particular nature of their work may very well put confidential and privileged information at their disposal, which may be misused.

There is a risk of conflicts of interests occurring and of creating a dependency between consultants and clients, which could compromise the integrity of the consultancy services and introduce a bias in the selection of future consultants (Transparency International, 2011).

Due to the limited capacity of the GACM and the short timeframe to carry out the procurement processes, a great number of activities are being outsourced. For instance, the GACM has outsourced staff that have no legal or labour obligation with the GACM; consultancy firms may advise on the design or revision of tender documents; and most probably, contractors will subcontract part of their activities.[6]

It is thus of outmost importance, that while entering in contractual relationships with consultants and other partners, particularly in connection to the procurement process, GACM makes sure its internal integrity mechanisms apply to them as much as it applies to GACM personnel. Alternatively, special integrity mechanisms could be developed specially for them as carried out by the US House of Representatives (Box 4.18).

Box 4.18. **US House of Representatives' ethics clauses for consultants**

Beyond integrity clauses integrated into consultant agreements, some organisations recommend that consultants be considered as employees and as such require that they abide to the organisation's code of conduct and overall ethical rules and regulations.

The US House of Representatives, for example, subjects consultants to the House's ethical clauses, including those pertaining to gift acceptance, undue influence exerted on the consultant, discrimination, etc. (US House of Representatives Committee on Ethics, n.d.). Consultants are required to execute an oath of confidentiality before receiving access to classified information. In addition to these rules, consultants are also prohibited from engaging in certain lobbying activities, such as lobbying the contracting committee on any matter. Consultants are also subject to the House's gift rules governing the acceptance of anything having monetary value such as services, travels, meals, tickets, sporting events, shows, etc.

While the House's rules do not require consultants to file public financial disclosure statements given the short term nature of their services, the Ethics Committee strongly recommends that each committee, before entering into a consulting contract, obtain some basic financial information on the individual's source of income, the type of income and the rate at which he is compensated, the identity of each client for whom he is providing services, the nature and value of any investment and liability held by the individual that could be affected by the services provided to the committee. These recommendations are intended to allow monitoring of the consultant's compliance with conflict of interest rules.

Source: U4 (2011), "Examples of integrity agreements for consultants and advisors", U4 Anti-Corruption Resource Centre, Chr. Michelsen Institute, Bergen, Norway, www.u4.no/publications/examples-of-integrity-agreements-for-consultants-and-advisors (accessed 22 June 2015).

In addition, the GACM code of conduct can be applicable to all those involved in the procurement process as it is the practice in Queensland, Australia (Box 4.19) or include specific provisions in the consultancy agreements, such as: *i)* confidentiality; *ii)* prevention of bribery; *iii)* declaration of interest; and *iv)* a declaration of ethical commitment, as is the case in Hong Kong (Box 4.20).

Box 4.19. **Code of Conduct for the Queensland (Australia) Public Service**

Application

This code applies to employees of Queensland public service agencies. Public service agencies are defined under the Public Sector Ethics Act 1994 as:

- a department
- a TAFE institute or statutory TAFE institute
- the administrative office of a court or tribunal
- an entity prescribed by regulation.

For the purposes of this document only, employees (other than judicial officials), are defined as:

- any Queensland public service employee whether permanent, temporary, full-time, part-time or casual
- any volunteer, student, contractor, consultant or anyone who works in any other capacity for Queensland public service agency.

The code applies at all times when we are performing official duties including when we are representing the Queensland Government at conferences, training events, on business trips and attending work-related social events.

Source: www.psc.qld.gov.au/includes/assets/qps-code-conduct.pdf (accessed 13 June 2015).

Box 4.20. **Ethical commitment clauses for inclusion in consultancy agreements: Hong Kong's ICAC Best Practice Checklist**

Hong Kong's Best Practice Checklist aims at providing organisations with a user friendly and step-by-step procedural guide, with recommendations on safeguards to minimise corruption risks, for the employment of consultants and monitoring of their services. Organisations are expected to adapt the recommended safeguards to suit their organisational structure, resources, risk exposures, and any statutory requirements applicable to the works projects.

Ethical commitment clauses for inclusion in the consultancy agreements have four major areas of focus, including: *i)* confidentiality; *ii)* prevention of bribery; *iii)* declaration of interest; and *iv)* a declaration of ethical commitment.

- The confidentiality clause commits the consultant not to disclose information such as the terms of the agreement or any report, document, specification, software, data, etc., to outsiders, whether they are furnished by the employer or generated by the consultant.
- The prevention of bribery clauses require consultants to prohibit their directors, agents, sub-contractors or staff involved in the agreement from offering, soliciting or accepting any advantage as defined in the Hong Kong's Prevention of Bribery ordinance. Consultants should also caution their staff from soliciting or accepting excessive hospitality, entertainment or inducement that may compromise their impartiality in relation to the assignment.

Box 4.20. **Ethical commitment clauses for inclusion in consultancy agreements: Hong Kong's ICAC Best Practice Checklist *(continued)***

- The declaration of interest clause commits the consultant to declare in writing any conflict of interest or potential conflict between their personal/financial interest and their duties in connection with the agreement.
- The declaration of ethical commitment clauses consist of a declaration of compliance with the confidentiality and prevention of bribery clauses in a form provided by the contracting authority when requesting payment of services. Payment can be withheld until the consultant submits the signed declaration.

The checklist provides sample forms that can be adopted or adapted where applicable. It includes sample codes of conduct with report forms on gifts received, declaration of conflict of interest, sample probity, anti-collusion and debarment clauses as well as declaration forms on compliance.

The checklist can be found here: www.icac.org.hk/filemanager/en/Content_1031/manworkconsult.pdf.

Source: U4 (2011), "Examples of integrity agreements for consultants and advisors", U4 Anti-Corruption Resource Centre, Chr. Michelsen Institute, Bergen, Norway, www.u4.no/publications/examples-of-integrity-agreements-for-consultants-and-advisors/ (accessed on 22 June 2015).

Enhancing transparency and access to information in the construction of the new airport

Going beyond the law: Proactive disclosure of public procurement and project information

Proactive disclosure of procurement and project information and documents promotes a culture of openness around the project and ensures that procedures and decisions may be widely monitored, commented upon and influenced by relevant stakeholders. Conversely, lack of transparency or selective information can hide corruption and manipulation, and is increasingly perceived as doing so. Knowing about the rationale behind an infrastructure project as well as the level of budget allocation and technical specificities can help the public better understand the Government's choice. Therefore, transparency should be seen as an opportunity to enhance trust and get buy-in for the project.

Giving the public a clear and consistent channel to access information could strengthen public trust in GACM's various projects. In Mexico, the law makes the proactive disclosure of information mandatory for a wide range of areas including on the structure of the entity and its procurement. In 2007, Mexico entrenched access to information as a fundamental right through constitutional amendments. The National Institute of Transparency, Access to Information and Data Protection (*Instituto Nacional de Transparencia, Acceso a la Información y Protección de Datos*, INAI)-former IFAI-was established by law to effectively guarantee citizens' access to information. INAI also ensures that information is proactively published and disseminated. According to INAI data, between January and September 2015, the GACM has received 80 requests for information, 10% of which have been appealed.

These numbers reflect the fact that the GACM has taken its obligation regarding transparency seriously. In this light, the Transparency and Accountability Unit at the GACM should perform the following functions:

- collect and disseminate the information of the "Portal of transparency obligations", and encourage the administrative units to update it regularly
- receive and process requests for access to information
- assist citizens in the development of applications and, in case, orient them towards the departments, entities or any other body that might have the information they request
- perform the internal procedures of each unit or entity, necessary to deliver the requested information, in addition to performing the notifications to citizens
- enable the public servants of the unit or entity as are necessary, to receive and process requests for access to information
- keep a record of the applications for access to information, their results and costs.

In addition, the unit puts forward to the Information Committee the internal procedures to ensure greater efficiency in the management of the access to information requests. This does not exist, however, inside the GACM. Due to the specificity of the project and the national security dimension, some information will not be publicly available. This unit together with the Information Committee could proactively establish guidelines on what kind of information will be disclosed. These guidelines could be published on the GACM website and could explain the main provisions of the Federal Transparency and Access to Government Public Information Act in plain language, especially that which is related to confidential information.

It may be helpful to consider the Guide to Open Government 2.0 (OGP, 2013) which establishes that an organisation should identify the core classes of information to be disclosed, including:

- *Contracts*, including licenses, concessions, permits, grants or any other document exchanging public goods, assets, or resources (including all annexes, schedules and documents incorporated by reference) and any amendments.
- *Related documents* such as pre-studies, standard bid documents, performance evaluations, guarantees, and auditing reports.
- *Key pieces of information concerning contract formation*, including the planning process, method of award, scope and specifications for each contract, criteria for evaluation and selection, bidders or participants in the process, their validation documents, and any procedural exemptions for which they qualify, any conflicts of interest uncovered or debarments issued, results of the evaluation, including the justification for the award, and the identity of the contract recipient and any statements of beneficial ownership provided.
- *Information related to performance of the contract*, including subcontracting arrangements, schedules and milestones, status of implementation, dates and amounts of stage payments made or received, service delivery and pricing, arrangements for ending contracts, final settlements and responsibilities, risk assessments, including environmental and social impact assessments, assessments of assets and liabilities of government, provisions in place to ensure appropriate

management of ongoing risks and liabilities, and appropriate financial information regarding revenues and expenditures, such as time and cost overruns.

Furthermore, in February 2015, the INAI and the GACM worked together in a programme to "Ensure transparency and access to information in the infrastructure project known as the new international Airport of Mexico City". Although, the Programme was never formalised the GACM and/or the INAI are working among others on the following actions:

- INAI provide training to public servants and citizens through its online platform and workshops.
- The GACM website will be able to transmit online the opening of bids
- Implementation of a request for information scorecard
- Implementing a model document for the management of Transparency and Access to Information networks. To respond to this action, recently the GACM hired an expert on managing archives.
- Implement a working group in which officials of the different entities comprising the airport sector participate. They meet upon request of the SCT.
- Publication of the asset declaration of the senior management of the institutions involved in the process of building the NAICM in order for citizens to be aware of changes on the assets of the top decision-makers. This has been a difficult action to be implemented as does not have reached consensus in the public administration.

Providing citizens with access to information is an important yet often time-consuming task. Offering access to information thus requires adequate financial and human resources to allow for a dedicated service with sufficient staff to fulfil the task. The GACM could consider reinforcing its structure to be able to keep up to its transparency and access to information requirements.

The public procurement information provided in the GACM website is insufficient

Although the GACM has been disclosing information, the quality and availability of data on its procurement processes remains uneven, therefore making access to easily understandable, up-to-date and complete information difficult for citizens and suppliers. While GACM has taken an important step forward by making a considerable amount of information publicly available and has advanced on this front since the beginning of the project, areas for improvement remain.

The GACM has published what has been procured (Figure 4.1). It seems that this information only relates to the construction of the airport *per se* and not on other related activities of the GACM. According to this information, no contracts were awarded for goods, while the annual plan for goods and services may indicate the contrary (see www.aeropuerto.gob.mx/gacm/programas-anuales.php). In addition to what is procured, GACM is currently publishing a list of contracts and suppliers. As of September 2015, only nine contracts and nine suppliers were published. Yet, when compared to the Mexican federal e-procurement platform (CompraNet), at least 83 contracts have been concluded.[7] The discretion in the publication of contracts lowers the perceived transparency of the project. The GACM could, as a consequence, publish all the procurement information not only related to the airport but also to the functioning of the GACM.

Figure 4.1. **Snapshot of GACM procurement information (USD)**

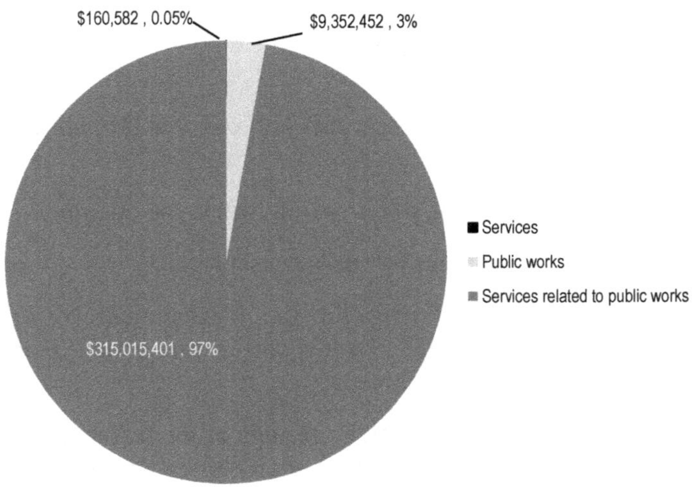

Note: The calculation in USD was based on USD 1≈MXN 17.05, as of 28 September 2015.

Source: Extracted from the GACM website, www.aeropuerto.gob.mx/gacm/que-se-ha-comprado.php (accessed 28 September 2015).

In addition, the GACM could publish procurement information by the type of procedure used in terms of numbers and in terms of value, as is normally carried out in many OECD countries (Box 4.5). Moreover, to avoid any misinterpretation, the GACM could consider providing clear definitions of the procurement procedures and the most common exceptions to public bidding that are foreseen.

Furthermore, the GACM website provides information about future procurements or procurement plans. However, this information, in PDF format, does not provide a clear timeframe for the procurement of goods and it is not possible to view the ongoing processes or how the procurement processes are conducted in relation to the procurement plans. The GACM could consider publishing the procurements plan in a usable format that can allow distinguishing from what was already procured, what is currently being procured and what will be procured in the future.

Although CompraNet may provide most of this information, it has been evidenced from previous OECD reviews that often CompraNet does not provide all the information related to the procurement process and that it is not considered to be very user friendly by internal and external users. CompraNet experiences technical difficulties in uploading or downloading information, making the process slow and inefficient. In this regard, GACM could proactively publish, on its webpage, all the relevant information, such as annual procurement programmes, tender procedures (solicitation documents, minutes of the clarification meetings and of the opening of tenders), contract awards history, modification to contracts and formal complaints (*inconformidades*), as carried out for example by New York City (Box 4.21).

Box 4.21. Checkbook NYC

In July of 2010, the New York City Comptroller's Office launched Checkbook NYC, an online transparency tool that for the first time placed the City's day-to-day spending in the public domain. Using an intuitive dashboard approach that combines a series of graphs and user-friendly tables, Checkbook NYC provides up-to-date information about the City's financial condition.

The website provides information about:

- budget
- revenue
- spending
- contracts
- payroll
- sub vendors.

Information can be found under contracts, including detailed information on contracts, contract modification, vendors, award methods and more.

Contracts include information on the contracting agency, prime supplier, current amount of the contract, original amount and how much has been spent to date.

CONTRACT ID	PURPOSE	CONTRACTING AGENCY	PRIME VENDOR	CURRENT AMOUNT	ORIGINAL AMOUNT	SPENT TO DATE
CT185620050034130	PUBLIC UTILITY	DEPARTMENT OF CITYWIDE ADMINIST...	NEW YORK POWER AUTHORITY	$7.19B	$7.19B	$5.80B
CT100220060028251	FUNDING AGREEMENT	MAYORALTY	MTA BUS COMPANY	$3.12B	$1.04B	$2.66B
CT182720141400213	MANAGEMENT, TRANSPORTATION A...	DEPARTMENT OF SANITATION	COVANTA SUSTAINABLE SOLUT...	$2.86B	$2.86B	$4.89M
CT100220070029782	HUDSON YARDS SUPPORT & DEVELO...	MAYORALTY	HUDSON YARDS INFRASTRUCTURE CO	$1.83B	$1.83B	$0.00
CT106920141428608	CHANGE OF OWNERSHIP OFFICE...	DEPARTMENT OF SOCIAL SERVICES	VANDERBILT ASSOCIATES OWNER LP	$1.71B	$1.71B	$10.36M

Information on contract modification includes, among other things, the percentage between the original contract amount and the current amount, as well as how much the contract has been modified.

Top 5 Contract Amount Modifications *Number of Contract Modifications: 4,435*

CONTRACT ID	PURPOSE	CONTRACTING AGENCY	PRIME VENDOR	CURRENT AMOUNT	ORIGINAL AMOUNT	SPENT TO DATE	DOLLAR DIFFERENCE	PERCENT DIFFERENCE
CT100220060028251	FUNDING AGREEMENT	MAYORALTY	MTA BUS COMPANY	$3.12B	$1.04B	$2.66B	$2.08B	200%
CT100220040015984	FUNDING AGREEMENT	MAYORALTY	DORMITORY AUTHORITY...	$556.88M	$120.00M	$533.46M	$436.88M	364.07%
CT182697B4876	AGREEMENT TO PROVIDE...	DEPARTMENT OF ENVIRO...	NYS ENV FACILITIE...	$410.30M	$79.60M	$374.54M	$330.70M	415.46%
CT185620020005358	BUILDING LEASE	DEPARTMENT OF CITYWI...	59 MAIDEN LANE ASSO...	$587.68M	$297.98M	$188.88M	$289.70M	97.22%
CT18269236727	DESIGN OF THE CROTON...	DEPARTMENT OF ENVIRO...	METCALF & EDDY OF N...	$299.50M	$44.23M	$288.57M	$255.27M	577.19%

Source: Checkbook NYC, official New York City website, www.checkbooknyc.com/contracts_landing/status/A/yeartype/B/year/116 (accessed 22 June 2015).

Lastly, to proactively disclose documents and data in a timely manner without having to incur excessively high costs, there needs to be a routine system of data collection that is easy to use and that makes data accessible to analyse. The OGP (2013) suggests the following:

- Where feasible, contracting information should be digitised and made available to the public on an online portal.
- Structured formats such as structured XML and inclusion of all relevant metadata allows for user- friendly searching and access.
- Digital information should be retained and made available in perpetuity.
- Where possible, use non-proprietary software applications.

Where possible, citizens should have the ability to subscribe to services to alert them of certain types of contracting developments through the use of email, SMS text, or other technologies.GACM's website can also be an important instrument to promote civil society scrutiny of the project

Social scrutiny or social accountability mechanisms, such as community monitoring, contribute to improving the quality and performance of a given project. They help empower local groups and enhance public participation, thanks to channels made for citizens to voice their concerns, provide constructive feedback, and flag wrongdoings and abuses (Transparency International, 2013b).

Allowing for social scrutiny contributes to strengthening the ties between citizens and their local or central government, which can have positive implications for reinforcing democratic governance. By constructing these linkages, social scrutiny can help improve the focus of public investment project, monitor the performance of the administration and promote responsive governance. Social scrutiny tools have the benefit of making the needs of the most vulnerable groups visible. More generally, it helps improve government transparency, and expose abuses and corruption (UNDP, 2010).

GACM could take into account that proactive disclosure of information cannot only be on information on public procurement. It can provide citizens and other stakeholders with necessary information about the whole project. During the fact-finding mission, complaints were raised about the lack of information on the project. For instance, the website could reach the actual construction stage and allow the public to monitor the advancement of work through photos and videos, as in the case of the Tappan Zee Hudson River Crossing Project in New York (Box 4.22).

Box 4.22. **Tappan Zee Bridge video-camera monitoring**

Public involvement is an integral part of the transportation planning process. Accordingly, the goal of the public and agency involvement programme for the Tappan Zee Hudson River Crossing Project is to ensure open, collaborative, and meaningful public and agency participation throughout the process. The project has its own website where the public can keep up to date on the project, where all non-confidential information is made available to the public and where advancement of work can be observed live through construction cameras.

Source: http://newnybridgegallery.com/webcam.php (accessed 14 June 2015).

Furthermore, webpage complaint mechanisms are increasingly recognised as a valuable tool to promote government accountability. Complaint mechanisms give citizens channels to provide feedback and submit complaints to public bodies in order to improve their work and services. Public institutions must consider a few key principles when designing complaint mechanisms, such as transparency, independence, accountability, accessibility, safety and user-friendliness (Transparency International, 2014b).

Making the complaint mechanisms look quite informal and accessible is a key to success, as it reduces potential user intimidation while still allowing public officials to have access to feedback on public services and policies. Making it simple for people to give feedback and empowering them to report mismanagement and abuse, without having to escalate it into a formal complaint mechanism can create a powerful feedback loop for public services. To be as user-friendly as possible, these feedback channels should be set up around what people already use and like (e.g. mobile phones, markets, prayer groups, schools). Technology opens up new avenues through which citizens can give their views, such as using SMS, and online social media channels (OGP, 2013).

Currently, under the GACM webpage there is a link to file a complaint; however, the user is redirected to the SFP webpage describing the procedure to follow. It is stated that the complaint can be done through email, postal mail, in person or by phone. Once this is done the complaint is directed to the OIC of the entity. The GACM OIC's and the SFP could work together to develop a complaint template that will be posted in the GACM website for suppliers and citizens to make their complaints on line. The GACM could follow the example of New York State Office of the Inspector General and have the template in different languages (Box 4.23). The complaint could arrive directly at the GACM OIC email address and could include a follow-up number for the user to follow up his/her complaint.

Box 4.23. **Online complaint form, New York State, Office of the Inspector General**

The Inspector General's Office is entrusted with the responsibility of ensuring that the state government, its employees and those who work with the state meet the highest standards of honesty, accountability, and efficiency.

It has created an online complaint form to report allegations of misconduct in state government. The complaint form is created to have as much information as possible on:

- Who is engaging in misconduct?
- Which state agency is involved?
- What wrongdoing occurred?
- When did it happen?
- Are there witnesses to the misconduct that we can contact?
- What laws or agency regulations have been violated?

The form also asks for information about the complainer, but he/she can request confidentiality. In addition, also the complainer can provide information about the documentation in his/her possession that relates to his/her complaint. The form is available in other six languages including French, Spanish, Chinese and Russian.

Source: New York State, Office of ,the Inspector General, "Online complaint form", http://ig.ny.gov/content/on-ine-complaint-form (accessed 22 June 2015).

Proposals for action

To enhance the integrity and transparency of its public procurement processes, GACM could consider taking the following actions:

- The GACM could promote a culture of integrity through:
  - raising awareness of corruption risks among its personnel, particularly among those involved in the procurement process
  - amending its code of conduct, taking into account that it will need to: *i)* outline to GACM personnel and partners what is expected of them in terms of conduct; *ii)* contribute to reinforcing integrity in the organisational culture by setting new norms; and *iii)* provide a disciplinary framework to sanction deviant behaviour
  - developing specific standards for procurement officials, for example through code of conduct for GACM procurement officials
  - ensuring that its code of conduct is known and create one code of conduct for all those involved in the procurement process including consultants, outsourced personnel and subcontractors
  - providing training for procurement officials on integrity, ethics and anti-corruption tools
  - increase the visibility and awareness of the Ethics Committee to have a better dissemination and enforcement of the code of conduct and subsequent adaptation of norms to new risks
  - developing a comprehensive conflict of interest policy, including the development of a Procurement Management Framework that lists situations which would be considered as a conflict of interest and provides guidance on the steps to follow
  - checking any potential conflicts of interest before the procurement process begins and allowing bidders to disclose any potential conflict of interest they may have with the contracting organisation or with the other bidders
  - assessing the possibility of discussing with its public officials which channels will provide confidence to report wrongdoing
  - implementing training and education on the notion of integrity and the purpose of reporting to encourage the correct use of reporting mechanisms and prevent misuse
  - engaging with groups of suppliers to explore ways to encourage them to develop their own standards and programmes to enhance integrity in their relationship with the GACM.
- The GACM OIC:
  - could ensure it does not only perform a control role but also serves as an advisory body for GACM management and procurement units to achieve greater effectiveness and efficiency of the procurement process.

  - GACM procurement units and the OIC could work closely with the GACM internal control committee and the SFP's *Mesa de acompañamiento* to ensure efficient and transparent procurement procedures.
  - The GACM OIC's and the SFP could work together to develop a complaint template on the GACM's website to allow suppliers and citizens to make complaints on line.

- The GACM could avoid integrity risks during the procurement process by:
  - Developing a corruption risk map of the organisation and its processes in order to identify the positions of officials that are particularly vulnerable, the activities in the procurement cycle where risks can arise, and the specific projects at risk. This will also allow the GACM to:
    - use a system of red flags following the development of a risk map
    - develop an integrity plan to facilitate the development of mitigation strategies following the mapping of specific corruption risks and thus ensure that all parties involved in the process are aware of existing integrity risks and mechanisms as well as their own responsibilities.
  - Continue with the involvement of civil society experts through the inclusion of social observers in key procurement procedures.
  - Reducing in its procurement manuals the threshold for the mandatory use of social witness for the procurement of public works, goods and services; as well as including in its procurement manuals other conditions under which a social witness needs to be included.
  - Developing standard bidding documents for the technical and economic proposals, statement of integrity, and disclosure forms for current commitments and financial situation.
  - Implementing the two-envelope approach to ensure that procurement decisions are taken according to the set criteria.
  - Implementing the four-eyes principle to limit public officials' discretionary power and ensure a certain level of deliberation and the protection of the public officials from suspicion.
  - Exploring the possibility to designate an integrity monitor that can follow all the procurement cycle.
  - Ensuring that its existing internal integrity mechanisms are known by and applicable to consultants, outsourced personnel and subcontractors as much as it applies to GACM personnel, through for example a code of conduct.

- The GACM could improve the transparency of its procurement activities by:
  - ensuring that it has the needed resources, structure and capacities to perform these functions
  - publishing all the procurement information not only related to the airport but also to the functioning of the GACM

- publishing procurement information by the type of procedure used in terms of numbers and in terms of value
- providing clear definitions of the procurement procedures and the most common exceptions to public bidding that are foreseen
- proactively establishing and publishing online guidelines in plain language on all the information disclosed
- publishing procurement plans in a usable format that can allow distinguishing from what was already procured, what is currently being procured and what will be procured in the future
- proactively publish, on its webpage, all the relevant information such as annual procurement programmes, tender procedures (solicitation documents, minutes of the clarification meetings and of the opening of tenders), contract awards history, and modification to contracts
- publishing the signed declarations of bidders on its website.

Notes

1. For more information, see http://dof.gob.mx/nota_detalle.php?codigo=5404567&fecha=20/08/2015

2, For more information, see http://reniresp.funcionpublica.gob.mx/ppcapf/consulta/consultaGeneral.jsf.

3. For more information, see http://dof.gob.mx/nota_detalle.php?codigo=5404568&fecha=20/08/2015.

5. The amount equals to 5 million days of daily minimum wage at Mexico D.F for goods and services and 10 million days of daily minimum wage at Mexico D.F for public works. The 2015 daily minimum wage in Mexico D.F is MXN 70.10, approximately USD 4.60.

6. Article 63 Section II of ROPSRM states that proposals which commit to subcontract part of the public works to SMES should receive points or percentages: "*a los licitantes que se comprometan a subcontratar MIPYMES para la ejecución de los trabajos que se determine en la convocatoria a la licitación pública, se les otorgaran puntos o unidades porcentuales de acuerdo a los lineamentos señalados en el párrafo anterior.*"

7 . This estimation was based on only those procedures that had all the information, including the type of procedure used, as of 28 September 2015.

References

Asian Development Bank, (2015), *Bidding Procedures*. www.adb.org/site/business-opportunities/operational-procurement/goods-services/bidding-procedures

CCAB, (2014), *Developing and implementing a code of ethical conduct*, www.ccab.org.uk/PDFs/Code_Guidance_final_SG_Amends2.pdf

Corporate Executive Board, CEB, (2015), *Why integrity pays*, www.executiveboard.com/exbd/legal-risk-compliance/integrity-capital/index.page.

Control Risks, (2011), *Assessing corruption risks,* https://www.controlrisks.com/~/media/Public%20Site/Files/Our%20Thinking/risk_assessment_published.pdf

Construction Sector Transparency Initiative, COST, (2012), *Press Release*. www.constructiontransparency.org/documentdownload.axd?documentresourceid=8.

Forbes. 2013. *The Real Cost Of Bribery*. www.forbes.com/sites/hbsworkingknowledge/2013/11/05/the-real-cost-of-bribery/

Hawkins J, (2013), *How to Note: Reducing corruption in infrastructure sectors. Evidence on Demand*, www.engineersagainstpoverty.org/documentdownload.axd?documentresourceid=4.

Kenny C, (2009), "Measuring Corruption in Infrastructure: Evidence from Transition and Developing Countries", *Journal of Development Studies*, 45(3), pp. 314-332.

OECD (2015), *Consequences of Corruption at the Sector Level and Implications for Economic Growth and Development*, OECD Publishing, Paris, http://dx.doi.org/10.1787/9789264230781-en.

OECD (2013a), *Public Procurement Review of the State's Employees' Social Security and Social Services Institute in Mexico*, OECD Public Governance Reviews, OECD Publishing, http://dx.doi.org/10.1787/9789264197305-en.

OECD, (2013b), *Ethics Training for Public Officials*, OECD Publishing, Paris. www.oecd.org/corruption/acn/library/EthicsTrainingforPublicOfficialsBrochureEN.pdf.

OECD, 2009, *OECD Principles for Integrity in Public Procurement*, OECD Publishing, Paris, www.oecd.org/gov/ethics/48994520.pdf.

OECD (2007), *Integrity in Public Procurement: Good Practice from A to Z*, OECD Publishing, Paris, http://dx.doi.org/10.1787/9789264027510-en.

Open Government Partnership, (2013), *Guide to Open Government 2.0*. www.ogphub.org/wp-content/uploads/2013/02/Guide-to-open-government-public-contracting.pdf.

Transparency International (2014a), "Implementing codes of conduct in public institutions", www.transparency.org/whatwedo/answer/implementing_codes_of_conduct_in_public_institutions

Transparency International, (2014b), *Local-level complaint mechanisms in developing countries*, www.transparency.org/whatwedo/answer/local_level_complaint_mechanisms_in_developing_countries

Transparency International (2013a), "Whistleblowing in Europe", www.transparency.de/fileadmin/pdfs/Themen/Hinweisgebersysteme/EU_Whistleblower_Report_final_web.pdf, p. 25.

Transparency International (2013b), *Community monitoring of humanitarian aid and service delivery,* www.transparency.org/files/content/corruptionqas/Community-monitoring-aid-service-delivery-.pdf

Transparency International, (2011), *Corruption Risk Assessment Topic Guide*, http://gateway.transparency.org/files/uploads/Corruption_Risk_Assessment_Topic_Guide.pdf

Transparency International, (2006), *Handbook for curbing corruption in public procurement*. www.transparency.org/whatwedo/publication/handbook_for_curbing_corruption_in_public_procurement

UNDP, 2010, *Fostering Social Accountability from Principle to Practice,* www.undp.org/content/dam/undp/library/Democratic%20Governance/OGC/dg-ogc-Fostering%20Social%20Accountability-Guidance%20Note.pdf

Wells, J. (2015), "Corruption in the construction of public infrastructure: Critical issues in project preparation", *U4 Issue* No. 8, U4 Anti-corruption Resource Centre, Chr. Michelsen Institute, Bergen, Norway.

Chapter 5

Communications strategy recommendations for the NAICM project

*Mega infrastructure projects require building broad social and political support. This effort calls for an effective and proactive communications strategy. In fact, a common weakness in many projects is the lack of a coherent communications strategy linking the needs, expectations, and concerns of the project's stakeholders. Until November 2015, the New International Airport of Mexico City (*Nuevo Aeropuerto Internacional de la Ciudad de México*, NAICM) had not developed such a strategy, nor the Airport Group of Mexico City (Grupo Aeroportuario de la Ciudad de México, GACM) had established a communications office with the mandates of building consensus and enabling more inclusive decision making. This chapter will describe the communications efforts carried out in relation to NAICM and how they can be improved to abide by international good practices.*

The need for a solid communications strategy

The New International Airport of Mexico City (*Nuevo Aeropuerto Internacional de la Ciudad de México,* NAICM) is at the core of the current administration's (2012-18) infrastructure plan. Given the potential long-term benefits of the project, building broad social and political support, which can only be achieved through an effective communications strategy, should be a top priority.

A successful communications strategy would help to improve the project perceptions among key players to achieve certainty, transparency and trust as the core vectors of the project (see Figure 5.1).

Figure 5.1. **A successful transition as a result of a communications strategy**

From:

- Rational, distant, technical language that does not connect with the audience
- Sending the same messages to all stakeholders
- Low community engagement
- Scepticism, uncertainty, and biased perceptions among key players

To:

- Attractive, engaging storytelling about the project and its positive impact
- Eliciting differentiated messages that address the aspirations and concerns of specific audiences
- Construction of shared meaning among communities in the project's vicinity
- Certainty, confidence, transparency, and trust as the core of the project

Source: Author's own work.

Political inequality in access to decision-making processes can lead to an unequal distribution in the risks, burdens, and benefits of megaprojects. The general public is often sceptical or negative towards such projects. In fact, citizens and interest groups may orchestrate hostile protests against the undertaking of major infrastructure projects.

The use of proper communication enhances sustainable infrastructure and facilitates good governance. Development communication, which is "the social process designed to seek a common understanding among all the participants of a development initiative, creating a basis for concerted action" strengthens the foundations for good governance by promoting open government, increased accountability, and the active engagement of participants in civil society (Hass, Mazzei, and O'Leary, 2007) (Box 5.1).

Communication also provides a crucial analytical device and management tool to promote sustainable infrastructure development in three respects:

- Improving the quality of infrastructure: enabling more inclusive and informed decision making at all stages of the project cycle; driving new thinking and innovation to create sustainable infrastructure; and establishing consensus based on service-provision priorities and delivery methods.
- Building consensus on infrastructure-related government reforms: raising awareness of corruption vulnerabilities at all stages of infrastructure development and establishing consensus on reform programmes, including the partnerships and tariffs needed to make services sustainable.

Box 5.1. **Why do communications matter?**

International experience shows that effective communication is of utmost importance to the development and completion of any project. According to the Project Management Institute, in organisations whose communicators are considered highly effective, 80% of projects meet their original goals, versus only 52% at their minimally effective counterparts.

The same source estimates that highly effective communicators are also more likely to deliver projects on time (71% vs. 37%) and within budget (76% vs. 48%). Executives claim organisations with effective and efficient communication methods are more likely to stay within scope, meet quality standards, and deliver intended business benefits.

A good communication process keeps stakeholders engaged and project teams motivated. Yet, true communication both inside and outside enterprise walls remains a rare commodity — much of which comes down to the fundamental difficulty of communicating with the right level of clarity and detail.

Source: Project Management Institute, www.pmi.org (accessed 17 September 2015).

- Taking concerted action to manage corruption risks on infrastructure: maintaining pressure for the implementation of anti-corruption reform and building popular consensus on specific efforts, improving transparency and visibility of actions taken.

A common weakness in many large projects is the lack of a coherent and effective communications strategy linking the needs, expectations, and concerns of the project's different stakeholder interests. Besides controversy, symptoms of underfunding communication functions include ad hoc approaches and a lack of up-front communication and strategic planning. Project managers must balance competing priorities for resources by upholding communications at each stage of the project cycle.

Another important line of argument to support resource allocation for communications is to link it to gains in corruption savings.

Main communications actions of the NAICM

As of August 2015, three milestones have required intense communications efforts:

- the initial announcement of the NAICM (September 2014)
- the agreement with the OECD (January 2015)
- the presentation of the procurement packaging strategy (July 2015).

The initial announcement

On 2 September 2014, Mexico's President announced the administration's plans to build the NAICM. The President explained that the public work's development would take place in five stages, with an investment of approximately MXN 169 000 million: MXN 120 000 million would go to the airport's infrastructure and the rest would finance various complementary works (i.e. preparing land for construction). The President assured the public that the project would be financed with tax revenue from Mexico

City's International Airport (AICM) together with tax revenue from the NAICM, once it becomes operational (Box 5.2.).

Box 5.2. **Analysis of the initial announcement speech (2 September 2014)**

1. Argument:
   - There is a clear sense of urgency.
     - The current airport has reached its operational limits.
     - It lacks the ability to carry on simultaneous operations, which is unacceptable for an airport in a city as globally important as Mexico City.
   - The decision was made on a technical basis.
     - We asked experts and specialists to conduct an analysis to find better alternatives.
   - We have selected the best people for the project.
     - Experts evaluated and qualified proposals.
     - We have selected prestigious architects for the design work..
   - The project will have many benefits.
     - Economic: 160 000 direct and indirect new jobs; hundreds of SMEs will benefit from contracts.
     - Social: A new Aeronautics University as well as housing projects for people working on the new airport.
     - Environmental: Clean energies and water-saving technologies in the buildings; the surrounding area will have new lakes and forests.
2. Tone: Positive. The airport will be one of the most advanced in the world. It will be a logistical and engineering challenge, but also a unique opportunity to showcase Mexico as a rising nation.
3. Language: Clear and understandable. Avoids technical jargon; conveys optimism and pride for the project.

Source: www.presidencia.gob.mx/articulos-prensa/palabras-del-presidente-de-los-estados-unidos-mexicanos-licenciado-enrique-pena-nieto-durante-el-evento-avances-y-retos-del-plan-nacional-de-infraestructura/ (accessed 17 September 2015). OECD assessment.

The administration mentioned this would be the world's most sustainable airport—a hallmark of Mexican innovation to be built to the possible extent by national contractors and engineers. Given its symbolic nature, the Federal Government committed to make the airport a world reference in terms of design, construction, and sustainable operation with clean and renewable energy, green technologies, and efficient ventilation and air conditioning units to optimise water and energy use. The airport's engineers also plan to take advantage of biogas from the *Bordo Poniente* dump as an energy source for the new airport.[1]

Immediately after NAICM's construction was announced in September 2014, government communications put the spotlight on the project's modern architectural design, costs, construction phases, and expected completion dates. Among the most stressed positive aspects, the following messages stood out:

- The economic growth, job creation, and mobility projects that will go hand in hand with NAICM.
- The unprecedented nature of this infrastructure project's architectural design.
- The eco-friendly aspects and the positive impact NAICM will have on the area, which currently struggles with high levels of environmental degradation.
- The fact that this will be one of the largest airports in the world, serving up to 120 million passengers a year (phase 2).
- The modernity of "the airport of the future": the project is expected to benefit from the collaboration of top national and international experts.

Agreement with the OECD

In January 2015, the OECD and the Ministry for Communication and Transport (*Secretaria de Comunicaciones y Transportes*, SCT) signed an agreement by which the OECD would "share its knowledge on best practices with Mexico's government in order to implement a comprehensive strategy during the NAICM's construction phase, particularly regarding integrity, transparency, accountability, procurement, and concessions."

The procurement packaging strategy announcement

On 8 July 2015, the SCT announced that the bidding process to award contracts for the construction of the NAICM would begin with preliminary works packages in September 2015. The communication highlights were the following:

- The NAICM is the most important infrastructure project of this administration and one of the largest of its kind in the world.
- The packaging scheme for the bids allows the Government to receive proposals from contractors with proven experience.
- Contractors will work using state-of-the-art technology, as well as the highest quality and fastest execution rates possible.
- Transparency is a top concern for the Government and social witnesses appointed by the Ministry of Public Administration (*Secretaría de la Función Pública*, SFP) will oversee the process.

During 2015-16, several relevant contracts will be awarded for the construction of the airport's main infrastructure, like the terminal building, fuel-storage facilities, arrival platform, and fuel-distribution lines. According to the official schedule, the second set of contracts will be awarded to build notably navigation systems, the central service tunnel, and audio-visual assistance. During the second half of 2016, bids will be open for fire stations. Contracts will be awarded for support buildings in August 2016 and for the first building phase of the surrounding road infrastructure in October 2016. Contracts for the multimodal transport centre and parking lots will follow in 2017.

Media coverage

The announcement of the NAICM project was significantly covered in the national media, with 1 218 mentions during September and October 2014.

The participation of the selected architect as head of the new airport's interior design, together with the announcement of the project's environmental impact studies, were the topics with the most media coverage.

Between April and May 2015, the media mostly covered the NAICM's Master Plan, financing, and investment, and, yet again, the architectural design and its sustainable strategy (the use of clean energy and green technologies). The media also showcased stories about how the new airport will have its own "mini city" in 2028 (*Aerotrópolis*, with malls and hotels). Descriptions about the construction and enlargement of highways, subway lines (metro), rapid transit bus lines (*metrobús*), and the creation of an express train that will go from downtown Mexico City to the new terminal were also featured.

During May and June 2015, the GACM and SCT insisted upon the project's social component. The Government emphasised the importance of the social benefits NAICM will trigger.

The GACM's Director General noted that NAICM would benefit youth, as the terminal's operation and construction process will be a great source of employment. The NAICM will be an economic detonator for the whole country, especially for the heavily challenged *Ex Vaso de Texcoco* Federal Zone.

Government officials have highlighted the positive social impact the new airport will bring. In the medium and long term, the surrounding areas have the potential to become hubs for social and economic development, with higher-education institutions, such as the Metropolitan University of Aeronautics and Aviation, as well as training centres for aviation-related professionals. Hotels, convention centres, shopping malls, and other amenities for travellers are being anticipated as part of the NAICM.

As the official announcement for NAICM's bid-packaging strategy took place in early July 2015, NAICM's media coverage shot up in said month, with 73 more mentions than those registered in June. All in all, 88% of the total coverage was informative or neutral, while 9% was negative, and only 3% percent had a positive tone.

The bids' packaging strategy alone received 148 media mentions, with an advertising value equivalency (AVE)[2] of MXN 7.1 million. Most of these mentions took place within three days of the announcement (7-9 July) and received little follow up in the media. Mobility and transportation solutions for the airport's new access routes to Mexico City are still key issues. The issuance of the first package in late September 2015 also attracted attention in the media.

By late July 2015, the future of the current airport's grounds became a central topic to many stakeholders. This issue poses a looming debate between federal and local (Mexico City) authorities, which will be responsible for the outcome, as discussed in further sections of this chapter.

The website

In the follow-up to a series of previous discussions initiated in February 2015 and as per the agreement signed with the SCT, the OECD made on 18 June 2015 seven recommendations to improve the GACM's operations in the website (www.aeropuerto.gob.mx).

These recommendations, which focus on transparency issues and access to information, have already been taken into account. However, further actions need to be considered.

The first recommendation was to include a *normatividad* (regulations) button on the website's Documents section, so that users could find the regulatory framework for the procurement process, the GACM, and transparency. This has already been incorporated (Figure 5.2).

Figure 5.2. **Website content regarding regulations**

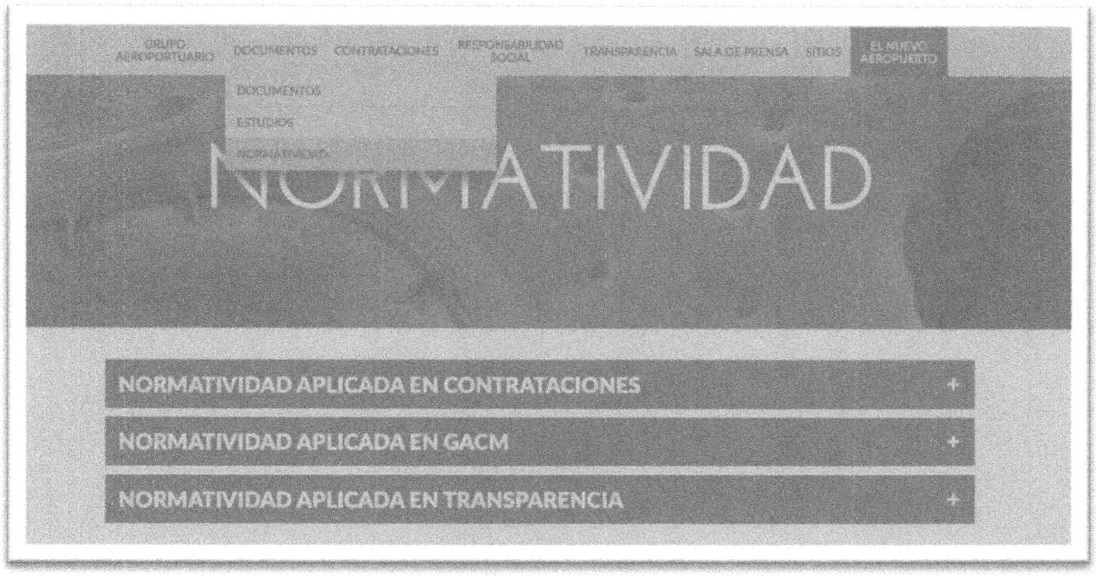

Translation: Regulations, procurement regulations, GACM regulations, transparency regulations.

Source: www.aeropuerto.gob.mx/gacm/index.php (accessed 1 August 2015).

The second recommendation, which is also already incorporated, was that in the *Most Important Purchases* section, there should be a small description of each item (Figure 5.3).

Figure 5.3. **Website content: The most important purchases section**

Translation: The most important purchases, services, public works, services related to public works.

Source: www.aeropuerto.gob.mx/gacm/index.php (accessed 1 August 2015).

The third recommendation was having direct access to the social witnesses' reports instead of having to go to the *CompraNet* webpage when reviewing the details of each procurement process. This recommendation was also implemented (Figure 5.4).

Figure 5.4. **Website content: The section on procurement procedures (ongoing, followed up, and completed)**

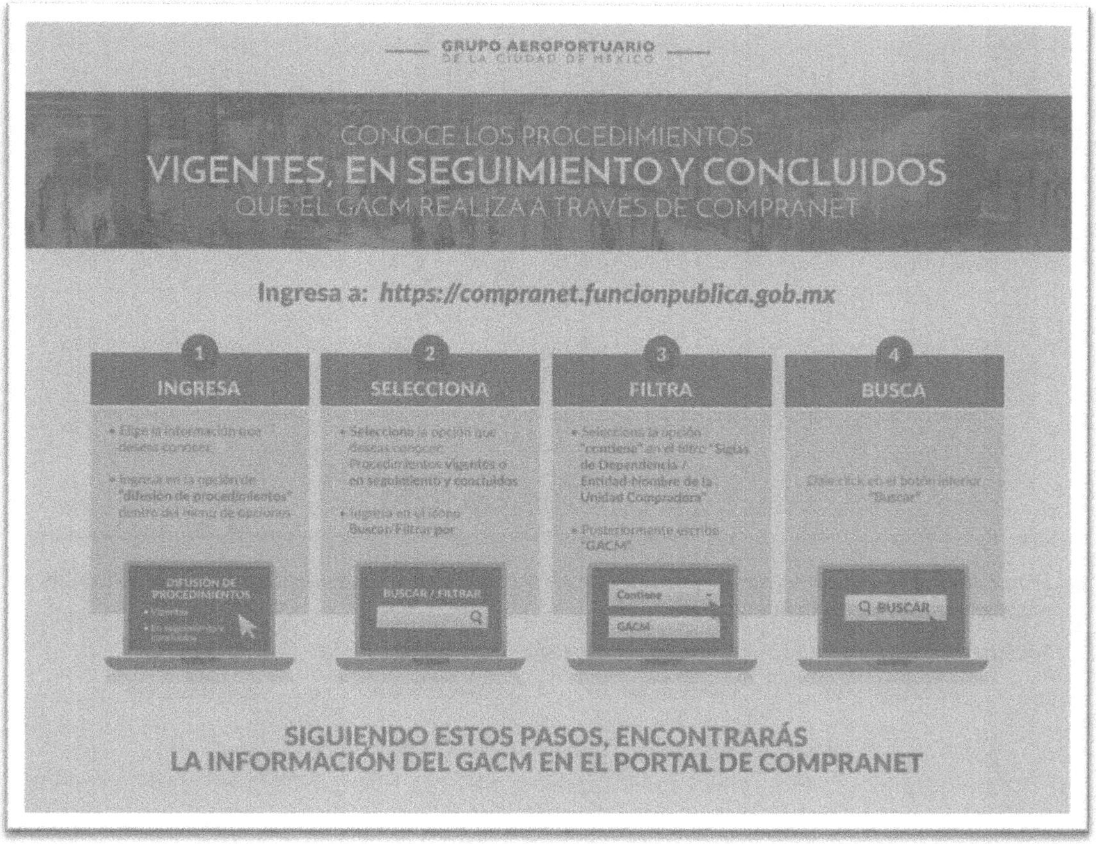

Translation: Get to know the procedures, current, under monitoring, and concluded, that GACM carries out through Compranet. Link to: https://compranet.funcionpublica.gob.mx. Enter, select, filter, search. By following these steps, you will find GACM's information in Compranet.

Source: www.aeropuerto.gob.mx/gacm/index.php (accessed 1 August 2015).

The fourth recommendation was to enlist the NAICM's resource-oversight organisations in the *Transparency* section and to link their icons to the organisations' official websites. This can already be seen in Figure 5.5.

Figure 5.5. **Website content: Transparency section**

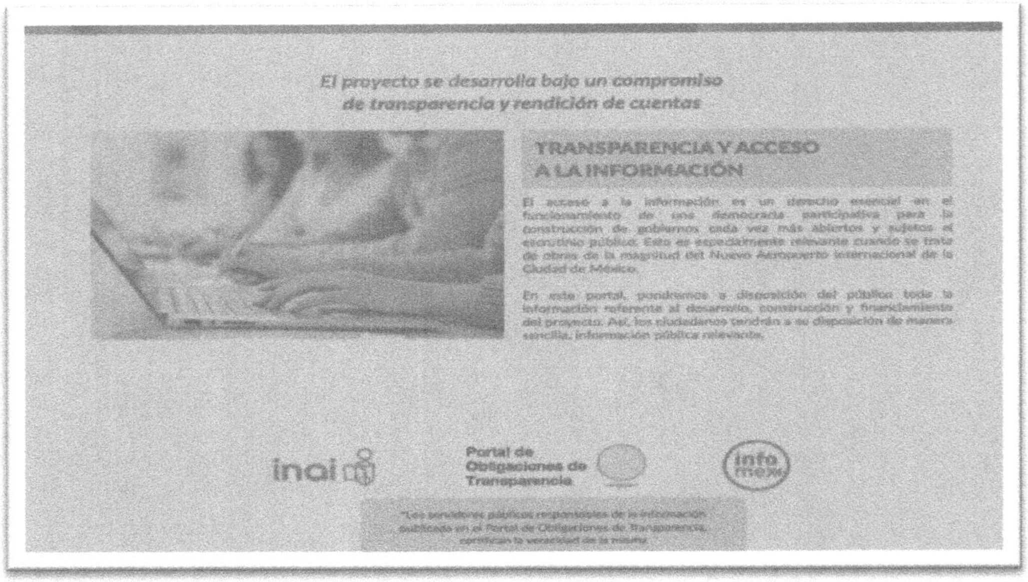

Translation: The project is carried out following a commitment with transparency and accountability, transparency and access to information.

Source: www.aeropuerto.gob.mx/gacm/index.php (accessed 1 August 2015).

Next, the OECD recommended that in the *Sites of Interest* section, a transparency label be included with a list of the responsible organisations and their descriptions. This is already in the website (Figure 5.6).

Figure 5.6. **Website content: Transparency label in the sites of interest section**

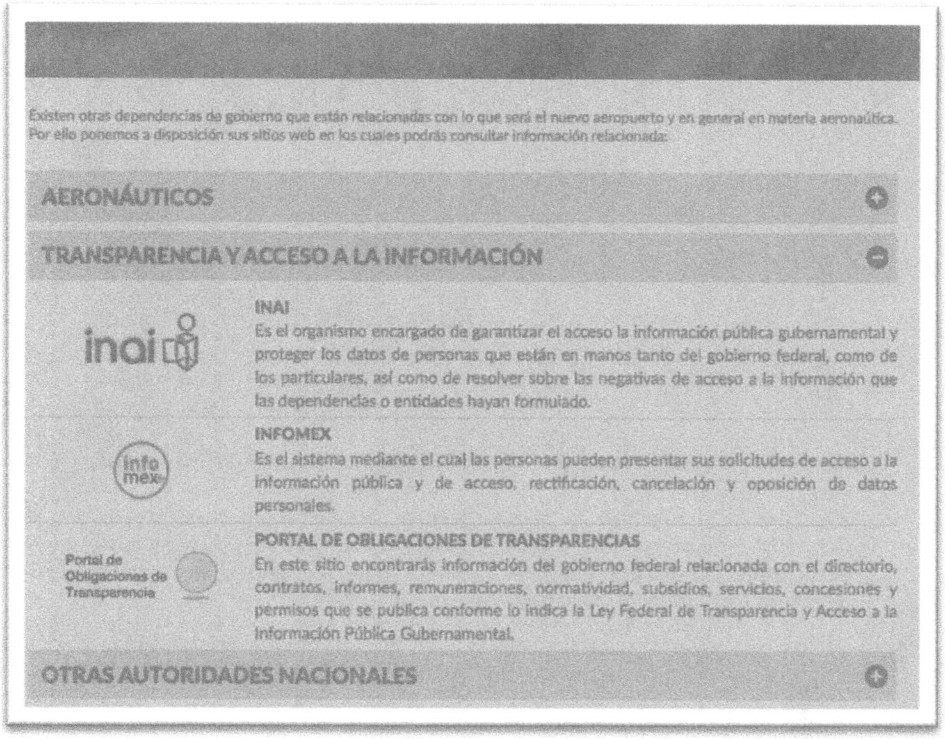

Translation: There are other government entities related with the new airport project and, in general, dealing with aeronautics. Hence, we make available their websites in which you may find related information: Aeronautics.

Transparency and access to information. INAI: It is the entity in charge of ensuring access to government information and protecting personal data in possession of the Federal Government, private individuals, as well as deciding on the challenges to denied requests to access information issued by government entities.

Infomex: It is the system by which individuals may submit their requests to access government information and to access, rectify, cancel, or challenge personal data.

Transparency Duties Portal: In this system you will find information from the Federal Government regarding staff directory, contracts, reports, salaries, regulations, subsidies, services, concessions, and permits, published in compliance with the Federal Law for Transparency and Access to Government Information.

Other national authorities.

Source: www.aeropuerto.gob.mx/gacm/index.php (accessed 1 August 2015).

In addition, it was recommended that the Site Map section include a guide question: What are you looking for? (*¿Qué estás buscando?*). The answers would be drawn from two previously established areas: *Get to Know the Project* (NAICM) and *Get to Know Those Responsible for the Project* (GACM). The recommendation has been incorporated (Figure 5.7).

Figure 5.7. **Website content: Site map section**

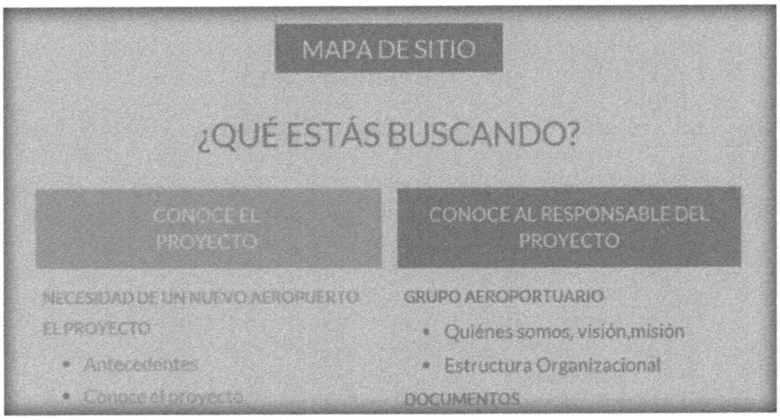

Translation: Site map, What are you looking for? Get to know the project: The need for a new airport, Background, Get to know the project, Meet those responsible for the project: Airport Group, Who we are, vision, mission, organisational structure, documents.

Source: www.aeropuerto.gob.mx/gacm/index.php (accessed 1 August 2015).

Finally, there was a recommendation to insert a Search tool. This has been implemented, but only works well if the user inserts precise keywords. Otherwise, the site displays the message, "No results found" (Figure 5.8).

Figure 5.8. **Website content: Search tool**

Translation: Site map.

Source: www.aeropuerto.gob.mx/gacm/index.php (accessed 1 August 2015).

The website fails to provide a direct form of contact. As of November 2015, no e-mail, contact number, or link to Twitter, Facebook, or any other social network has been found on the website.

Perceptions of key stakeholders

For this section, the OECD conducted interviews with key stakeholders in the private sector, non-governmental organisations (NGOs), and officials from local and federal governments. The OECD also conducted a thorough analysis of the media. The views expressed here candidly reflect what was said in those interviews, as well as the expressions and content of media coverage, both positive and negative, with the aim of contributing to the improvement of the communications strategy.

Private sector

The private sector's response to the NAICM project has been mostly positive, both in terms of business opportunities and long-term competitiveness for Mexico. For instance, a representative from a major construction company claimed that the country has the experience and capabilities to successfully build a project of this magnitude, and that it will also benefit from international experiences and technology.

The Mexican Chamber of the Construction Industry (CMIC) asserted that its affiliate companies had the disposition and capacities to "face the challenges a project of this magnitude implies".

The president of IATA claimed that the new airport would allow Mexico to become the main hub between Asia and Latin America. IATA is optimistic about the new airport's announcement and has proclaimed the association's will to advise NAICM planning.

In public statements, the president of the World Travel and Tourism Council (WTTC) stated that the construction of the new airport is a "wonderful investment" that will allow Mexico to both improve its global position in tourism infrastructure and produce economic benefits. The director of Airports Council International (ACI) also recognised that NAICM would improve the region's transit capacity for passengers.

One important concern mentioned in interviews with private sector representatives was the risk that public officials might not ensure fairness in bidding and contract processes.

Pilot and Flight Attendant Union

As of August 2015, the Government has not formally invited the Pilot and Flight Attendant Union (ASPA) to join the dialogue. Nevertheless, ASPA expects its input will be taken into account as the project progresses. ASPA leaders view the NAICM project very positively, as the current airport has reached its operational limits. They believe increasing transport capabilities from 34 to 50 and then 120 million people per year will boost the economy and generate revenue from tourism and business travellers. ASPA and the *Colegio de Pilotos* (a different pilot association) can provide technical opinions to improve the new airport's efficiency, and both are willing to share their expertise.

ASPA leaders consider the NAICM a "national priority" and a "state project," which means that its importance goes well beyond any given government administration. According to ASPA leadership, today only 0.5% of the Mexican population has access to air transportation, given its relatively higher costs compared to bus and car transportation. The NAICM will expand supply, making prices more affordable. ASPA considers that the NAICM project will benefit from an open dialogue between the Government and stakeholders.

Mexico City government

The Mexico City government officials interviewed for this report affirmed that there is a clear need for a new international airport. They openly support the project, as they recognise its benefits for the city and the nation as a whole.

The city government has, among others, two main concerns: how the NAICM will affect urban mobility and what is going to happen to the land where the current airport operates. With regards to the NAICM's impact on urban mobility, the city's authorities believe there is still a long way to go in terms of communication and dialogue with the Federal Government for the implementation of a shared mobility plan. City authorities believe mobility should be as high a priority as the construction of the airport itself.

As mentioned above, the second concern is how the lands of the soon-to-be vacated airport will be used. This is a unique opportunity, as this well-situated terrain amounts to about 1% of the city's total area. This area, twice the size of New York's Central Park, could become a development hub for the city's housing, education, economic activity, public spaces, and environmental recovery. The local government maintains that once the old airport closes, the land will no longer be under federal jurisdiction. Thus, the Government has opened consultation and public debate to collectively determine the area's future uses. SCT claims that, in any case, the old airport area would not be available for use until 2023, implying that any discussion on its use is premature. Political dialogue should continue to avoid these issues turning into political and legal controversies.

NGOs and think tanks

NGOs and think tanks are some of the stakeholders that have expressed the most scepticism regarding the Government's communications strategy. According to most of the NGO leaders interviewed for this report, the complex political context surrounding the project has spurred these doubts.

Some of their main criticisms of the communications and outreach strategy are as follows:

- The Government is perceived as non-proactive in its communications and outreach efforts. Some NGO leaders recognise that they have established good communications channels with GACM senior staff, but they perceive that this is the result of good willingness rather than of a well-defined policy.
- NGOs believe making public documents and studies available would be the right way to make this project more open and transparent. In their opinion, public information about the construction of the New International Airport is insufficient for a project of this relevance.
- Details about how the Government awarded the design and construction of the main terminal and other key contracts were scarce.
- In this context of distrust, NGO leaders believe the Government should strive to make the procurement process highly competitive and transparent. Nevertheless, they claim many contracts awarded by direct invitation and details have not been made public, sometimes because of reasons related to national security.
- It should be noted that in August 2015, the National Institute of Transparency, Access to Information and Data Protection (*Instituto Nacional de Transparencia, Acceso a la Información y Protección de Datos*, INAI) ordered GACM to disclose preliminary studies, executive plans, and contracts that had been classified due to national security. The INAI also shortened the generic construction plans' classified period from 12 to 3 years. Information about the future military facilities in the new airport[3] will remain classified.

- Some NGO leaders are confused as to why the Government chose to create GACM as an autonomous public enterprise, only to make it dependent of the SCT as if it were just another branch of the ministry. This has not been perceived as managerial good practice.
- Besides procurement and contracts, NGO leaders believe several other issues have not been properly assessed, such as land engineering, water and waste management, environmental impact, air security, energy management, urban mobility, and potential social conflicts (see Box 5.3).

Box 5.3. **Top concerns expressed by NGOs**

1. **Transparency and trust.** Communications and outreach efforts have to be more systematic and proactive in order to create and reinforce trust.
2. **Mechanisms of access to public records.** More technical studies and financial projections need to be available for public scrutiny.
3. **Financial sustainability.** The fall in oil prices will inevitably lead to cuts in public budgets. There are concerns about the availability of government resources to pay for the project given the Government's austerity measures.
4. **Timetable and execution capability.** The Government is seen as optimistic in its assertions that the airport will be ready by 2020.
5. **Urban mobility plans.** NGO leaders believe that the mobility plans are not in place, and they should have been ready before construction started.
6. **Surrounding communities.** Negotiations with local social leaders could foster distrust. Openness, consultation, and dialogue with local communities would better serve the Government's efforts to prevent conflicts.
7. **Political conflict.** As the 2018 elections come closer, changes in the political landscape could evidently put additional pressure on the project. The future use of the current airport also looms as a potential disagreement between the city and federal authorities.
8. **Public security.** The authorities seemed to have overlooked the fact that the NAICM will be located in a high-crime area. Plans for regional security are needed.
9. **Air safety.** Some specialists consider that the area poses challenges that need to be fully addressed to ensure air safety. Birds are the top concern, and special measures will need to be taken.
10. **Inter-institutional co-ordination.** NGO leaders perceive that agencies such as CONAGUA, SEDATU, and SEMARNAT are not exactly on the same page as the SCT and GACM.

Source: Interviews carried out by the OECD Secretariat with NAICM stakeholders.

Political parties

- *Institutional Revolutionary Party* (PRI). The PRI has not publicly supported the NAICM. PRI legislators have called the NAICM a federal project but have no defined position. It is therefore uncertain to assess whether it could be a form of tacit political support.

- *National Regeneration Movement, commonly known as Morena (Spanish acronym).* Morena is opposed to the construction of the new airport, as well as to many other initiatives coming from the current administration. It has pointed out that enormous investments in the current airport will go to waste (i.e. Terminal 2 was only built six years ago).
- *National Action Party* (PAN). The PAN called for the creation of a special commission to monitor the NAICM. Senators from this party, as well as those from the Party of the Democratic Revolution (PRD), requested that the Ministry of Communications and Transport provide a report on the financial projections, bidding process, and environmental impact of the NAICM's construction. The head of the PAN in the Chamber of Deputies clarified that his party is not against the project but did want guarantees for transparency, technical support, and peace with the area's residents. The legislative commission the PAN proposed would oversee the procurement processes, environmental care, and sustainability.

Front of Towns to Defend their Lands (Frente de Pueblos en Defensa de la Tierra, *FPDT)*

FPDT is a peasant organisation based in the municipality of Atenco, whose pressure halted the construction of the then new to be Mexico City airport back in 2001. They warn that the project will plunder the land, water, and natural resources that sustain their communities.

The organisation opposes the urbanisation that will stem from the new airport project. On 15 April 2015, the FPDT protested against the NAICM at a Senate-organised forum.

On 22 June 2015, the media reported that 78 FPDT-affiliated people living in the areas surrounding the NAICM's location sued the Government before the Supreme Court to get an injunction to halt the project. So far, no court order has been issued, which has allowed the NAICM to move forward.

Journalists

Journalists and columnists agree that the NAICM is a very ambitious project that should have been undertaken a long time ago. They have highlighted several positive communication efforts, deeming information on the airport's new location adequate.

The President's initial announcement of the project was also viewed positively, although journalists did express concerns about the proposed timetable. In their opinion, the Government lost momentum after the official kick-off. "After the announcement ceremony, there were more questions than answers," one interviewee said. Some journalists believe this is due to the lack of a more proactive strategy to keep the NAICM news feed updated.

Media professionals believe the GACM needs a communications team and a strategy. The SCT is sometimes seen as an entity that is busy handling a wide agenda of projects, even though the NAICM would deserve its own spotlight.

Credibility and trust are also challenges. The interviewed journalists consider that given the size of the project in financial terms, more proactive efforts from the Government are required. Some see the lack of regular press conferences and official communication channels as a possible sign of opacity. Others consider that the lack of proactive communication has excluded important opportunities to engage society in the project. One editor of a leading newspaper said, "the NAICM could generate an interesting, positive story almost every day, but this is not happening."

Most journalists consider that it is time to analyse whether SCT is the ideal spokesperson for the NAICM project. Some think the head of GACM could be a trustworthy spokesperson, but know that this decision could bring about political discussions. Thus, some suggest that it would be wise to have a third person with knowledge and credibility in media circles to act as a spokesperson, provided that he or she has autonomy, staff, and an adequate working budget.

Polls

According to a poll published in *El Universal* newspaper (September, 2014), 88% of people in Mexico City have heard about the NAICM project. Among these, 64% approve of the project and 19% are against it. Those who approve the project do so because the current airport has surpassed its capacity (33%) or because of job creation (21%), better road infrastructure (11%), better public services (10%), or the NAICM's positive effects on the city's image (6%).

Those against the project reject it because of lacking transparency in the use of resources (29%), other priorities in the country (13%), the effect on farmers in the area (12%), the belief that this is an unnecessary expense (10%), or because the site is not a good place for the airport's construction (10%). A total of 76% of respondents believe the NAICM will generate economic growth, while 18% is convinced that it will have no impact.

Many respondents believe the construction of the new airport will have a negative impact on the city's groundwater recharge (46%) and that it will increase the probability of flooding (47%).

When asked what should be done with the site of the current airport, 17% think a reservoir or ecological zone should be created, while 16% favour a park, and 15% prefer a residential area. Finally, 88% said they would support the Government if it decided to transform the whole area into an ecological zone.

Challenges ahead

The NAICM is regarded with scepticism among specific stakeholders. This may have to do with the fact that the Government has limited its communications strategy to informing the public of its doings, with varying degrees of detail. However, a project of this importance should not take its audiences for granted; thus it is of the utmost importance that persuasion takes a central place in communications efforts.

To better understand the meaning of persuasion, the "Communications Hierarchy" can serve as a guide.

A basic communications strategy that answers the questions "who, what, when, where, and how" informs its audiences about the general purpose and direction of the organisation's actions. This does not mean, however, that the public actually believes or supports what is being done. What it means is that an explanation or recount has been emitted and, hopefully, received. The NAICM communications are currently at this basic level.

The next step in the hierarchy is to create understanding. This requires the communications strategy to answer an additional key question: "Why?" For the NAICM, it means that spokespersons cannot just take for granted that every audience understands why it is necessary or urgent to build a new airport, why it will be built in a particular place, or why the project is positive for Mexico and its citizens in the long run. The benefits of the NAICM have to be constantly explained in a way that allows people to share a common meaning about the project in the belief that it will bring the country many benefits.

The next step in the hierarchy is to reinforce values, or to communicate in a way that appeals to those who already see the project in a positive light. In this case, the communications strategy needs to create messages for all those actors who are pro-NAICM (besides the Government), so they can disseminate said messages among the general public, acting as third-party, *bona fide* spokespersons.

The next step of an effective communications strategy would be to change attitudes. This requires conveying messages in a way that can actually change people's perceptions. In this case, persuasion would make the case for the NAICM and the Government's ability to carry out the project in an efficient and transparent manner. Even the most sceptical audiences can react differently if they perceive that the Government is committed to doing things right.

Finally, the goal of a successful communications strategy is to elicit action. This happens when audiences are effectively persuaded and respond by doing something that has been asked of them. To achieve this, communication has to be built around the audience's interests and concerns rather than around the spokesperson's agenda.

To achieve these steps, a persuasive communications strategy needs:

- to go beyond conveying facts, helping people understand their roles in the project
- to positively appeal to the audiences' emotions
- credibility and trust as core elements
- clear, understandable language
- logical explanations supported by evidence
- storytelling that frames the project so people understand why the new airport is necessary.

With these elements in mind, the speeches issued by SCT, the project's leading entity, were analysed, yielding the following results:

- Language is mostly abstract and technical: "connectivity", "competitiveness", "hub", "architectural sustainability" and other terms that are unknown to wide audiences are frequently used.
- Logical explanations are the messages' main content. However, the Government uses too much quantitative data. Figures are not used to reinforce the message: they are the message.
- There is no appeal to the audience's emotions. Concepts that can elicit positive feelings towards the NAICM, such as "pride", "modern", "beauty", "clean", and "friendly" need to be used repeatedly.

- There has been no compelling storytelling effort to create a sense of urgency and support for the NAICM. It is assumed that everybody shares the Government's story: that an airport is badly needed, that the 2000-06 administration failed to build it, and that the current government is going to do it right, in record time, and with many benefits.
- The message has not reached the communities around the NAICM site. There are mentions that "160 000 jobs" will be created and that "public parks, and health and education facilities" will be built. These vague statements do not create "shared meaning" for the NAICM as a project and fail to highlight that surrounding municipalities' living conditions will change for the better.
- The Government's discourse uses a "trickle-down" approach: the Government assumes that if shops and office buildings are built, jobs for the locals will naturally follow, but local communities may not share this vision. It is important to create a shared vision of the future.

Assessment of the Internet site

Overall, the NAICM website (www.aeropuerto.gob.mx) is clearly structured and boasts an attractive design. Still, there is room for improvement in terms of content. This communication channel could be more proactive and ambitious, considering the magnitude of the project. An area that clearly needs improvement is the regularity of its updates: the website has not posted videos of the latest press conferences, or of the most recent SCT and GACM leaders' interviews.

The website could also benefit from interactive features, such as e-mail and contact details to help interested people find more information or deepen public knowledge on the project. Some newspapers have used more attractive ways of providing information about the NAICM (videos, infographics, etc.), which could be used as models for the website.

The airport-dedicated website is static and needs to provide frequent real-time updates on the project's status. The website could capitalise on interactive features and tailor information to attract younger audiences. It is quite positive that an English version has been developed, with information for foreign audiences.

Communications responsibilities and capabilities

Unlike most government agencies, GACM's organisational structure does not yet include a communications office. Its organisation chart includes an administrative board, a directorate general, and four main corporate directorates, but at the present time, none of these directorates is officially tasked with conducting social communication.

The SCT has the power to exert political control over GACM and has *de facto* taken control over the project's communications and outreach efforts. There is no specific, independent, and formal communications strategy for the NAICM. According to SCT sources, this is because GACM still lacks the human and financial resources to have its own communications office. Consequently, communications efforts are framed within the SCT's communications policy.

According to interviews with sector officials, an *ad hoc* group has formed between the GACM, SCT, the project management firm, and its external communications and public relations agency. This group meets twice a month to review positive and negative coverage of the NAICM and recommends future courses of action, mostly for the SCT and GACM. It has been said that the project management firm has a strong preference for communicating technical details, while the SCT and GACM are more concerned with the political and policy aspects of communication actions. One observer described this group as a "good orchestra with competent musicians, but no director".

This group has created a good mechanism to track the NAICM's news coverage and the PR agency has helped the project manager to improve its communications. There has been a proactive approach to give business journalists information on a regular basis so they can write pieces on the NAICM. However, these actions are not part of a wider communications strategy, limiting their scope and impact. The GACM needs more resources and more autonomy from the SCT in order to implement a good strategy.

Internal communications

One aspect that was constantly mentioned during the interviews with public officials was that different stakeholders inside the agencies involved had different views of the project. Thus, their communications placed emphasis on different messages. This is common in large projects. The way to address this issue is through an internal communications strategy.

In general, the three most important barriers for efficient internal communications are the following:

- *Time.* People working in a project usually have their schedules filled up with tasks that are essential to the completion of the project and devote less time to communicate what they are doing and why.
- *Hierarchy.* The top members of an organisation are usually the busiest, and it is difficult for them to regularly meet with all the members of the team to provide a clear understanding of where the project is at a certain point in time. People can also feel that they are not empowered to talk to their superiors if they lack formal channels to do so.
- *Agendas.* In complex projects involving inter-agency communications, different people can have a diverse vision of the project depending on their own interests. This could make communication more difficult.

These barriers need a conscious effort from the team leadership to be overcome. A good internal communications strategy can help to that end. Such a strategy needs, as a minimum:

- a clear message aimed to reach all members at all levels in all the teams involved in the project
- clear mission and vision statements that remind the organisation members what the ultimate purpose of the project is and how the future looks once the project is finished
- a policy ensuring that information flows efficiently across all members of the organisation and facilitates that any member can have his/her concerns and questions addressed.

Additionally, an internal communications strategy may use the following tools:

- *Regular meetings:* The team needs to be assembled regularly only with the purpose of understanding where exactly the project is at a certain point and what the next steps are. It is essential that during these meetings, people are encouraged by the project leaders to express their concerns and opinions.
- *Regular update emails:* All members of the organisation should receive a brief, electronic weekly/bi-weekly newsletter with the most important news about the project. This newsletter can serve not only to keep them abreast of facts and recent developments, but also to convey messages from the project leadership that can serve to motivate the team and recognise their work and effort.
- *A real and/or virtual mailbox.* Project team members should be able to ask questions and receive answers from their leaders in a regular fashion. Sometimes, distance and time do not allow for everybody to raise a concern or pose a question, so a mailbox can serve to encourage people to speak freely.
- *A catalogue of all project documentation available for reference.* The Intranet of the project can concentrate all the relevant documents that the members of the organisation may need at some point. This allows everyone to be on the same page and to have a common place of reference.

A key element in internal communications that any organisation needs to keep in mind is the fact that every member of the organisation is a potential spokesperson. When every member of the organisation knows the mission and vision, and has the necessary information and facts at hand, he or she can be an effective spokesperson in their social and professional circles. That is why internal communications not only need to keep people informed, but also motivated and engaged. That is why clear messages that help everyone understand how their work contributes to the project are essential.

Internal communications at the GACM

During a round of interviews with the GACM staff, it was clear that decision-making in crucial areas as well as day-to-day interaction can enormously benefit from a well-planned internal communications strategy. Five main obstacles for internal communications were identified:

1. *Staff and time constraints.* Almost all areas agreed in that the GACM is understaffed, given the magnitude of the NAICM project. This results in work overload, which leaves little time for meetings. One of the areas even holds internal briefing meetings on Saturdays.

2. *Office location.* GACM uses half a floor in a large corporate building as its headquarters. However, there is not enough space to house all the staff. Consequently, offices of Administration and Infrastructure are both located in separate buildings. While Infrastructure has its offices near the airport construction site, Administration is located about one hour and a half from it. This reduces the opportunities for one-to-one communications. Distance and traffic reduce the incentives for the staff to meet more often.

3. *Lack of equal access to technology.* Only 11 members of GACM staff have regular positions as public officials. The rest of the staff has been hired through temporary contracts, illustrating the questions over GACM's capacity discussed in the other chapters. This means, for instance, that only a few people have access to the

"@gacm.mx" official email account that complies with the Federal Government's transparency and security requirements. The rest of the staff uses their personal email accounts. This has consequences for internal communications, as they cannot be included in the same Intranet. There is also a need to increase access to ACONEX, a document-sharing electronic platform that has been used by some members of the staff. With regards to this platform, interviewees said that despite its usefulness, not every area inside GACM is willing to use it, due to "generational barriers" (older senior staff have found it difficult to use) or because they have not been properly trained in its use due to time constraints.

4. *Language.* Most of the staff from the project management firm does not speak Spanish. While some members of the GACM staff are fluent in English, others are not. This has been cited as another significant communications barrier.

5. *Differences in organisational culture and agendas.* GACM is a newly formed agency, and its staff comes from diverse backgrounds in the government, private sector, and academia. It is not strange that they have different views and management styles, which has created barriers to communication. In words of a senior member of the staff "GACM is a new, fresh corporatised agency, but given our diverse backgrounds we already have the internal communication problems of an old government one."

Proposals for action

External communications

The main proposal is to establish a formal NAICM communications strategy with goals, means, actions, budget, and responsible actors. It is imperative for SCT, GACM, and the project manager to have clearly divided communications and information responsibilities. As part of that communications strategy, the following measures are necessary:

1. Empower GACM as the leader of day-to-day communications and outreach efforts, while the SCT could limit itself to taking the stage when key milestones are reached. This would put communications in the hands of the agency that is formally responsible for the project and prevent grey areas of responsibility.

2. Create a formal communications and crisis management committee to be led by GACM, with members from SCT, the Office of the Presidency, and the project manager. Crisis management manuals and plans should be developed.

3. Undertake media training and crisis-management workshops.

4. Appoint a project-dedicated spokesperson. Ideally, the spokesperson would have solid technical knowledge of the project as well as the interpersonal and communications skills necessary to create and maintain a highly positive relationship with all of the project's stakeholders, both inside and outside the Government.

5. Change the language from technical and rational to persuasive and emotional. The NAICM has the potential to become a symbol of pride for Mexico. Everyone involved has to convey that pride in the project.

6. Conduct public-opinion studies and focus groups to understand stakeholders' aspirations and concerns. Quantitative and qualitative studies would allow the GACM to understand which areas need outreach efforts the most.

7. Create tailored messages for different audiences according to their nature (NGOs, community leaders, the business sector, local governments) and attitude (those supporting the airport, those who are neutral, and those who are openly against it). Likewise, develop tailored messages for each stage of the project (see Box 5.4). Use different channels to convey those messages.

8. Strengthen the functions of outreach and community liaison of the Corporate Directorate for Planning, Evaluation, and Outreach. NGO leaders are a particularly important audience, as they have a constant demand for information and data. They expressed their need to have a formal contact inside the GACM.

9. Define a calendar for private meetings with key stakeholders to keep them abreast on the evolution of the project. A recurring perception among key stakeholders is that communications are very irregular, with big announcements followed by weeks and months of "silence".

10. Steer clear of information voids. Define a calendar for press conferences. Use videos and social networks to provide weekly updates on the project. For instance, the spokesperson can have a Periscope account to show the public that work is being carried out according to plan. YouTube time-lapse videos are another great tool to show progress. The Facebook account can be used to tell positive stories about the people working on the project as well as about people living in the surrounding communities.

11. Do not underestimate the risk that radical groups may pose to the project. As the 2018 federal and local elections get closer, these groups will have incentives to seek support from political parties.

12. Strengthen efforts to reach out to the local communities surrounding the NAICM. People in the vicinity of the airport will be powerful spokespersons for or against the project, and therefore need to get all of the GACM's communications and support.

Box 5.4. Key messages for each stage of the communications strategy

Stage 1: Preliminary works

Objective: Creating a sense of vision and pride for the new international airport.

Key message suggested:

- "Mexico is building its new doorway to the world".

Narrative*:*

- Current airport is no longer functional / comfortable / convenient.
- Current airport is not a source of pride / good image of Mexico.
- We can do better than this.
- We are working to do better than this.
- We are building the nation's new doorway to the world.

Stage 2: Construction

Key message suggested:

- "Mexico is building one of the top airports in the world".

Narrative:

- We are changing the face of Mexico City to receive visitors from all over Mexico and the world.
- When people come and see the new airport they will see and feel the new face of Mexico.
- Mexicans can do great things when we work together.
- This airport will be a source of pride and welfare for Mexico City and the nation.

Stage 3: Operation

Key message suggested:

- "Mexico has a new symbol of progress: the NAICM".

Narrative:

- Mexico has changed a lot in the last eight years.
- The new airport is the symbol of the new Mexico.
- The new airport is the face of a renewed nation.
- We want you to come, look, feel, and taste the new doorway of Mexico to the world.

Internal communications

1. Appoint a responsible person for internal communications. This can be a part of the functions of the external communications office, but the same person cannot be in charge of both. Internal communications needs its own strategy and implementation.

2. Define the communication tools and channels. Despite its relatively small size, the GACM staff faces the challenge of talking a common language. A leadership group can be appointed to ensure that information flows among areas that have expressed concern about organisational bottlenecks. This group can define better

practices to ensure that all concerns and views are taken into account in the selection of the communication tools and channels.

3. Invest in the creation of a document-sharing platform for all the staff. ACONEX is a platform brought by the project management firm, but opinions about its usefulness and user-friendliness are divided. It would probably be necessary to think about an alternative that suits the needs of all the areas inside GACM. The issue of credentials for access to the platform needs to be addressed, so every member of the staff has access according to his/her needs and seniority.

4. Define a calendar and format for internal communication meetings. Meetings have proven to be successful as the preferred communication tool inside some areas, but when it comes to interaction among different areas, they are not as successful as desired. There is a need to create criteria (templates and rules) for meetings among different teams, so they are not time-consuming and deemed ineffective by staff members.

Notes

1. The Bordo Poniente is a 500-hectare dump in the former lake of Texcoco area, which received rubble from thousands of buildings that were destroyed in the 1985 Mexico City earthquake. It soon became the main dump for the city's solid waste and received more than 12 000 tons of trash per day until it reached its full capacity. It was officially closed in 2012. However, there are no effective plans to correctly manage the 70 million tonnes of accumulated waste. The Bordo is considered a serious environmental hazard, as the winds push trash particles to populated areas. Some of these trash particles are less than 2.5 microns large and can adhere to the lungs.

2. AVE is the amount in dollars a story would cost if it appeared as paid advertising. AVE is determined by multiplying the length of the story by the respective publication or station's advertising rate, based on the Mexican Media Publicity (MPM) advertisement media guide.

3. See http://inicio.inai.org.mx/Comunicados/Nota%20INAI-071-15.pdf for more information.

References

Dean, F. (2011), *Ten Steps to Writing A Vital Speech: The Definitive Guide to Professional Speechwriting,* Create Space Independent Publishing Platform.

Hass, L., L. Mazzei and D. O'Leary (2007), "Setting standards for communication and governance: The example of infrastructure projects", World Bank Working Paper No. 121, Washington, DC, http://elibrary.worldbank.org/doi/pdf/10.1596/ 978-0-8213-7169-5.

Chapter 6

Plan of action for the implementation of the OECD recommendations relative to the NAICM project

Effective delivery of large infrastructures is one of the most demanding accomplishments in global project implementation due to the efforts it takes in terms of governance, multi-level co-ordination, planning, financing and construction under ambitious timelines and budgets.

This chapter presents a plan of actions for an adequate implementation of the NAICM project in the areas covered by this report, namely governance, procurement, integrity and communication. Considering the priorities set for each of the proposals it also proposes key actors inside and outside the GACM for its adequate implementation.

Governance

Proposal for action: The governance model of the project needs to be strengthened to allow timely decision making, accountability, and inclusiveness, as well as to effectively allocate risks.

Actions	Managing unit
Clearly define and allocate responsibilities among corporate directorates	DCA
Map services outsourced and consultants with accountability measures	DCA
Develop new accountability mechanisms for GACM officials	DCA
Establish the wider governance map of the project	DCP
Establish a monitoring group with NGOs, academia, think-tanks, etc.	DCP
Formalise a partnership with INAI	DCP
Formalise a partnership with COFECE	DCP
Pursue the establishment of an *ad hoc* interaction mechanism with SFP (i.e. a special unit in SFP)	DCP
Develop a strategy to reward good performance by suppliers, aligned with procurement regulations	DCA

Proposal for action: Corporate governance should be reviewed to align with good international practice defined in the OECD Guidelines on Corporate Governance of State-Owned Enterprises.

Actions	Managing unit
Consider writing a letter/statement of expectations to the GACM Board to communicate government expectations on its performance	Office of the President
Develop the vertical co-ordination scheme for the NAICM project, following good practices of corporate governance	SCT-GACM
Put together a committee to nominate members of the GACM Board and propose them to the pertinent authorities (or some alternative, transparent and merit-based nomination mechanism)	SCT
Design a training programme for the introduction of new board members	DCP/DCF
Regulate the participation of alternate members in board meetings	DCA/DCF
Establish an internal audit function	DCA
Develop an annual mechanism of evaluation for the board	DCP-DCF

Proposal for action: While co-ordination among central government stakeholders seems to be working well, this is not necessarily the case with others.

Actions	Managing unit
Formalise the functioning of the high-level co-ordination group, including the participation of the Federal District and the State of Mexico	Office of the President
Establish the Metropolitan Council for the NAICM, with the participation of the state, municipal, and delegation governments involved	Office of the President and SCT-GACM

Proposal for action: GACM capacities need to be strengthened, and a collaborative working environment should be developed.

Actions	Managing unit
Diagnose the different functions and skills that need to be reinforced and estimate HR needs on this basis, leading to an adjustment of the organisational structure	SHCP-SFP-SCT-DCA
Review salary levels and employment stability to improve the working environment and avoid high levels of stress and/or turnover	DCA-DCF
Establish protocols/traditions to celebrate the achievement of major milestones of the project	DCA

Proposal for action: Continuous and open dialogue with stakeholders, involving them in planning, decision making, and oversight, is a key feature of successful megaprojects.

Actions	Managing unit
Develop a strategy to engage stakeholders in planning and decision making, including mechanisms such as public meetings, targeted meetings, mailing lists, informational materials, media outreach, and repositories	DCP
Develop a strategy to engage stakeholders in the oversight of the project, including public information and complaints management, third-party monitoring agreements, social witnesses, community monitors, and social contracts	DCP

Proposal for action: Periodic financial and procurement reviews must be undertaken to respond to changing conditions.

Actions	Managing unit
Establish an analysis methodology and KPIs to assess the achievement of secondary policy objectives through public procurement	DCA-SFP
Update the financial analyses and alternative scenarios for the funding of the project	DCF

Procurement

Proposal for action: GACM could foster transparent and effective stakeholder direct participation to ensure a co-ordinated approach to the project by co-ordinating procurement expertise in the decision-making process.

Actions	Managing unit
Map the involvement of the different stakeholders in procurement processes	DCP
Create a project-oriented steering committee federating the different expertise	DCI
Define the critical procurement milestones for each package to ensure their assessment by the steering committee	DCA
Develop follow-up mechanisms of decisions taken by the steering committee	DCP

Proposal for action: In designing appropriate award criteria and adequate frameworks proportionate to need, GACM could facilitate access to procurement opportunities to competitors of all sizes and help identify proposals offering the best value for money.

Actions	Managing unit
Identify major evaluation criteria and overall weightings common to all packages	DCI and purchasing areas
Identify detailed evaluation criteria and weightings tailored to the specifics of each package	DCI and purchasing areas
Develop standardised response frameworks for bidders	DCI and purchasing areas
Define formulas used to score proposals received	DCI and purchasing areas
Identify stakeholders responsible for the assessment of proposals received	DCI and purchasing areas

Proposal for action: Sound contract design, including renegotiations, adjustment management mechanisms, and post-implementation contract management could allow GACM to drive efficiency throughout the entire procurement cycle.

Actions	Managing unit
Ensure that expertise required to draft contracts adapted to the nature of the project is secured	DCI
Design draft contracts tailored to the sequencing of the packages	DCA
Introduce in the contracts service level agreements (SLAs) key factors contributing to the successful completion of the works	DCI
Include renegotiations mechanisms in contracts	DCA
Periodically assess contractors performance against contractual provisions	DCI and DCP

Proposal for action: GACM could implement procurement strategies aiming at facilitating access and increasing attractiveness of public procurement operations, while pursuing other policy objectives.

Actions	Managing unit
Map existing barriers to entry into the competition and carry out a cost-benefit analysis of such barriers	DCA
Assess the feasibility of removing existing barriers to entry into the competition	DCA
Implement into each package strategy positive evaluation criteria for specific policy objectives rather than administrative qualification requirements	DCA
Lower transaction costs for bidders and GACM whenever possible/desirable by grouping distinct packages	DCA
Include into packages recurring follow-up activities for works requiring ongoing maintenance to increase attractiveness of public procurement operations	DCA

Proposal for action: GACM could engage in transparent and regular dialogues with suppliers, business associations and experts to decide the most efficient procurement process, its openness and design effective technical specifications and appropriate award criteria.

Actions	Managing unit
Develop a strategy to engage suppliers, business associations and experts in procurement processes	DCP
Define the structure of the dialogues with business and experts communities, including the participation of social witnesses	DCP
Widely communicate this strategy to business and expert communities	DCP
Advertise and carry out information sessions prior to the finalisation of each package strategy and documentation to assess market capabilities	DCA and DCI
Include feedback received into each package strategy and documentation	DCA and DCI

Proposal for action: GACM could consider all available means to foster participation of SMEs in the NAICM project.

Actions	Managing unit
Develop a strategy to engage SMEs in procurement processes	DCF/DCP
Define appropriate weightings for proposals committing to subcontract part of the works to SMEs according to the nature of the works carried out and to market capabilities	DCA
Encourage the creation of consortia of SMEs for packages where required resources are proportionate to SMEs capabilities	DCP and DCF

Proposal for action: GACM could implement risk management strategies, allowing for the identification of threats and mitigation measures.

Actions	Managing unit
Set up a formal risk register for procurement processes and define corresponding roles and responsibilities within GACM	DCP
Map all potential risks affecting procurement processes	GACM
Assess their severity, likelihood and consequences	GACM
Identify corresponding mitigation measures which are, or could be, implemented	GACM
Periodically re-assess the existence and qualification of risks and the effectiveness of mitigation measures	GACM

Enhancing the integrity and transparency of the procurement process

Proposal for action: The GACM could promote a culture of integrity.

Actions	Managing unit
Raise awareness of corruption risks among its personnel particularly among those involved in the procurement process	GACM-DCA and SFP
Amend its code of conduct taking into account that it will need to: *i)* outline to GACM personnel and partners what is expected of them in terms of conduct; *ii)* contribute to reinforcing integrity in the organisational culture by setting new norms; and *iii)* provide a disciplinary framework to sanction deviant behaviour	GACM-DCA and SFP
Develop specific standards for procurement officials, for example through code of conduct for GACM procurement officials	GACM-DCA and SFP
Ensure that its code of conduct is known and as much as possible applicable to all those involved in the procurement process, including consultants, outsourced personnel and subcontractors	GACM-DCA and SFP
Provide training for procurement officials on integrity, ethics and anti-corruption tools	GACM-DCA and SFP
Increase the visibility and awareness the Ethics Committee to have a better dissemination and enforcement of the code of conduct and subsequent adaptation of norms to new risks	GACM-DCA and SFP
Develop a comprehensive conflict of interest policy, including the development of a Procurement Management Framework that lists situations which would be considered as a conflict of interest and provides guidance on the steps to follow	GACM-DCA and SFP
Check any potential conflicts of interest before the procurement process begins and ensure that bidders can disclose any potential conflict of interest they may have with the contracting organisation or with the other bidders	GACM-DCA and SFP
Assess the possibility of discussing with its public officials which channels will provide confidence to report wrongdoing	GACM-DCA and SFP
Implement training and education on the notion of integrity and the purpose of reporting to encourage the correct use of reporting mechanisms and prevent misuse	GACM-DCA and SFP
Engage with groups of suppliers to explore ways to encourage them to develop their own standards and programmes to enhance integrity in their relationship with GACM.	GACM-DCA and SFP

Proposal for action: GACM and SFP could empower a strategic and strong OIC.

Actions	Managing unit
The OIC could ensure it does not only perform a control role but also serves as an advisory body for GACM management and procurement units to achieve greater effectiveness and efficiency of the procurement process	GACM-DCA, SFP, and OIC
GACM procurement units and the OIC could work closely with the GACM internal control committee and the SFP's *Mesa de acompañamiento* to ensure efficient and transparent procurement procedures	GACM-DCA, SFP, and OIC
The GACM OIC's and the SFP could work together to develop a complaint template on the GACM's website to allow suppliers and citizens to make complaints on line	SFP and OIC

Proposal for action: The GACM could avoid integrity risks during the procurement process.

Actions	Managing unit
Develop a corruption risk map of the organisation and its processes in order to identify the positions of officials that are particularly vulnerable, the activities in the procurement cycle where risks can arise, and the specific projects at risk. This will also allow the GACM to: • use a system of red flags following the development of a risk map. • develop an integrity plan to facilitate the development of mitigation strategies following the mapping of specific corruption risks and thus ensure that all parties involved in the process are aware of existing integrity risks and mechanisms as well as their own responsibilities	GACM-DCA and SFP
Continue with the involvement of civil society experts through the inclusion of social observers in key procurement procedures	DCA
Reduce in its procurement manuals the threshold for the mandatory use of social witness for the procurement of public works, goods and services; as well as include in its procurement manuals other conditions under which a social witness needs to be included	DCA
Develop standard bidding documents for the technical and economic proposals, statement of integrity, and disclosure forms for current commitments and financial situation	DCA
Implement the two-envelope approach to ensure that procurement decisions are made according to the set criteria	DCA
Implement the four-eyes principle to limit public officials' discretionary power and ensure a certain level of deliberation and the protection of the public officials from suspicion	DCA
Explore the possibility of designating an integrity monitor that can follow the entire procurement cycle	DCA
Ensure that its existing internal integrity mechanisms are known by and applicable to consultants, outsourced personnel and subcontractors as much as it applies to GACM personnel	DCA

Proposal for action: The GACM could improve the transparency of its procurement activities.

Actions	Managing unit
Ensure that it has the needed resources, structure and capacities to perform these functions	DCA
Publish all the procurement information not only related to the airport but also to the functioning of the GACM	DCA
Publish procurement information by the type of procedure used in terms of numbers and in terms of value	DCA
Provide clear definitions of the procurement procedures and the most common exceptions to public bidding that are foreseen to be used	DCA
Proactively establish and publish online guidelines in plain language on all the information disclosed	DCA
Publish procurement plans in a usable format that can allow distinguishing from what was already procured, what is currently being procured and what will be procured in the future	DCA
Proactively publish, on its webpage, all the relevant information such as annual procurement programmes, tender procedures (solicitation documents, minutes of the clarification meetings and of the opening of tenders), contract awards history, modification to contracts and formal complaints (*inconformidades*)	DCA
Publish the signed declarations of bidders on its website	DCA

Communications

Proposal for action: Establish and implement a formal NAICM communications and outreach strategy.

Actions	Managing unit
Empower GACM as the leader of day-to-day communications and outreach efforts	Office of the Presidency-SCT (Decision). GACM (Management)
Create a formal communications and outreach office inside GACM	GACM
Appoint a director / spokesperson	GACM
Create a formal communications and crisis management committee	Office of the Presidency, SCT, GACM, and related entities
Prepare crisis management manuals and train the spokesperson for media and crisis management	GACM Office of Communications
Conduct public-opinion studies and focus groups to understand stakeholders' aspirations and concerns	DCP and Office of Communications
Create tailored messages for different audiences	DCP and Office of Communications
Strengthen the functions of outreach and community liaison	DCP and Office of Communications
Define a calendar for private meetings with key stakeholders to keep them abreast of the evolution of the project	DCP and Office of Communications

Proposal for action: Establish and implement an internal communications strategy.

Actions	Managing unit
Appoint a responsible person for internal communication	DCA
Define the communication tools and channels	DCA
Create an Intranet to gather all relevant information that will be available for the team	DCA
Define a calendar for internal communication meetings	DCA

Annex A

The EXPO MILANO *ex ante* control mechanism

Following several corruption scandals that occurred in 2013 and 2014 in the procurement and construction processes of EXPO2015 Milano, the President of ANAC (*Autoritá Nationale Anticorruzione* – National Anti-corruption Authority of Italy) was committed functions of supervision and guarantee of the fairness and transparency of the procurement procedures related to the implementation of the event in June 2014. As part of this assignment in July 2014 ANAC established a special operational unit (UOS) to monitor the projects of the EXPO 2015.

With the establishment of the UOS several rules, procedures and control mechanisms were set as to monitor and exercise "*a priori*" control of the procurement processes (Linee Guida ANAC 17.07.2014).

The establishment of *ex ante* control mechanisms, although not a common practice for Supreme Audit Institutions in OECD countries (only Chile, Italy and Portugal exercise it with regularity) seems adequate for the enforcement of additional integrity measures, necessary to be addressed at the date development stage of the project, and after the recent events.

In fact, this approach could prove useful mainly in specific contexts, such as EXPO 2015, that have already been affected by instances of corruption which have not only contaminated existing tenders but also threaten to undermine future contracting procedures. Indeed, to be effective, *ex ante* controls of documents concerning the award and performance of public contracts for works, services and supplies of goods, by an entity separate from the contracting authority, cannot cover all public tenders but must focus on individual, specific cases with a "high risk of corruption". For these reasons, using this control system in specific cases, as per Article 19 of Law Decree 90/2014, establishing a UOS within ANAC responds to multiple public interest objectives: it enables the creation of an innovative system of *ex ante* third-party controls on the legality of tender documents, with particular regard to Italian laws and regulations on transparency; it strengthens and safeguards the probity and transparency of the award procedures used; it potentially functions as a way to dissuade future instances of corruption, given the explicit checks on the propriety of each procedural step in the tenders; it helps to restore confidence among operators in the relevant market about the transparency and probity of award procedures and the subsequent management of tenders.

However, it is worth noting that the *ex ante* control of documents concerning award procedures and the performance of public contracts for works, services and supplies of goods, by a party separate from the contracting authority, could exacerbate the time it takes to complete tenders. The entities responsible for assessing risk must ensure that the *ex ante* control clearly identifies the best ways to ensure control effectiveness, without having an excessive effect on the swiftness and efficiency of the administration of the tender. The establishment of a threshold by ANAC for the exercise of the prior control mechanism is a good step forward to balance the efficiency of the process.

Since its establishment in July 2014, the UOS developed a comprehensive framework for controlling the public procurement procedures of EXPO 2015. This framework includes:

1. the definition of *Linee Operative* (Operative guide)
2. the setting up of seven models of checklists
3. the publishing of *Linee Guida* (Guidelines)
4. the setting up of the *Raccomandazioni* (Recommendations).

Since July 2014 and up to the opening in May 2015, UOS revised all public procurement procedures of the EXPO using this framework. When there were unconformities in the processes, UOS requested additional information to EXPO S.p.A, prior to the clearance. UOS also met regularly with the procurement technical units of EXPO 2015, either in Rome or in Milan, holding more than 20 meetings until that date. The average response time of UOS is five working days between the arrival of the process and the issue of the response, in order to allow the processes to continue without major interruptions or delays, which can be considered as an internationally accepted good practise for review bodies.

Table A.1 presents a summary of the work developed by the UOS as of 16 March 2015, detailed by type of procedure and outcome. At this date, the UOS had reviewed 153 procurement processes, with a total procurement value of around EUR 589 million, with 60% of the processes related to tenders. In 136 processes UOS received the process from EXPO, and for an additional 17 it took the initiative to request clarifications and information from the contracting authorities (CA).

Table A.1. **Procurement procedures reviewed by UOS**

	No.	With comments from UOS (unconformities and legal issues)
Procedure/tenders	92	80
Settlement agreements	2	0
Additional agreements	4	4
Sponsorship	3	3
Request for information	17	0
Conventions	4	4
Tender committees	8	5
Awardings	18	13
Random controls[1]	2	0
Intermediary note	3	0
Total	153	109

Source: ANAC, 16 March 2015.

In 109 (72% of the cases analysed) of the procedures, the UOS detected unconformities or potential failures to meet legal requirements, and requested the correction of the process in one or several aspects. The processes analysed include checklist validations and information about the procurement procedures, usually with a technical note issued by UOS about the type and object of procedure, commenting on the awarding criteria, the conditions of the supply of the goods or services and contract details. They also included a note issued by the co-ordinator of the UOS control section with remarks and recommendations whenever necessary. In some cases these recommendations included the analysis of the object of the contract, identified incongruences, the changing of the awarding criteria, the elimination or changes in the technical specifications in order to increase competition or the improvement of requisites to assure the quality of the delivery of the goods or services. The analysis was always formalised in a letter with the assessment of each procedure sent by the President of ANAC to EXPO.

For 107 procedures, Expo 2015 S.p.A. has adopted the corrections formulated by the UOS and/or eventually provided the explications and the additional documentation required.

Notes

1. Art. 6.2, Linee guida del 17/07/2014.

Annex B

Comments by the OECD on the NAICM websites (based on the status of the websites as of 5 May 2015)

GACM portal (www.aeropuerto.gob.mx/gacm/index.php)

- In the section "Documents", we suggest maintaining the label "regulatory framework" (*normatividad*) but changing the title to "regulatory framework applicable to GACM" and creating a new label reading "regulatory framework applicable to procurement and public works" to upload the laws on acquisitions, public works, POBALINES, bylaws, etc. Alternatively, these regulations could go into a sub-heading under "Procurement".
- The section "Procurement" (*Contrataciones*) displays incomplete lists of what has been purchased and of suppliers. These lists need to be updated periodically to keep their relevance, indicating the time of the latest update. In addition, definitions of *servicios relacionados* and other categories would be useful. The lists shall include all procurement and not only selected tenders.
- When you go into the detail of each procurement process, some information is missing (i.e. the report of social witnesses). There is a link to CompraNet but it takes you to the main page and not to the specific processes.
- Likewise, it would be useful to display current (ongoing) and future public biddings. Currently, accessing ongoing biddings requires going to CompraNet. The GACM website could display some basic information and provide the link to the CompraNet fiche. Furthermore, this section would benefit from a short, plain-language explanation regarding the procurement process and the use of procurement procedures and exceptions. The Procurement Manual, when ready, would also make a good addition to this section.
- The section on "Social Responsibility" could be complemented with some basic information and "killing facts" from the NAICM website (widely explaining the economic, social, and environmental benefits).
- The section "File your complaint" (*Presenta tu Queja o Denuncia*) could be more user-friendly in order to encourage complaints. More details on how this may be achieved and examples will be provided in the integrity chapter of the review report.
- The section under "Transparency/Access to Information" is clearly still to be developed. In the meanwhile, you can provide links to the Transparency Duties Portal (POT) and INFOMEX. Links can remain in the future, but the ideal is to have a one-stop point where you can get the information you are looking for. Uploading the different regulations concerning access to information (law, bylaws, SFP manual, etc.) would also be a plus. In addition, you could make

explicit the information that will not be public, justifying the exemptions allowed by the Law for Transparency and Access to Information. Finally, you may want to provide the physical address of GACM's Unit for Access to Public Information (not clear if it is the same as the GACM general offices).

- In the "Press Room" label, under videos, we suggest adding the date after the title of each event.
- In the "Interesting Sites" (*Sitios de Interés*) label, you may want to add a category for sites related to transparency (i.e. POT, INFOMEX, and the section provided in this website itself). Even if links were provided in the "Transparency/Access to Information" section, their importance calls for proactively leading users to these sources.
- The site map provides the skeleton of both the GACM and the NAICM websites. We think this is correct, in order to guide the user to the information he/she is looking for. However, the map could be highlighted, indicating as well that it refers to both sites. A different title, more user-friendly (i.e. What are you looking for?), could also be helpful in this regard.

NAICM portal (www.aeropuerto.gob.mx/index.php)

- We suggest a banner on the top linking to the "Procurement" section of the GACM website, as well as one linking to the "Transparency" section.
- The SCT portal (www.sct.gob.mx) provides the link to this website, while the GACM portal contains useful information as well. There is a need for a search tool that guides the user to the right portal for the information he/she is looking for. Both the GACM and NAICM websites have good information, but it is not evident which one you should look at first. It rather seems that the answer depends on the information you need.

ORGANISATION FOR ECONOMIC CO-OPERATION AND DEVELOPMENT

The OECD is a unique forum where governments work together to address the economic, social and environmental challenges of globalisation. The OECD is also at the forefront of efforts to understand and to help governments respond to new developments and concerns, such as corporate governance, the information economy and the challenges of an ageing population. The Organisation provides a setting where governments can compare policy experiences, seek answers to common problems, identify good practice and work to co-ordinate domestic and international policies.

The OECD member countries are: Australia, Austria, Belgium, Canada, Chile, the Czech Republic, Denmark, Estonia, Finland, France, Germany, Greece, Hungary, Iceland, Ireland, Israel, Italy, Japan, Korea, Luxembourg, Mexico, the Netherlands, New Zealand, Norway, Poland, Portugal, the Slovak Republic, Slovenia, Spain, Sweden, Switzerland, Turkey, the United Kingdom and the United States. The European Union takes part in the work of the OECD.

OECD Publishing disseminates widely the results of the Organisation's statistics gathering and research on economic, social and environmental issues, as well as the conventions, guidelines and standards agreed by its members.

OECD PUBLISHING, 2, rue André-Pascal, 75775 PARIS CEDEX 16
(42 2015 22 1 P) ISBN 978-92-64-24832-8 – 2015-18

www.ingramcontent.com/pod-product-compliance
Lightning Source LLC
Chambersburg PA
CBHW061210240926
51846CB00006B/1177